FEARLESS
MAJOR GIFTS

FEARLESS
MAJOR GIFTS
Inspiring Meaning-Making

Charles LaFond

Church Publishing
NEW YORK

Unless otherwise noted, the scripture quotations contained herein are from the New Revised Standard Version Bible, copyright © 1989 by the Division of Christian Education of the National Council of Churches of Christ in the U.S.A. Used by permission. All rights reserved.

Church Publishing
19 East 34th Street
New York, NY 10016
www.churchpublishing.org

Cover design by Jennifer Kopec, 2Pug Design
Typeset by John Turnbull

Some names of donors throughout this book are for purposes of illustration and are not those of actual people.

Library of Congress Cataloging-in-Publication Data

LaFond, Charles D.
    Fearless major gifts : inspiring meaning-making / Charles LaFond.
        pages   cm
    New York : Church Publishing, 2017. Includes bibliographical references.
    ISBN 9780898690293 (ebook) | ISBN 9780898690286 (pbk.)
    Church fund raising. | Deferred giving—Religious aspects—Christianity.

BV772.5 (ebook) | BV772.5 .L343 2017 (print)
254'.8—dc23

                2017028908 (print) | 2017038596 (ebook)

This book is dedicated to the millions of people in the course of history who have summoned up the courage to ask for a major gift from another person.

From the first cave lent to a stranger running from a sabertooth tiger
to the jars given to hold the Dead Sea Scrolls;
from the use of a stable behind an inn for a pregnant traveler
to the cave donated for the grave of a crucified savior;
from the request of a boy with five loaves of bread and two fish
to the request of a fortune from a rich young ruler;
from the jewels and authority given by an emperor and his mother
to the land given for the first hospitals and monasteries;
from the food given to a saint who fed the poor,
to the cathedrals and furnishings given by wealthy merchants;
from royal grants to hospitals to ten dollars donated from a child's
*   allowance,*
from a dowager's bequest to a pensioner's
in time of war and times of peace,
in the Great Depression and the Great Awakening,
from the wall given in Capernaum by the Zebedee family,
to the Hebrew Temple walls erected by the Anitpater family;
in every conceivable time of blessing, creation, joy, and crisis
good people have asked for major gifts and other good people have
*   discerned an answer.*

CONTENTS

Foreword *by Kathy Coors*   xiii

Preface   xv

Acknowledgments   xix

A Giving Story: Maude and Meaning-Making   1

Chapter 1: Major Gifts   9

What Is a Major Gift?   9

Created in the Image of a Generous God   10

The Meaning-Making Mandorla   11

We Have Enough, We Need to Give   13

Talking about Money and Membership Growth in Church   15

The Mission of Major Gifts   16

Tips: *How to Get People Comfortable
with Asking for Major Gifts in Your Church*   20

Resource: *Membership Growth as a Financial Resource—
Ask the Congregation to Stand Up*   21

Resource: *How to Help Your Congregation
Get Over Fear and Anxiety*   23

Resource: *How to Set Major Gifts within
an Effective Annual Pledge Program*   24

Resource: *What to Look for in a Leader
for Major or Planned Giving*   25

Resource: *A Worksheet on Feelings about Asking for Money*   26

Quick-Start Suggestions   27

Study Questions   28

Prayers   30

A Giving Story: Bill and Helen—People Leading the Way   31

Chapter 2: People and Relationships 37

Different People 38

Different Generations 39

An Aging Congregation 39

How We Make Choices 39

The Great Generation 40

The Silent Generation 40

Baby Boomers 42

Generation X 42

Millennials, or Generation Y 44

On Women as Major Donors 45

    Tips 47

    Resource: *A Bible Study on the Rich Young Ruler*
(Mark 10:17–22) for Stewardship Leaders 49

    Quick-Start Suggestions 50

    Study Questions 51

    Prayers 52

A Giving Story: Jason—Curating a Mission 53

Chapter 3: Mission Integrity 59

The Garden Metaphor 59

How to Train Your Leadership 62

An Intentional Introduction 63

Anxieties and Persistence 64

The Importance of the Pledge Campaign for Major Gifts 65

Choosing Leadership in Major Gifts 66

Noticing Passions and Curating Conversations 67

The Role of Vulnerability 67

The Sacramentality of Conversation 69

Mission Integrity 70

En-Theos 71

Be Whole (Not Perfect) 72

Being Good Ancestors 73

Integrity and Effectiveness 73

A Major-Gifts Case for Support 75

Spiritual Underpinnings of Leadership 76

Resource: *Job Description—Stewardship Commission*   78
Resource: *Job Description—Major-Gift Committee Chairs*   78
Resource: *Wow Cards*   79
Resource: *A Case-Development Exercise for Confidence and Joy*   79
Resource: *The Community Interview*   80
Resource: *Summary of Discernment Tools*   81
Resource: *A Ministry-Effectiveness Survey*   82
Resource: *Member Questionnaire*   83
Resource: *The Art of Hosting Meaningful Conversation—*
A Method for Leveled Engagement   84
Resource: *A Sample Letter Asking for the First Visit*   87
Resource: *A Sample Donor-Engagement Continuum*   88
Resource: *A Sample Parish Meaning-Making List*   91
Quick-Start Suggestions   93
Study Questions   96
Prayers   97

A Giving Story: Caroline—The Unexpected Donor   99

Chapter 4: Asking for a Major Gift   103

Jesus Is the Word Made Flesh   103
On the Beauty of Presence-Making   104
On Listening   104
On Co-creativity, Ideas, and Vision-Casting   105
Capacity and Interest: Making Your Prospect List   106
Prospects and Suspects   108
Living-Room Visits: Test the Vision and Listen Carefully   109
Ask for a Donor's Opinion before Asking for a Donor's Money   111
It's Like Hosting a Friend   112
The Individual-Engagement Process   113
Why Is the Work of This Chapter Important?   114
How to Do This Work   116
The Premature-Request Double Checklist   117
Are You Ready to Make the Major-Gift Request?   119
Setting the Appointment   120
Preparing for the Request of a Major Gift   123
The Request for the Gift: An Outline   124

A Final Word Regarding the Major-Gifts Request   143
   Resource: Example—*How to Identify*
   Your Major-Gifts Prospect List   146
   Resource: *A Sample Presentation Outline*   147
   Resource: *A Sample Phone Script to Ask for the First Visit*   148
   Resource: *How to Plan for a Good Living-Room Visit—*
   A Summary   149
   Resource: *Sample Schedule for a Major-Gift Visit*   150
   Quick-Start Suggestions   152
   Study Questions   153
   Prayers   155

A Giving Story: Kenton   157

Chapter 5: Obstacles to Raising Major Gifts   163

Compassion for Human Fears   163
Facing Resistance   167
   Resource: *An Exercise on Feelings about Money*   168
   Resource: *Leadership Red Flags*   168
   Resource: *Facing Resistance to the Major-Gift Program—*
   An Apology for the Return on Investment of Time   169
   Resource: *An Example of the Need*
   for a Flexible "Case for Support"   171
   Resource: *Facing Resistance from the Pulpit—*
   Pat's Sermon about the Realities   173
   Quick-Start Suggestions   174
   Study Questions   174
   Prayers   175

A Giving Story: Chuck and Janet—Planning a Gift   177

Chapter 6: Planned Giving as a Part of
Major-Gifts Programming   181

Managing Your Planned-Giving Major-Gifts Program   184
Starting Up a Planned-Giving Program   185
A Final Word on Planned Giving   188
The Annual-Giving Pledge Card   189
   Resource: *Sample—The Planned-Giving Committee Mission*   191
   Resource: *Sample—A Strategic-Plan Outline*   191

Resource: *Sample—A Communications Plan*   194

Resource: *One Planned-Giving Donor—An Example*   195

Resource: *A Valuable Testament to Your Mission
Being Known in Your Town*   196

Resource: *Sample Tracking System
for Requests for Will Inclusion*   197

Resource: *Sample Planned-Giving Participants'
Welcome Letter (for New Members)*   198

Resource: *A Story of Missed Opportunity—
Mrs. Symington's Last Question*   199

Resource: *Sample Donor Wall*   200

Quick-Start Suggestions   200

Study Questions   202

Prayers   203

A Giving Story: David Ball—The Chairperson   205

Chapter 7: Programming and Stewarding   209

Why Is the Work in This Chapter Important?   209

About Programming   210

About the Stewardship of Received Gifts   211

Toward Regeneration   213

Resource: *A Sample Weekly Major-Gifts Report to the
Major-Gifts or Stewardship Committee*   215

Resource: *A Sample Letter—What to Do
When Stock Is Being Given*   217

Quick-Start Suggestions   218

Study Questions   219

Prayers   220

Conclusion   221

About the Author   223

FOREWORD

by Kathy Coors

. . . .

When Charles asked me to write the foreword to this book . . . I was shocked. Panic took over as I said to myself, "I am not qualified to do this." Then a softer, gentler message emerged—"This must be a God thing." God doesn't call on the qualified, God qualifies the called.

Like Charles, I am a fundraiser and am part of a family whose blessings allow for significant philanthropy. I feel confident connecting with people and understanding what motivates them to give, and I model that motivation as well. Asking for money is not hard once you figure out what brings the donor joy. People get excited, even thrilled, to support a cause that connects with their heart, no matter the size of the gift. Charles figured me out after one honest conversation, and, because of that, my husband and I gave one of our largest donations to the church.

Donors give to the person representing the cause—they give to a person they like and with whom they connect. Charles is more than a likeable guy; he clearly understands how to link the donor's heart with the church's mission. The process requires psychological insight. If a potential donor is not self-aware as to what would motivate them to give, Charles helps the donor to discern their philanthropic cause.

This book is inspiring and uplifting. He dissects and explains for those working in church fundraising how to get to "yes," but he also reminds the church to tread lightly so that the donor is making meaning joyfully, voluntarily, and in real discernment. This book will give the reader common-sense tools to use in any-sized church and seeking any-sized gift; it will help bolster the reader's confidence that they can ask boldly for large donations within a carefully curated process.

We have an obligation as children of Christ to serve others as the hand and eyes of God on Earth, and we are called upon to give in our own unique ways. Everything we have comes from God. Fear is usually the one thing that locks up a person's heart and makes them grip their finances tightly. We humans fear that we don't have enough, or we fear that something terrible is coming down the pike and, if we give, we might end up destitute. This fear needs to be brought out of the dark place in our psyche and into the light, exposing it for the lies it tells our soul. My husband and I tithe 10 percent of our gross income. Following God's command to share our gifts with others has blessed our family beyond our wildest dreams.

I have yet to hear, "Oh, I wish I had not given to those kids suffering from cancer." Yet the secular world tells us an abundance of material goods will make us happy. This is the great fallacy that keeps us on the hamster wheel of life as we race after obtaining a house with a certain square footage, a car with a special emblem, a bigger diamond ring . . . If we live according to this worldly version of happiness, we will race from one fleeting thrill to the next temporary high, only to end up empty inside at the end of each day.

The truth is this . . . our life only gets better when we figure out a way to share our financial gifts with others. My husband and I have been asked well for the right gifts, and we have been asked very poorly for the wrong gifts. We wish that everyone who asked for major gifts had first read this book.

This book will bless those, like me and my husband, who carefully give money away for God's mission on Earth. It will help the church to ask for money appropriately, in discernment and with tender care. It will midwife gifts and help us all to make meaning with our money. And as a side benefit, it will, perhaps, raise the money the church needs for its small part in healing the world.

Clergy are not taught to ask well and carefully for major gifts from a context of relationship-building and engagement. This is holy work—benefiting both the donor and the church. It must be done well. I believe this book will help clergy and congregational leaders to learn the art, science, and theology of major-gifts fundraising.

ACKNOWLEDGMENTS

This book is dedicated to the many people like Nancy, Merle, Tami, Chuck, Janet, Kathy, Helen, Bill, and Iva Mae. These are just some of the many hundreds of men and women who exemplify the passage in Luke's Gospel in which we are told that Jesus' mission was funded by "the women who followed him and gave out of their resources" and whose philanthropy exhibits the calling to love humans.

This book is also dedicated to The Reverend Canon Pat Malloy, who befriended me when I needed a friend the most. He then preached a courageous major-gifts sermon that launched a tidal shift from "the old days" to "a new day." He told the congregation the truth about our need for major gifts and then let me get to the fund-raising. They broke out into a standing ovation. Somebody had just told them the truth, and they were up for the challenge. It was the first stewardship sermon (other than mine) that I had heard from the pulpit in four long years. As a result of his hard work, and mine, and that of others, we increased the annual giving campaign by 50 percent in three years. This occurred during a transition, a painful season in which the cathedral's membership plummeted and we were between deans. We raised the money we needed for a new organ and a bunch of other needed renovations, and we are now watching an apartment for fifty homeless families growing up out of our former parking lot, the construction of which was ending as this book was being written. It is also my pleasure to thank my editor, Milton Brasher-Cunningham; publisher, Nancy Bryan, who so kindly encouraged me when in the midst of a difficult season in my life; and John Turnbull, whose polish eased your reading of the work, making me seem a better author than I am. Thanks also to Ryan Masteller of Church Publishing and to the editor of the first *Fearless* book on annual campaigns, Stephanie Spellers, who lent me courage for the series.

Together, seventy men and women, along with me and others, have transformed philanthropy in our parish church in just four years. It is my great hope that this book will help transform philanthropy in your own church and that, with that transformation, you bless the lives of major donors and those in your towns and cities. This book is for the many helping to make meaning with their money and for the many people whose suffering is reduced by the ministries of churches fully funded by major gifts. Be fearless. Raise major gifts. Make meaning.

A GIVING STORY:
MAUDE AND MEANING-MAKING

When I stopped being attached to my fears, something like freedom blossomed inside me and I relaxed. I had never asked for money before. It intimidated and embarrassed me. I had never really asked for much more than a hundred dollars from a few close friends for sponsorship in a marathon or for a breast-cancer walk. Maude changed all that. Maude and God.

One day I asked for twenty thousand dollars from someone I thought perhaps unable to make such a large gift over five years to a capital campaign; she ended the meeting by pledging one hundred thousand dollars over the five years. Never again did I prejudge a person's willingness and capacity to make a major gift, and never again was I tempted to short-circuit the meaning-making a donor has in mind. She was wealthy precisely because she did not look or seem wealthy. She was generous precisely because she had meaning she wanted to make in honor of the life she lived with her husband and that they lived with the YMCA in their town.

I know you might be afraid of asking for major gifts. I hope this book eases those fears. I know people want to make meaning with their philanthropy. I hope this book emboldens you and channels your efforts efficiently and effectively to ask for and receive major gifts. You do not need expensive campaign counsel. You often do not need fundraising professionals; in fact, they can get in the way. You just need a strong cup of tea, some extra sugar, a scone, and this book. You can do this. Your clergy can do this. Your vestry can do this.

After three years of planning, the capital campaign for the YMCA of Metro Richmond, Virginia, was underway. I was young—in my late twenties, with more hair and fewer love handles—and appropriately terrified as the YMCA's new vice-president. We had twelve branches in Richmond area, and all of them had some stake in the campaign to renovate buildings and build new ones. Though I had been a fundraiser for a few years, I had never personally asked for a major gift.

The job of vice-president had been given to me by a man who remains a dear friend, Journey Johnson, the chief executive officer of the YMCA in

Richmond. A tall, handsome man with the kindness and honesty of a saint and the brain of a strategist, Journey had taken a chance on me. A big one. I had never raised major gifts, but he saw my ability to connect with people and he felt that was all I needed—that, and passion for the YMCA and its mission of personal wellness and what wellness could accomplish in families and towns. I had the ability to connect quickly and easily with people, and I had a deep passion for human wellness. I can see now that I was trying anything I could to avoid a clear call to ordained ministry, figuring that God would not argue with the YMCA and a career in development. God did not argue. God waited. God has lots of time.

Journey was enthusiastic and a YMCA leader through and through. If you failed, he took your hand and gently discussed a better way for next time. If you succeeded, he was full of praise. He was a great leader and a man of deep and abiding faith. I wanted to please him.

We met together as I prepared to ask for my first major gift for one of our branches in south Richmond. The request was for twenty thousand dollars to be paid over five years: four thousand dollars per year. Journey always called me "Sir Charles" because of the slight British accent I inherited from my mother, and because I liked to dress in tweed. I told him I was terrified to ask Maude Pardon for the money, and he said, "Sir Charles, you can do this. She loves you, and you love her. She wants to give this gift to honor her husband's founding of that YMCA. Help her to make meaning with her money, her love of the YMCA, her town, and her husband's memory."

When he said, "make meaning," I was like one of those cartoon characters who gets struck in the head with a big gong—a great idea—complete with vibration lines all around their body. In that moment, my life changed a bit. I could see that asking for this gift was a pastoral ministry as much as it was fundraising. I was not yet ordained, but I was engaging in ministry— the ministry of helping people to make meaning out of their passions and their money.

Journey said, "You can do this, Sir Charles. Just be yourself, sit and talk, and then ask for the gift. She is ready to be asked. She has done all the work of planning this campaign for three years. She is ready; in fact, she is anxious to kick off this campaign in her YMCA. So help her. Do you think she could give twenty thousand dollars?"

I said I thought she could.

"Then go," he said, "pray outside her house, and then sit in her living room and ask." He then said the second wonderful thing: "What's the worst thing that can happen?"

He was right. She had founded that YMCA branch with her husband in their basement around a card table with three other town leaders. She had gone there to walk and lift weights for dozens of years and sat on every committee they had. She was the grandmother of that YMCA, cherished and adored by the staff and community who frequented it. She had been the first person, six years previous, with whom we discussed a capital campaign. She had been involved in all the campaign planning. She was ready to be asked. What was the worst that could happen?

I drove to her home and sat in her living room on a couch with a lace headrest. The house was simple—a few pieces of furniture and lots of photos of her family. She smiled at me the way my grandmother used to, with utter joy in my being there. When she picked a bit of fluff from my blazer, I was worried she might lick her thumb and remove a smudge from my cheek or tamp down my cowlick.

"So, here we are. Would you like some coconut cake and milk? I made it for you," she said with a Miss Marple–like combination of sweetness and razor-sharp intelligence. She was a little old lady from central casting, with a fragile frame and a sweater draped over her shoulders. I agreed to the cake with gratitude (I love coconut cake), and she bustled off to the kitchen while I sat in her small living room where the light made shafts in the dusty air. While she worked in the kitchen, I tumbled into a fear storm. "What if she's not able to make a major gift?" I thought to myself. "What if her children expect an inheritance, or need the inheritance for their credit-card debt?" The questions began to stack up in my mind: What if she has no pension, or if her retirement planning was not very good? What if she wants my boss, Journey, to be the one asking? He was the CEO after all. What if she needs to be asked by someone who is also giving twenty thousand dollars? I was giving only twelve thousand dollars over five years. For a guy in his late twenties, I was making a sacrifice, but it did not match what I was asking her to do.

My legs went weak, and my palms became sweaty. A knot formed in my stomach, and I began to doubt my ability to ask for this first major gift. I even wondered if I should just make this a social call and not even try. She bustled in with cake and milk, making my hasty escape impossible and saying, "So, let's talk about my gift to the campaign."

I swear on a stack of Bibles and YMCA fitness manuals that she said that because she thought I was terrified. As an old lady with lots of human experience, she saw my fear and immediately set about to make me feel at ease and to set the conversation in motion. My doubts stayed with me, but the fear left. The cake was amazing. The milk was cold. Her smile was warm. So I launched in.

I did as I had been taught by my mentors at the YMCA and reminded Maude of the long history of their founding of the YMCA in our town. I recapped the previous six years of planning for the capital campaign into which we were now stepping at long last. We laughed about the first day we saw the date of the capital campaign and had both agreed that six years of planning seemed like an eternity. Yet, here we were launching the campaign. We agreed that we had needed very bit of that long runway to imagine possibilities, assemble donor prospect lists, host conversations, make plans for new buildings, involve donors in editing plans and, finally, to lay out the $12.4 million campaign for fourteen YMCAs—all of which had brought us to this moment, filled as it was with cake and milk, to talk about the first major gift for the first branch.

There was a long silence, and Maude seemed to tear up. She was reliving so many years as we, together, told the story of how we both had ended up there in her living room that sunny spring day. I let the silence hang in the air like incense after a festal liturgy. She was hard at work appreciating the wonderful story we had just told each other, drinking deep of those founding days in her basement with its bare light bulbs and linoleum floors. She was remembering her husband and his early vision of the YMCA in their small town. She was re-membering—busy knitting together those memories and making meaning of them while I kept eating my cake.

Suddenly she lifted her chin and beamed at me. "We're ready aren't we?" she said with great enthusiasm. Once again, I felt the clear signs of panic. My heart began to race, my palms sweated a second salty layer. My face flushed; my mouth went dry despite the dulcet strains of coconut and butter. I had interpreted her comment, "We're ready, aren't we?" to mean, "We are ready for you to ask me for a major gift, and I am ready to decide that you are an incompetent idiot for asking me for too much money." But that is not what she meant. I made that up because I was afraid of asking for the gift. We create these stories and we weave them around reality like a scarf around a neck—or a noose—to make our fears feel justified. My inner voice said: "See Charles? I told you. She bakes a great cake and is a nice lady, but she's on to you. When you ask, she will be furious and then you will be fired and then you will be poor and then you will be homeless and die horribly in a gutter." It is amazing how fear works on us, especially when we are asking for money.

But, in blurting out, "We're ready, aren't we?" after the long silence, she was saying, "We are ready to launch this campaign!" And she continued, "It is time to launch this campaign. We have all worked so hard to get to this day. Thank you for helping the process along. My husband would be so proud!"

At this point, she choked up and excused herself by asking if I would like a second piece of cake. Before I could politely decline, she was in the kitchen shouting, "Oh, I am so glad. It is good cake. It's a family recipe from a Good Housekeeping magazine from before you were born."

"Oh, great," I thought. "Now I am an idiot, and I am young and inexperienced. This is not going well."

And yet, it was going very well indeed—for both of us. Maude returned with more cake and more milk and sat closer to me on the couch. She asked again how the cake was, and, with a mouth full, I mumbled that it was stunning (which came out as "shmumung"). She laughed, and my anxiety began to flake off like ice from branches in the afternoon sun. I finished piece number two, cleared my throat, fought a deep desire for a nap, and prayed "Sweet-baby-Jesus, help me to ask this nice lady for twenty thousand dollars." Suddenly, I found courage and went for it.

"Maude," I began tremulously and with no small sugar high, "given our conversation about the long years of preparation and your decades of leadership along with your honorary chairmanship of this campaign at your YMCA, would you give a leadership gift to launch the campaign at the Manchester YMCA that you and your husband founded downstairs forty years ago?"

Her YMCA was working to raise nine hundred thousand dollars. I was going to ask for twenty thousand—and hoped for four other gifts of that size to launch momentum. "Would you make a pledge of TWEN-TY-THOU-S-AND-DO-LLAR-S, paid over five years to launch this campaign?" I remember pronouncing the words "twenty thousand dollars" like an American speaking to a French tourist—loudly and slowly with the big lip movements of a gasping trout.

Her eyes got big. "Damn," I thought. "Damn. I blew it. Journey is going to kill me when I get back to the office—unless I first die from diabetic shock. Clearly, I have just insulted her. She was expecting me to ask for two thousand. Oh God, what do I do now?"

She rose to her feet, and I prepared to be asked to leave and never, ever come back. But she said, "Well, yes. I think I can do that. I need to talk this over with my children, but they are all adults and have good careers of their own. They do not need my money." She looked at me and said, "Charles, you need just one more small piece of cake."

I didn't, really, but I was so relieved that I shook my head up and down at the possibility of her making the leadership gift—which she interpreted as my wanting a third piece. Did I mention that each piece weighed about ten pounds? She disappeared into the kitchen.

"Well," I thought, "it looks like I did okay. I may not lose my job today. And I won't need to eat until Pentecost."

She came back with the third piece of coconut cake and another glass of milk. My current high blood sugar almost thirty years later probably stems from that one afternoon on that green couch. She sat next to me and said, "I have been thinking about this request you have made. Twenty thousand dollars over five years. That's a lot of money, but my husband would have been proud to make this gift and so am I." She paused. "Yes, Charles. I will make this pledge. Thank you. Thank you for asking and for helping me to figure this out."

Thank you? Seriously? Thank you? She was thanking me? I couldn't believe it. I just asked for and received my first major gift. Twenty thousand dollars. I had a 100 percent success rate so far. Hurray for me. I could hear "We Are the Champions" playing in my mind. I was bowing to roaring crowds. I could see myself accepting the YMCA award for best fundraiser of the millennium. Then I heard something which pulled me out of my narcissistic reverie.

"So, Sweetie," she said, "Why don't I just give you the first twenty thousand now in a check. Then I can pay the other twenty-thousand-dollar payments over the next four years and the gift will be paid for."

I think I stopped breathing. I definitely saw my right hand trembling.

Mrs. Purdon looked at me like I was a small child that had just written my first word with the "E" written backwards—proud, with a soupçon of compassion.

"Yes," she said with a hand on my knee, "one hundred thousand dollars, paid twenty thousand per year for five years, will be a wonderful way to honor our life with the YMCA. Will there be a plaque or something?"

I was expecting to annoy her by asking for twenty thousand dollars, and she had been planning on a much larger gift. She adjusted my expectations kindly, gently, so as not to make me feel like the moron I considered myself to be. We went on to discuss the terms of the gift—a named room for her husband, his image on the plaque, and a short story about the founding in the basement. We even talked about using a piece of the basement linoleum floor mounted on the plaque to show where the YMCA was founded.

As I left her home, I took another look around. The light had shifted; there were deeper rays now, at a longer slant. Her furniture could not have been worth more than five thousand dollars— a few chairs, a table, and end table. She lived simply. She had reused her tea bag while I ate her cake. She had money not because she was wealthy. She had money because she lived simply and saved so that she could do something with it that made meaning of the sixty-year marriage to a man who loved his YMCA and raised his family in it.

At the door, she paused. "Thank you," she said with wet eyes. My eyes were wet, too. "Thank you for eating all that cake. I was as nervous as you were. I needed the time to think about it all. I feel so happy that I can make this pledge. It will be a very powerful tool when I start asking my friends for pledges to this campaign. And the gift will help me to make meaning—to make something I want to make. It will help me to leave something good behind for a community that has loved me and my family for so long."

I remember climbing into my car and loosening my belt, full of gratitude for a woman who really understood what was important in life. On the way back to the office, I called Journey on one of those massive car phones from the late 1980s. We virtually high-fived each other, not because we had just raised one hundred thousand dollars and secured the leadership gift that would secure the rest of the branch's campaign. We were elated because we had helped Maude to make meaning; as a side benefit, we had secured a new YMCA gym for kids who needed one.

The story is not over. I am told by the now-retired YMCA branch executive director that people still talk about the day Maude gave her pledge. For years she told the story of how her YMCA was founded in her basement on that grey linoleum. Then she would tell the story of that day we—well, I—ate cake and began the capital campaign with her pledge. She called it her "hundred-thousand-dollar hug."

There are many other wonderful stories like this one. Each chapter begins with one. Be inspired by them. You can do this. And you must, because these donors want and need your help to make these major gifts—to make meaning with their money. The process outlined in this book will help you to ask for a major gift carefully, respectfully, and based in a real relationship and in the real desires of the donor to make a major gift.

This is beautiful work. Once you help to midwife your first major gift, you will wonder what all the fuss was about. Do not be afraid. All manner of things shall be well.

CHAPTER 1

••

The Meaning
of Major Gifts

What Is a Major Gift?

When a member of the congregation makes an annual pledge, they are supporting the ongoing work of the church: keeping the lights on, the building
heated, the ministry to the poor and marginalized accomplished, the clergy
paid, the grass mowed, the walls painted, hymnals in the pew racks, and
coffee in the kitchen.

A major gift, on the other hand, goes beyond annual pledge support.
Year after year, pledge campaign after pledge campaign, annual budget after
annual budget, the annual offerings of members of the congregation invest
in the ongoing ministry and mission of the church. The careful stewarding
of those pledges provides a runway for the possible request of a major gift:
something beyond our regular giving.

A major gift is money given for a special project above the annual pledge. It
might be two thousand dollars for much-needed new carpet, or ten thousand
dollars to pay for a new ministry the church feels called to pursue. It could be
one hundred thousand dollars for a new organ, or a gift of stock to the church
endowment fund. The question of whether the gift is "major" has more to do
with the capacity of the donor—a donor might feel that their $220 special gift
is "major" if they are on a low fixed income. And indeed it is—to them. But
for the purposes of managing a church, it is essential to delineate an "average"
major gift, and that is usually one, in our economy, of five figures.

My working definition of a major gift is any gift above a pledge. It usually represents 5 percent or more of the donor's annual income. Sometimes
a major gift is a gift-in-kind, such as a new grand piano, or new carpet-

ing made possible by a member of the congregation who owns a carpeting company; however, it is best to keep gifts in cash unless you want the "gift in kind" and you would otherwise have budgeted for the gift item. Perhaps the simplest definition is to say a major gift is defined as a major gift by the donor. Usually, major gifts fall into one of three categories:

Annual pledge campaign: In any pledge campaign, there will be "major pledged gifts" that are larger than the average; still, to the donor, these will simply form part of an annual pledge, made as part of a pledge-campaign challenge effort to reach a fundraising goal. Some major gifts come as pledges to the church simply because they are large or because they come from major or "deeply committed" donors. These should be asked for in the pledge campaign but carefully, as major annual gifts.

Major/capital: These are large gifts, the subject of this book, made to a meaning-making major-gifts program or to a capital campaign. They are five to twenty times the amount of money normally pledged to the annual stewardship of finances campaign.

Planned: These are gifts made with planned giving tools (a will, a Charitable Remainder Trust, etc.) and that are bequests to a church after death made through an estate or simple will-inclusion. A gift can be made during life using a trust tool. Always consider your "planned giving members and prospects" to be "major donor prospects." Most of us give our biggest major gift at our death, even those who lived within modest budgets throughout most of their lifetimes.

Most major gifts, as stated above, are five to twenty times larger than the normal annual pledge. They are generally made in response to a capital campaign, a special need, a major-gifts needs menu (a wish list) produced by the church, or as part of an estate plan. In asking for major gifts, one assumes the expectation of bounty rather than scarcity. Churches tend not to receive major gifts because churches don't ask for major gifts—not because major gifts do not exist in the parish. Every pledger, and every non-pledger, is a prospective major-gift giver. The only way to know who is or is not a prospect for a major gift is to do the work of "qualification" and discernment, which we discuss later.

Created in the Image of a Generous God

How we come at the topic of major gifts is important. Before we get too far in this conversation, we need to realize that what we are doing is spiritual work with logistical implications, not the other way around.

I have a niece who loves the planet. She loves nature and Jesus, and she works as an environmental scientist in Virginia. I have given her some gifts over the years that have run the gamut between successful and dismal failure. She loved the scarves. She loved the baked goods. The pin made out of a real butterfly wing, however, was not a hit. Recently I gave her Mary Oliver's new book *Upstream*, a series of meditations on the land and wildlife around Oliver's home. It would be a big hit, I knew, because Lara was placed on this earth—was called—to care for it, to lobby for it, to protect it. God made her to care for our planet.

Just as Lara was designed to care for the environment, you and I were designed to give some of what we have away. We were designed for it the way my fountain pen was designed to leave ink on a page, to leave beautiful lines of azure blue ink on thick, ivory stationery. And all humans—*all humans*—were made in the image of a generous God: a God who loves, a God who creates, and a God who gives extravagantly. God gives. God creates. God loves. We, who are made in God's image, are designed to do those same three things: give, create, love.

What I love—I mean really love—about raising major gifts in churches and nonprofits is that people want to give, and I get to help them do so. It is truly magical work. When we raise major gifts in church, we are simultaneously helping people do what they were designed to do as people created in God's image, as well as helping them to experience the joy in giving part of themselves away as members of the Body of Christ. At the same time, we are helping the church that benefits from the gift. Can you see how theologically economical this work is? Through a series of conversations ending in a specific request for funding, we can help both the donor and the church become more of who God intended them to be. There are very few win-win scenarios left in life, but this is one of them. Each time you and I effectively ask for and raise a major gift, we are blessing both the giver and the receiver, as well as ourselves. In short, this is a ministry of midwifery. We are midwives—attendants or servants—to a process. This work is a great honor and, as some would say, good karma.

The Meaning-Making Mandorla

When I was raising money for nonprofits in the 1980s and 1990s, we would have a major capital campaign every ten years or so. It was that way in many churches, too. While I worked for the YMCA, I was also president of the Richmond Region of Episcopal Churches. I founded the Stewardship Institute to train churches in the Diocese of Virginia in effective financial development. We did good work together. But today, nonprofits are more likely

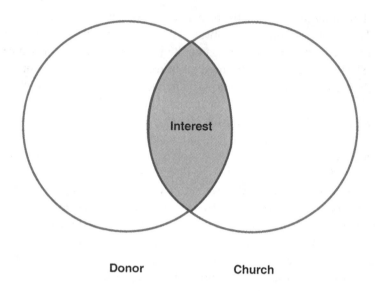

Donor   Church

to have major-gifts programs rather than capital campaigns—a transition most churches have not made.

And that is what this book is about: how can churches begin and maintain ongoing major-gifts programs that emphasize meaning-making, focusing on the donor's need to give rather than simply focusing on the needs of the institution to receive? In this way, we make a list of major-gifts needs (like a wish list) and then simply publicize it so that, at any time, this year or next, three years from now, or tomorrow a person desiring to buy something on the list may do so. If you do this work right, you are always in a major-gifts fundraising mode and always encouraging stewardship in the hearts of people which responds to that fundraising. The church does fundraising, and the church teaches stewardship. The people do stewardship, and they practice giving.

There is still a place for the occasional capital campaign, but, major gifts, asked for and received year-round, grow out of intentional conversations at the intersection of a person's need to make meaning out of their money and the church's needs for special funding. Imagine two circles. In one, we have a donor's interests: Mary Smith, let's say, has a passion for gardening, her church, health care (her husband died prematurely of a heart attack), and reaching out to those experiencing homelessness. In the second circle, we have her church, which has a list of needs generated by its mission. Let's add another wrinkle: Mary is concerned about where she and her husband will be buried. The church does not have a specific ministry to those experiencing homelessness, but they do have plans for a columbarium with a common grave in the center of a beautiful garden in the church's courtyard. Mary's "mission" overlaps with the "mission" of the church. Three things she loves (her church, gardens, and a columbarium) create an opportunity for a major gift to her church in a mandorla (see figure on page 12), the almond shape caused by the intersection of the two circles. This word *mandorla* is the word from which we get the word *almond*.

In a different scenario, Ms. Johnson has a deep commitment to those experiencing homelessness. Her granddaughter is mentally unwell and suffers in homelessness from time to time, because she has a hard time holding a job. Her church is hoping to begin a ministry to the homeless and to offer hot meals during the winter, but they need to renovate their kitchen to do so. Ms. Johnson's circle of mission overlaps with the circle of her church and they, quite wisely, involve her in the plans for the new kitchen and ask her for a major gift to help fund it. The shared mandorla, made by the overlapping circles of meaning-making, is where her willingness to give and the church's desire to receive exist.

We Have Enough, We Need to Give

Most of us have enough money to be able to give some of it away. Often, the issue is not our ability to give, but our reason for choosing to do so. For a single mother with three children and three modest jobs paying less than the minimum wage, a gift of a hundred dollars might be a massive decision, but she might choose to do so if she found meaning in what that hundred dollars would do for her children. A person of greater means, on the other hand, might be able to give a million dollars more easily, in terms of their comfort and security, but they too are looking to make meaning out of their offering. At the heart of making-meaning, our giving exhibits the truth that we, as those created in God's image, have an inherent spirit of generosity. But we need a bit of help, and so the church needs to do the good work of helping.

This book is about providing that help.

When we talk about asking for money, often our anxiety grows with each zero, but that is just a mental construct. Asking a ten-year-old for ten dollars is not so different than asking a billionaire for a million dollars. The heart of the issue has little to do with our anxiety as the ones who will do the asking. In other words, it is not about you; it is about the donor. Always. Only. If the donor has a capacity combined with an interest to give a major gift, then it is not about the size of the gift, nor about the asker; it is about making meaning for the one giving the money.

Most people in churches don't like the idea of raising money—or asking for it. I was one of those people a few decades ago. I did not want to get that personal with anyone. My parents taught me not to discuss money, sex, or politics with people at church (religion, ironically, was also on that list . . .). The weather? Sure. But not money. So imagine my surprise when, while on a church leadership team, I needed to ask someone for a major gift for my church. The clergy of my church asked me to ask Mrs. Symington to give five thousand dollars for a new baptismal font. She was a member of the committee for church furnishings and had been a part of the design team for the new font. I was tied up like a pretzel—and I was a professional fundraiser. I found it much easier to raise money for the YMCA. That was my job after all. But asking for money in church seemed so personal.

I drove to Mrs. Symington's home from church one day. She welcomed me in her home, and we discussed her two years on the committee. She told me all about her work to have designs drawn up for the new font. She showed me the drawings done by an artist friend of hers. The font had a simple, beautiful wooden frame that held a massive pottery bowl in watery glazes of blues and a pool of violet glass in the bottom. The bowl could be removed for draining and cleaning. It was simple and elegant. She knew I was a potter and asked me if I could make the bowl. I said I would love to, but we would need to have the frame made: a pedestal in mahogany with carved images representing the baptismal vows. I asked her if she would give the five thousand dollars needed to pay for the pedestal, and she was delighted.

"I must say, I thought we would have to do a lot of raffles, bake sales, pot-luck suppers, and yard sales to come up with the money, but sure . . . it is so much easier if I give the money myself," she said. She was bright and cheerful. Then she darkened like a storm cloud sailing in over the sun on a February day. "Water killed her you know," she said looking far away, somewhere past the walls of her home, out into her past.

I froze. Something had shifted in the room. There was a sort of electricity. She welled up in tears, and she said it again: "Water killed her."

Gently, as if I were approaching a fawn in the woods, I asked, "Ms. Symington, water killed who?"

"Whom dear. Water killed whom!"

Working hard not to be annoyed by the poor placement of a lesson in English grammar, I rephrased my question, "Whom did water kill?"

"Much better dear," she said like a Victorian school mistress. Quietly. Like she was trying to distract herself.

"Water killed my Violet. She drowned in a motel pool when she was young." After a short pause, she added, "It had a blue, tile bottom—the pool, I mean. And there was a great oak nearby."

Fighting back tears, I asked, "Mrs. Symington, do you want the baptismal font to be made of oak?"

"Yes, please. Yes, please," she squeaked, and then smiled a bit. Then wept.

She gave the money for the font, and I made the bowl. Two of them, in fact, in case of breakage. She was happy to make this gift, and I was happy to make the bowls. By placing a chunk of glass on the rim at four points, the glass melted down into the bottom of the bowl in the kiln, creating a glassy blue cross on the bowl against a smoky rutile glaze. We remained friends until the day she died. She never said anything more about her daughter's death, and I never asked, but the font was beautiful and the gifts made us happy to give. Something about that gift healed her. She left the church a large bequest for youth ministry. She told me that the gift of the font inspired the inclusion in her will a year later. "I can't take it with me," she had said, sparkling.

When we ask for major gifts, we are asking people to do something they are designed to do, want to do, need to do, and they are called to do. The art of major-gift fundraising is the art of midwifery. The science of major-gift fundraising is the science of process, which we will look at later in this book.

Talking about Money and Membership Growth in Church

We need to cultivate an ongoing conversation about money and membership in the day-to-day life of the church. One reason our churches do not raise money very well is that few of our clergy were taught how to do this work in seminary, which is a great tragedy. Clergy are not taught membership marketing either, and yet each new member is a new heart, a new soul, a new set of volunteer hands and, let's be frank . . . a new pledge. Seminaries teach pastoral care, liturgy, biblical scholarship, preaching, teaching, and other sacramental work. However, most stop short of teaching their students how to raise membership and how to raise money. The problem, of course, is that it does not take long for new clergy to find out that their church needs to raise money and needs to draw in new people. The inability or discomfort of clergy who do not want to, or are not able to, raise money in their churches limits the mission and ministry of the church. It's that simple. Clergy who cannot raise money often become bishops who cannot raise money, which further amplifies the dysfunction and further cripples mission and ministry.

Another reason our churches do not raise money very well is that the subject is often considered taboo. If we are not allowed to talk about it, then we're not going to do it. Satan always succeeds when he keeps a topic in secrecy. It is essential that we change this culture of shame and silence around fundraising in our churches. Very few lay leaders know how to raise money. If you have people in your congregation, a worthy mission, and effective, trustworthy leadership, then you have everything you need to ask for and receive major gifts—but it takes considerable humility, tenacity, compassion, honesty, and intelligence to learn to talk about and raise money in a church. And yet, remember: we were designed for it. Giving is who we are, not just what we do.

The Mission of Major Gifts

It may be tempting to think that your church can't raise major gifts. Perhaps you feel that you don't deserve the money you would be raising, or perhaps you think that you don't have people in your church who can and will give a major gift. I encourage you to reconsider. J. K. Rowling, the author of the Harry Potter children's book series, went from being a single mother on welfare to the wealthiest woman in Britain in just a decade.

We read in scripture of a God who accomplishes amazing things in what seem like impossible situations. Hopefulness is a fruit born of our faith in that God. Indeed, we do need to deserve the money we are raising. We need to carefully curate the conversations that will lead to major gifts, as well as summon up the humility and courage to ask for them. It is beautiful work, because it helps people to give their money to mission in which they want to invest, and it helps churches to fund that mission. A major-gifts program should be an ongoing program (not a campaign) in any church, no matter how small. Even in a church with six people, one of them will usually be able and willing to give a special gift if there is a vision, a need, and a means by which she or he is asked for the gift. Often churches abandon their responsibility to raise major gifts because they are frightened or because they lack the training.

We read in the Gospels that Jesus raised resources for his ministry from the women who followed him along "The Way" (Luke 8:1–3; Mark 15:40–41). I expect that the women watched Jesus love people, heal people, inspire people, and even challenge people to fund that work, so they gave. Perhaps they gave because Jesus asked them for the money. Perhaps they gave simply because they wanted to participate in Jesus' mission and ministry. Regardless of the reason behind the gifts, we know from the Gospels that Jesus raised major gifts from the women who followed him.

You will face resistance at times. There will be people in your congregation, perhaps even people in leadership, whose discomfort about money and fundraising may cause them to resist or even block major-gift work. Do not let them. This is holy work. This is work Jesus did. This is work that helps people feel good about the mission of the church and the meaning they are making out of their money. This is work which enables ministry by providing resources. Do not let fear or the lack of spiritual depth hold the mission and ministry of your church hostage simply because one or two people do not like talking about, or perhaps giving, money.

I often ask clergy, "If a parishioner came to you and said, 'I think that talking about sin is unpleasant. It makes me feel uncomfortable. I want you to stop talking about in our church.'" Would you agree to do so? What if someone came and said, "All this talk of love in our church is getting on my nerves; you need to stop talking about love." Would you do it? The answer to both is, "No." Why, then, would we pull back from talking about money simply because some people do not like the conversation? What I have learned in more than thirty years in church leadership was first taught to me by the rector of the church in which I was a curate in Charlottesville, Virginia. Harold, a priest much like George Herbert, taught me that the congregation sees their clergy as great prophets, when, and only when, the congregation sees their clergy as great pastors. If you love your congregation—if you show up when someone is in pain, or in need of care—then, when it comes time for the prophetic call to discuss money in church, the congregation is more likely to listen because of the trust you have developed in one another. It is that simple. Occasionally, clergy or bishops will ask me to teach them how to be better fundraisers. I politely decline because I am aware that I would first need them to be better clergy. Best just to pray for their flock and move on. On the other hand, *I love* working with able clergy, because they have set the stage to raise great major gifts for their equally great vision.

In like manner, congregations should not let resistance from the clergy, or from powerful leaders in the congregation, hold them back from the good work of major-gift fundraising. If your clergy are not willing to make the time to visit and ask funds from major donor prospects in your congregation, then it may be time to find new leadership. It is just that simple. When Jesus encountered resistance from Peter in their mission, Jesus faced Peter down, calling him "Satan" (which I must admit seems quite harsh), named the resistance out loud in front of the rest of the group, and demanded that they continue on their mission together. Peter fell in line, although that was not the only time Jesus' gentleness failed him. Over and over again, Jesus required that people following him summon up the courage to do difficult things. Jesus then modeled that courage with the ultimate sacrifice.

Some church leaders will be resistant to raising money, because they are insecure about their ability to do so. They may come up with excuses about how little time they have, how busy they are, or how few major donor prospects are available. Do not believe them. Love them, but do not believe them. And, for goodness sake, do not enable them by letting them hold you back. They may need a hug. They may need a sabbatical. They may need a fundraising class, or a scotch. Or a personality makeover. They may need a job description with measurable objectives in fundraising. Give them what they need to be successful, but do not let them resist this work because, if they do—and if you do not do this work—you are failing the donors who want and need to give the money away, and you are failing the people whose lives will be improved and blessed by the mission of your church.

We hope that while reading this book, you will catch a vision for how rich the harvest is and, yet, how few the laborers. The truth is that we only have a couple of decades left in which the Great Generation and the Silent Generation will be able and willing to give major and planned gifts to their churches. The older Baby Boomers will have some willingness to make major gifts, but they will not give the way their parents and grandparents gave. So we really have quite a short time line—less than one full generation (thirty years)—to get this work done and done well. Most of what we can raise to secure our church's mission will be raised in the next fifteen years. Yes. I said *fifteen years*. But the good news is that this is not hard work. In fact, this is wonderful, heartwarming work.

Anyone called to church leadership has imbedded into their leadership calling this second calling: a call to ask for money. Like the call to pray, to heal, to preach, and to companion, the call to ask for money in the funding of our mission is integral to our work. Yes, some people are going to be better at it than others, and some will enjoy the process more than others, but nobody in church leadership in this millennium is able to decline this work. To abandon this part of your mission and ministry is to commit two acts of great relational and missional violence.

First, when we avoid major-gifts work we abandon the people of our churches to the messaging of our culture. Advertising is aggressive, bright, compelling and occasionally manipulative. "Buy this, you need that, purchase this on sale, you are ugly without that, you are not successful without this . . ." The people of our churches are beaten about by every wind of advertising in a persistent hurricane of marketing. Our message is different. Our message says, "What meaning do you want to make in this life—this one, precious, wonderful, painful, marvelous life of yours? What meaning do you want to make with your money? How can the mission of our church meet your meaning-making? How can we partner to make the world a better place by making the church able to better serve the poor and the marginalized?"

Second, when we avoid major-gifts work, we also abandon our mission to the confines of our budget. That does not seem to be the way Jesus worked. Remember the feeding of the five thousand? They thought they had no food; they knew they had a bunch of hungry people. They asked Jesus, and he said, "You feed them." As they proceeded to do so, the food appeared and appeared and appeared. In one Gospel, even soft grass appeared in the wilderness so they would have a place to sit. God is all about bounty. God also seems intent on co-creativity. God's vision for our churches is not that we squeak by with light bills barely paid, cheap toilet paper, and clergy on quarter-salaries. God's vision is that our churches change the world as way stations for the workers in the vineyard. If you are like me, you may wonder why we spend billions on war machinery and yet see churches closing. Though it may feel like there is not much we can do to change those systems, we can raise money for mission and thus heal the world through well-funded churches worthy of a Savior who died that we might live.

This is gorgeous work. It is beautiful to ask people to fund mission and ministry. Yes, some people will not be able to give the major gift we ask of them. When that happens, we can ask ourselves if we asked too soon, or if we were careless when considering the match between donor and project, or if we were recklessly overoptimistic about what they could give. But these are all forgivable. We are called to do our best. And, when the right person has been asked for the right gift by the right person, something beautiful happens. For the donor. For the mission. Something breathtakingly beautiful. Make that beauty happen. Learn this work. Raise major gifts. Heal the world.

How to Get People Comfortable with Asking for Major Gifts in Your Church

- Host some potlucks in the homes of congregants and have conversations about fundraising and major-gifts work. Get their input.
- Let people talk about their fears. Most people simply want to be heard. Listen to them. This does not mean that simply because they are afraid, you do not do this work. By listening to them, you will soften resistance.
- Use the free exercises, teaching videos, and document models found at fearlesschurchfundraising.com to encourage people to name and discuss their fears about money. There's no need to reinvent the wheel.
- Ask people, "Where in your life have money and fear intersected?" Discuss that mandorla, that almond-shaped space of money and fear.
- As part of a sermon, in small groups, or in adult formation, ask members of your congregation to imagine what your church could accomplish with a 100 percent increase in funding; this increase could come from improved stewardship by the congregation and improved fundraising by the church. Get them to write their dreams down. Scriptures tell us that without a vision the people perish. Scripture also tells us to write the vision. If people in your congregation have a vision for greater mission and ministry, and if they can write it down so they can see it, and if they can discuss their vision with each other, excitement will grow, enthusiasm will deepen, and resistance to major-gift fundraising will melt away.
- Create a small advisory committee (two or three trusted people) who can develop a list equal to 10 percent of the active members in your congregation from whom major gifts could be raised.
- Make sure that major-gifts goals are included in every annual strategic plan and that these goals are measurable. If your clergy or key lay leaders are asking for major gifts, then define how many visits and how many requests are expected each month. What gets measured gets done.

What to Look for in a Leader for Major or Planned Giving

1. Choose a person who is beloved by the congregation, has been active for a very long time, and is well-known to have given a major gift under the right circumstances.
2. Recruit only people who are absolutely trustworthy and who are well-known for their integrity, philanthropy, gentleness, and kindness.
3. If possible, the major-gifts leader should be someone who has remembered the church in their will and who is a major-gift donor.
4. Recruit people who do what they say they will do. Others will imitate them and be motivated.
5. Recruit people who have and can clearly articulate a spiritual practice that is daily or at least regular (prayer, study, mindfulness.)
6. Recruit people who regularly attend weekly worship.

A Worksheet on Feelings about Asking for Money

Answer the following questions as quickly and honestly as you can:

1. How do you feel about asking for a gift equal to or greater than your annual salary?
2. In what way does it help to know that Jesus asked for major gifts from the women who followed him?
3. What most frightens you when you think of asking for a major gift, assuming that all of the proper steps have been followed, the donor has been properly rated and cultivated, and they are ready to be asked for this gift, about which they are excited and that they want to give?
4. What will it feel like to ask for a major gift and receive that gift?
5. What will it feel like to ask for a major gift and not receive the gift?
6. What anger do you hold against wealthy people?
7. It would be normal for you to experience indignation if you ask for a gift from a wealthy person who declines. How might you process that anger?
8. Imagine that you have asked for a gift for something you truly care about. Imagine that you yourself have made major gifts to this project. And then imagine that the major donor gives you twice as much of a philanthropic investment as you had hoped. How does this feel? Imagine that you are raising money for a project that will ease the suffering of human beings. How does it feel to raise that kind of money, and, having done so, how does it feel to ease human suffering?

QUICK-START SUGGESTIONS

Getting started with a few suggestions in each chapter will be essential to combating fear and resistance. If you read this book and find it intriguing but do not act on it, then this book runs the risk of being added to the shelves of books, class notes, and conference handouts that just sit there staring at you like a school mistress over wire-rimmed glasses. The best thing you can do when beginning something new, regardless if you are a small church or a massive one getting started with a major-gifts program, is to get going immediately. This section of each chapter will help you do just that. In time, you can go back and add some of the other ideas from each chapter, but I will offer a few tasks in order to help you build a major-gifts program in your church, diocese or judicatory office, or nonprofit agency.

Perhaps you have a tinge of excitement and want to get started. Here are a few quick-start suggestions:

1. Form a study group as you read this book and meet monthly over a wonderful dinner at each other's homes to discuss how this book might inform your ministry of meaning-making through major-gift philanthropy.
2. Make setting up a major-gift program a subject of your prayers. With all due respect to the gnosticism and dualism that imply that money is worldly, unholy, and not of God, I suggest that God would like to hear your hopes and fears about this work.
3. Identify one small thing that you would like to ask someone to give to some worthy cause. Make that gift yourself. Then speak to that person and ask them to give as well. Enjoy a small and early success. Then discuss that success with people whom you hope to engage in this mission of helping people make meaning of their money.
4. Work with your clergy to secure four of the fifty-two weeks of sermons specifically to discuss money and giving from the pulpit. Do the same in four adult forums. Stewardship emerges from good formation. Hold the clergy accountable to include money in preaching and teaching. Make this work part of their evaluation or mutual ministry review.

STUDY QUESTIONS

Each chapter in this book offers study questions so that you or a group may dig deeply into the material and work with it. When leading a study or discussion on chapter one, you will want to begin gently. Do not underestimate the level of fear that exists around these subjects for many members of your congregation. The leader of this discussion needs to be a very "well" human: balanced, kind, soft-spoken, clear-minded, and every bit as much a pastor as a prophet.

Go slowly at first, and if this is a group study (i.e., a committee or commission preparing for its work in major and/or planned gifts), allow lots of time for people to express their fears and concerns openly. That conversation is healing. Do not give over too much time to ranting and complaining, which will be a temptation since this subject touches issues of power. When that happens, we humans tend to rise up to dominate or reduce ourselves so as to be a victim. Allow neither. Simply hold the space you need to hold while your leaders get their heads around these tasks and, thus, reduce their fears of them. If there are heated or fear-based conversations, stop and hold the silence for a period of prayer. God will soothe. Then begin again.

Here are some possible study/discussion questions for chapter one:

1. What can we do, as a church, that will be made possible by major gifts to our mission? What possibilities excite you?
2. What transformation can a major gift make for our church? How do we bless people by helping them grapple with generosity and philanthropy?
3. How do you see major-gifts financial development and stewardship in our church to be a mission and ministry?
4. What do you feel, in your gut, about asking for a major gift? How might you find help and support in this work?
5. What are you afraid of when it comes to your own work around major gifts?
6. What does scripture, prayer, community, and liturgy do to assist and strengthen you in this essential work of mission?
7. How can major gifts help people in our church make meaning with their money?
8. How is asking for a major gift like building any other relationship? When you want a friend, you learn things about that person: what they like, their interests, hobbies, and passions. How can you dial

down the drama of asking for major gift and simply see it as getting to know someone, and helping them do something they want to do?

9. What kinds of projects in your church could you imagine worthy of asking for major gift? Make a list. Use classic discernment techniques by crossing out unworthy things and highlighting your favorite things to which people could give.

10. Spend some time with the story in Mark's Gospel in which Jesus encounters the rich young ruler (10:17–22). Use *Lectio Divina* and try to imagine the scene in every detail. What do you notice in your imagination? What are the messages on people's faces? Who is nearby? What is the sunlight like? What do you hear them saying? How does the scene make you feel?

11. Look hard at, or discuss, your annual pledge campaign. (If you are not sure what one should look like, consider reading my first book, *Fearless Church Fundraising,* or going to the website of the same name at fearlesschurchfundraising.com.) If you send out a letter in the fall, and then hope for the best, you don't even have an annual pledge campaign. Look hard at what you have and ask if it is robust enough to generate the money you need for your mission and to generate a few major-gift donors.

PRAYERS

A Prayer to Begin the Work of a Major-Gifts Ministry

Lord God, you brooded over creation and spoke the world into being. You spoke your own meaning-making in creation, then again, throughout the scriptures, and then again when you spoke yourself into flesh. Give us compassion for our fears as we consider asking for major gifts. Help us to see that this work is part of the co-creativity into which you invite us. Give us compassion for people who want to make meaning with major gifts and who need help to give the money away. Finally, Lord, give us the grace and humility to deserve the money we seek. When we ask and receive "no" as the answer, bind our wounds and remind us that "no" is just "no for now." Encourage us through your Holy Spirit to get up, dust ourselves off, and get back to work with joy. *Amen.*

A GIVING STORY: HELEN AND BILL—
PEOPLE LEADING THE WAY

Helen and Bill, two members of my congregation, called to ask for an appointment to speak with me. In our society, when parishioners call the church to speak to the minister, something must be up. I was prepared for any number of pastoral issues. A husband and wife were asking for the appointment, so I assumed marital problems or perhaps a health diagnosis. My morning prayers included Helen and Bill, and I asked God to guide me into effective and compassionate pastoral care. We sat in a beautiful room in the far corner of the church building with overstuffed chairs, tall bookcases, and a long couch that, I will admit, on long days occasionally became a place for a short nap with Kai, my dog.

Helen and Bill began to tell me they wanted to make a major gift to the church. They had some ideas. As they began to list their ideas, I had to recalibrate my expectations of the meeting. Rarely do people make an appointment with clergy to ask to make a major gift.

They sort of looked like each other, as happily married couples do after a lifetime together. Helen sat up straight, hands folded on her lap, like a teacher or governess, with a slight twinkle in her eye that betrayed mild mischief and deep intelligence. Bill was every bit the academic. A university president for decades, he had the kind face of someone who had achieved success not by climbing, but by simply being a great teacher, fundraiser, and scholar. He had raised more than eighty million dollars in his career and had sat with many major donors, asking them for major gifts enabling students to learn and become good, kind, honest leaders. And now they sat with me, offering a major gift of their own.

Now I admit that this is rare. Most of the time, a clergyperson or layperson will have to work hard even to get a first visit with a possible major donor. Then they will have to establish a series of meetings to further define what the donor wants to accomplish and further involve them in that to which they would like to give. Finally, one summons courage, goes to their home, and asks for a major gift, having made many visits to establish relationship and determine their interests—their meaning-making. Not so with Bill and Helen. They came to me. They had the money they wanted to give away, and they knew they wanted to give it to the church. I remember feeling grateful that there were people like them on the planet and that I got to speak with them. They lived very simply, a dozen pieces of furniture, a teapot, some books.

We recently had a very large and expensive Bible on display at the cathedral—hand-illuminated prior to its printing. It was beautiful. Because Bill had been scholar of medieval texts, a gift toward this Bible made some sense to him. It was part of his meaning-making. Helen resonated with the idea. We had long sought a major donor to purchase the Saint John's Bible—an illustrated, calligraphic text to use as a teaching and liturgy tool, a purchase that our leadership had discerned for our parish and that was on our meaning-making major-gifts list, publicized to our parish as one of a couple dozen items. Brochures of the wish list were placed all over the church. People were deeply aware of the list. But the Stewardship Commission's Major-Gifts Advisory Committee had other ideas that needed funding as well. We wanted a learning garden, but most of those funds had been raised. The parish also needed some capital renovations, but that was not the kind of gift Bill and Helen had in mind.

Helen leaned forward and asked about the annual pledge campaign. I explained it was well-planned and would launch in a few weeks. I also told them our biggest donor had moved out of town, and the campaign would be more difficult this year. Bill and Helen asked, with the kindness of parents, if we would reach our pledge goal, and if I would be okay. We were, after all, coming to the end of a long transition between clergy leadership, and morale was a bit low. We were also heading into a divisive presidential election, which I knew would distract the congregation as their inboxes became flooded with election material that could push our annual pledge campaign materials out of sight.

Bill and Helen decided to make a large, pace-setting leadership gift as the first pledge of the annual pledge campaign. It was a bold move, unglamorous, kind—like them. Bill explained that if the congregation heard that one of its member families had increased its annual pledge by tenfold, it might inspire others to do likewise. We were making the bold move for the first time of asking our congregation to do the math. We were asking them to raise their pledges this year by one percent of their annual incomes. It was a bold move, but with a deficit of almost one-third of our budget, we needed to get that deficit down to zero. In the end, that one gift inspired a 25 percent increase in the pledge campaign that year. It worked.

I accepted their major gift, which was also an annual pledge, because

I knew that their courage would inspire other families to increase their pledges. Pledges across the board increased substantially because Bill and Helen allowed us to tell the story of their decision to substantially increase theirs.

As we were closing the meeting, Bill leaned over and said, "Charles, I have been a fundraiser for most of my career. I am retired now and would be glad to help you to raise money in this church—especially planned and major gifts."

I do not often show emotion when providing pastoral care. And, in a way, this was pastoral care, because this couple wanted and needed to make meaning with their money. After our meeting, Bill and I got together frequently to discuss philanthropy in our church. I asked him to lead our planned giving, since we both knew it would be through the planned gifts of the next fifteen years that we would be able to secure the financial future and stability of our church. He agreed to the work.

A few weeks later, Helen came to church, leaving Bill at home reading, because he was not feeling well. While she was at church, Bill died in his reading chair with a book on his lap. As I cared for Helen in her grief and shock, I had to find ways to care for myself because I, too, was in deep grief at the loss of a man who had become like a father to me and with whom I had made so many exciting plans for the future of philanthropy in our church. That was, and may always be, one of the most painful funerals over which I have ever presided. I still miss Bill.

A few months later, as Christmas neared and the searing pain of Bill's death had softened a bit, Helen was able to make a slight smile. I had worked hard, under difficult circumstances, to reach the pledge-campaign goal; it had gone well, in part, because of Helen and Bill's gift. But we still had a ways to go, and it was two days before Christmas. The presidential election was over, but its aftermath was just beginning. I had no idea how to raise the final 8 percent of the budget.

I was honest with the church, thanking them for the many increased pledges, but admitting that we were still not quite at our goal and that we would have to surpass our goal if we were to have any chance at closing the budget gap and eradicating the deficit. One faithful member of the congregation called me to say she was willing to make a one-time major gift, which amounted to 10 percent of what we still needed to raise. I asked if she would make it a challenge grant and let me try to find three other families to each match her gift so that the four gifts would challenge the rest of the congregation to match them.

Two days before Christmas, I piled into my car with that one major gift and only a few hours to find three more. I drove a few blocks away and was welcomed into the home of another generous woman whose simplicity of life and depth of spirituality indicated that she might give the second challenge gift. Over sherry and lemon squares, cashews and tea, she made the second challenge pledge.

Who would be my third visit? Helen. I would go and ask Helen. She welcomed me into her home, both of us feeling the dull grief of a house absent of her husband. There was his reading chair. There were photographs of him. There was his widow, forcing a smile as a courageous act of hospitality to me. I reminded her that only four months earlier she and Bill had made the first pledge to our annual pledge campaign—a gift ten times that of their previous pledge. A lot had happened in those four months. When they made their pledge, both Bill and Helen indicated that they could do it annually. Since they had paid their pledge early, I asked Helen if she would join the other two women in making one of the four challenge gifts we needed to reach the pledge-campaign goal; this would be her *second* major gift to the annual pledge campaign in only three months.

Warmly, gently, and kindly, Helen explained that, with Bill's death, she was managing finances for the first time in her life. It was new to her, so she would have to check to see where she stood financially. The next day she called and made the pledge.

Four courageous women gave major gifts to the pledge campaign and assured the financial stability of our church in a year when we might otherwise have failed to reach our goal, and for very good and numerous reasons. The congregation, gorgeous and faithful as they were, rallied. Gifts came pouring in. Slowly, the four matching challenges encouraged hundreds of other gifts. We met our needs. We balanced our budget.

We accomplished a balanced budget—closing a high six-figure annual deficit to zero—because a few people wanted their church to thrive. They gave major gifts, and they challenged others to do so. These last few years for our parish had been hard, following terrible relational misconduct and the deep wounds it left. We had to raise a lot of money to recover a dozen years of reckless spending, a drop in members of more than 40 percent, and minimal fundraising or relationship-building. We had to slash our budgets in order to return our church to solid financial footing. But it was accomplished because human beings sat with each other over tea, over sherry, over cookies, and even over grief. We sat with each other and asked one another to make gifts. And we gave to one another generously, kindly, courageously. And you can do it, too.

Wherever you have people committed to a church and its mission, you will also have people capable of making major gifts. Someone just needs to ask. When you do—with humility, passion, and the promise that it is a great investment in God's kingdom in your place—they will give. And their giving will astound you. You will be humbled by it. And you will be a fearless church fundraiser. There's nothing wrong with that. In fact, inspiring stewardship and managing fundraising are some of the most beautiful ministries you will ever do.

CHAPTER 2

• •

People and Relationships

Knowing people—really knowing them—is the only way to raise money.

If there is nothing else you take from this chapter, filled as it must be, with generalizations, this one thing you must know: giving emerges from a solid and deep relationship that is built over time, tested by conversation and based in honesty. A new rector will not raise much money for two years as he or she builds those relationships. A brash, careless church leader who rushes into living rooms with shallow humor, charm, and glad-handing will fail to raise money. It takes time, conversation, and many visits of different kinds to set the stage for an effective major-gift request. Try to speed up the process and you will fail *always*. So this chapter is dedicated to understanding and listening to your donors. If you want a six-figure gift . . . then you need to spend the many hours of listening that such a gift requires. Knowing something about how different generations give will also help. But let's begin with neurology.

It has long been thought that the part of the brain that "lights up" when we give money away is the part of the brain that thinks about giving—a particular place in the prefrontal cortex. Current neuroscience has investigated the specificity of the locations of pleasure stimuli in our brain, and new studies show that the part of our brain that "lights up with stimulation" when we make a major gift is *not* the part of the brain that usually lights up with a generous act. Indeed, the specific part of the brain that *is* stimulated when we make a major gift is the same part that lights up when we receive a surprise gift, win the lottery, get a loaf of bread from a neighbor, or walk into a surprise party.

We are biologically designed to receive spontaneous joy from giving. It is a feature of our species that promotes survival, so it is engrained in our being, like running from a tiger or removing a hand from a flame. Knowing this science helps me ask for major gifts. In no way do I want to imply that I have no anxiety in the major-gift request process. Vulnerability creates tension from time to time. If the major gift is asked for properly, after the donor has been involved and informed over time, and if the gift requested falls into the meaning-making mandorla—that overlap between the missions of the donor and the needs of the church—there is nothing but joy, even if the gift is not as large as one might have hoped.

Different People

People are different from each other, so they give in different ways and to different things. They also change their giving patterns as their lives and interests change. In one season of life, a person might be fascinated by and give major gifts to digging wells in Africa. In another phase, that same person might give to cancer research because of the diagnosis of a very close friend. Later, that same person may choose to give a major gift to a library or to their church as they begin to end their life and desire to leave something behind, a marker to say, "I loved this."

The reason a chapter in this book is dedicated entirely to people and relationships is because major gifts and planned gifts are all about people. Anyone poor at building and maintaining relationships will be terrible at fundraising. What people love, what people think is important, what people find fascinating, what people want to make happen in the world—these things are the cornerstone of a major- or planned-gift program, and so a good fundraiser must know what a donor is interested in. What I see over and over again in churches is that people are so afraid of and unprepared for the work of raising money (primarily because nobody ever taught them how to do it or because they lack the humility to listen) that they run into the work panic-stricken like a bull in a china shop, asking too quickly or in the wrong way, approaching the wrong person and for the wrong thing. Busyness in committee meetings may feel productive, but thoughtful strategy and tender care for human lives and relationships are the only ways to raise money. It takes spiritual intention. Strategically figuring out the best way to approach someone for a major gift is in no way unspiritual. It takes time. There are no shortcuts to baking bread. The ingredients in the process have to be dealt with in order and with great precision and care in order for the bread to come out right. Similarly, the process of raising major gifts needs to be dealt with in order, with great respect for the ingredients and outcome, and with similar precision and care in order for the donor to come out of the process joyfully, and for the church to come out with the major gift it needs for its mission.

Therefore, we need to face the significant cultural changes that have occurred over the last two decades and that have changed how money is raised everywhere.

Different Generations

Throughout history, generations of people have always been different from those before and after them. All you have to do is watch a few episodes of *Downton Abbey* to see how different generations see the world differently. One generation wears a corset, while another one wants loose flowing clothes. One generation believes you should stand when a lady enters the room, while another generation does not see the point. One generation has no time for women's votes, while another generation is passionate about voting rights. Anyone involved in communications, such as clergy and advertising executives, will tell you that, if you do not understand the generation to which you are speaking, your words will not connect with their hearts. I offer, therefore, a brief consideration of generational giving. If you want more information, William Strauss and Neil Howe have written many books on generational differences. For now, and for this purpose, I briefly look at each generation and mention a few things to keep in mind when approaching them for major and planned gifts.

An Aging Congregation

Well over half of the people in the Episcopal Church are more than sixty-five years old. In many of our churches, especially those in rural areas, the median age is in the seventies. Having this wonderful wisdom in our churches is a great gift. These are people who can, if they are asked well, give significant major and planned gifts.

How We Make Choices

More than 90 percent of our values are set and established before we are teenagers. We adjust our values slightly in our teenage years, but they are locked in as we enter our twenties. After that, only big events in our lives change our values, for better or for worse.

Knowing the general values of a particular generation is helpful when asking for major gifts. This is not manipulation; it is communication. A brochure, conversation, video, or message that works for one generation may not work for another, even though the project for which you are raising money has great appeal to everyone, which means your approach and some of the tools have to be tailored to different generations. Let's look briefly at these different generations so you know how to best approach, communicate, ask, and thank the people making major gifts. And since planned gifts are just planned major gifts, let's look at both.

Since most of the capacity for major and planned gifts dwells with our older congregation members, we need to begin there. If you bury ten members of your congregation and do not receive ten planned gifts, then someone has, for the past decade, dropped the ball. It is important and valuable for any church vestry or leadership body to ask this telling question: "How many funerals have we done in this church in the past twelve months?" and then, the even more telling question: "How many planned gifts have we received in these past twelve months?" The answers to these questions will tell any clergy or vestry of their church's effectiveness regarding major and planned gifts from the Great Generation (people in their nineties) and the Silent Generation (people in their seventies and eighties). The answers in most churches, over the last decade, have been disappointing. I hope this book will inspire major and planned gifts over the next ten years, such that the answers will be more heartening.

The Great Generation

There may still remain some from the Great Generation active in your church and in their nineties. They are generally beautiful souls, many of whom have spent their whole lives in their church. If you have been doing good major- and planned-gift work among them over the last twenty years, you probably have an endowment that will secure the mission of your church into the future. If you have not done this work, then I am glad you are reading this book.

The Silent Generation

The most impactful gifts that you can receive in your churches and dioceses will come from the Silent Generation. Members of the Silent Generation have attended thousands of meetings and have been deeply invested in the future of the church. They are disciplined, detail-oriented, and conflict-averse. They value privacy, so the conversations necessary to raise a major gift will need to be given time. When you visit these people, turn off your cell phone and be willing to stay for a couple of hours. They like things on paper, so a proposal letter should be in the pocket of the one asking for a major gift. They also value the few friends they have left on the planet. They will want to know what their friends are giving to the project. This generation will want to hear directly from the leader of the project. They like to be visited in their homes, but they like church hierarchy so a conversation in the rector's office can work, too. They appreciate formality, requests for their wisdom, and time to think. Unlike some of the younger generations, they have a great personal dedication to their church buildings and congregation.

The Great Depression formed this generation's early years and their parents' middle years. After World War II, they had children and were prosperous. Fair play, church hierarchy, a respect for authority, conformity, teamwork, and honor are important to them. This generation is, at the time of this writing, retired and in their seventies and eighties. As a rule, they enjoy financial security. They value friendship, are generally modest, and have great concern for the poor and the marginalized. They enjoy the younger generations but are more modest in their speech and quiet in their giving.

They gravitate toward congregations that are inclusive. They dislike the rigid conformity demanded by their parents. They communicate well and effectively, are detail-oriented, and value working toward a goal. The work you do with this book to ask for major planned gifts from this generation will go a long way to help establish a solid financial future for your church or diocese. If you are willing to spend time in the living rooms of these people, then your work may result in a major gift after three to eight two-hour visits and after finding projects that they feel strongly about supporting. They will be very generous to a congregation where they feel involved and where they can trust their leader's authenticity and honesty. If you have an inauthentic or dishonest minister or bishop, you will find it very difficult to raise major or planned gifts in part because of the wisdom and intuition of this generation and that of the millennial generation, both.

The Silent Generation values privacy. You will need to take time to have conversations with them. They like clearly defined roles and prefer money to be cared for with deep scrutiny. They enjoy socializing, handwritten notes, and face-to-face meetings. They like personal stories, and they will want to know the budget details of any project. They will want to do their fair share, which is quite a large one. Asking this generation for gifts should be a top priority in any church.

If a minister or bishop is not in the living room of a member of the Silent Generation three times a week discussing their potential philanthropy, then those gifts will go to schools, museums, hospitals, and other nonprofits. A good vestry or bishop's standing committee should have fundraising clearly outlined in their job descriptions and should require monthly reporting about cultivation and solicitation visits made within that month. What gets measured gets done. Do not let the resistance or incompetence of your leader hold your church or diocese back from the financial resources it needs for its mission.

This generation has creative ideas; however, because our society tends to marginalize people over sixty-five, they often feel disregarded. The irony is they have the money to give major gifts to fund new, exciting, creative, and impactful programs.

Baby Boomers

The Baby Boomers grew up with strong and stable institutions and were parented by a prosperous and safe generation. They began a spiritual renewal and revival in the church and are currently in leadership. It was this generation that began to imagine a personal spirituality their children would inherit. They have not had as easy a time with their finances as their parents. Many of them are hard-working, with complex schedules and two incomes to make ends meet. Unlike their parents, who focus on a project's budget, this generation wants to understand why you are raising money to begin with. They want to know what impact it will have on human life. Their primary interest in philanthropy, should they have any money to give, is aimed toward the care of children and the environment.

This generation is less likely to want to meet in their homes and would prefer a local diner or coffee shop. They have opinions, and they will express them; they need time to do that. They crave meaning and its intersection with spirituality. They will give to the church but are less likely to give to buildings and more likely to invest in programs and services that meet human needs or provide for deepening spiritual life. This generation will give major gifts to accomplishment-based initiatives and will depart from their parents' values by finding little value in perpetuating tradition in the church.

Generation X

Generation X is pressed to fund their children's educations, or at least save for them. They grew up having to fend for themselves, because their parents were singularly dedicated to their work. They have lived through difficult financial times and experienced governmental distrust. They grew up somewhat skeptical of religion, and that skepticism has increased exponentially as they have aged. They are disinclined to associate with any one church on the basis of doctrine. They change careers quickly, locations frequently, and churches regularly. They have considerable debt, because their parents' generation had fewer financial resources than previous generations. They like to try things out, experiment, and then quickly move along.

This generation is comfortable with technology and demands transparency of nonprofits. They generally follow the choices their friends are making over the choices their parents made. They are increasingly materialistic and are less likely to attend and pledge to a church. They consider coffee shops, as well as fitness clubs or nature trails, to be places of deep spiritual reflection. They want authenticity, are skeptical of institutions (especially religious ones), and are not, in general, well-formed or educated spiritually, theologically, or even socially, in a traditional sense. Like their parents, their philanthropic interest is in the care of children and the environment.

Because of low incomes, high debt, and their stage of life, Generation X has little time or money to give away, let alone to the church. The irony is they crave and seek community; when they find it in the church, they stay, volunteer, and give what they can. When members of Generation X join a church and find their experience to be authentic, kind, and trustworthy, they will end up becoming the leaders and funders of that church over the next few decades. But they will not give at the level of their parents and especially not at the level of their grandparents, making near-term membership growth as important as resource development. Each generation that takes over from their parents will drop their pledging by about 50 percent. The Boomer will give 50 percent less than their Silent Generation parents gave. The GenXer will give 50 percent of what their Boomer parents gave, and so on.

When being asked for a gift to a church, they want to know the details and the expected results. They will use their computers to search, check, and double-check the information you offer.

In order to successfully ask a member of this generation for a major gift, the church will first need to make sure the person knows their gifts and talents are as appreciated as the time they give to the church. Your affirmation and repeated and creative "thank you" will midwife a financial contribution. Generation X cares deeply for the poor and the marginalized. If you can show tangible results from your project, they are more likely to invest.

They will use technology for their giving and they will give planned gifts, but it will take some time and effort to incline them to spend the five hundred dollars necessary to make their wills. Younger people do not usually write wills unless they are taking a vacation and worry about the care of their children. When they get to the life stage of will preparation, they will be in their fifties or sixties, so asking them point-blank to write their will and include your church is a dedicated conversation. Gathering Generation X into small groups and discussing the importance of financial planning and of having both a financial and living will can be a profoundly important ministry. The side benefit may be that they will include your church in their estate planning. Most planned giving from this generation (and indeed most generations after the Great Generation, and perhaps the Silent Generation) will be based on a percentage of their estate.

Generation X is not interested as past generations have been in doing its fair share in church pledging or major-gift donations, nor will it be interested in perpetuating the institution for its own sake, making clergy nervous about their own future. Generation X does give more than its fair share to the environment and to education, but church is not where their philanthropy will naturally land, making dedicated requests all the more crucial. They are extremely good communicators and like to be spoken to with clarity and honesty. Like all human beings, they like to be asked for their opinions and need to give feedback on a project over time. What makes them different from everyone else is that knowing their opinion is valued *determines* their inclination to make a gift. If you do not bring them in on the ground floor of a project for which you one day want to raise money (and this goes for all the generations), then you will find they are polite but unwilling to give a major gift to the project about which you are so passionate.

Place these people on leadership teams, increase your skills around technology, and be willing to host meetings online, at least some of the time. They are the first generation in the history of the church that feels little obligation to either attend, raise the children in, or give to the institutional church. That is a game-changer for us and raises the stakes such that we only really have a decade or two to raise the money with which we will, ultimately, need to make do. If we do not work hard now to involve and evangelize this generation, then the church's carelessness will result in its eventual financial starvation.

Millennials, or Generation Y

Much of what I said about the Greatest Generation can be applied quite easily to Millennials. They schedule their time carefully, set high goals, and enjoy problem-solving. It would be unwise to ignore this generation when recruiting leadership. Unlike Generation X, they are optimistic and group-oriented. Like their grandparents, they yearn for a calm interior life and meaningful spiritual practice. They will attend retreats, as well as evening, candlelit, quiet services. They are desperate to find places in which they can turn off their cell phones, tablets, and computers in order to experience psychic peace, free from the constant messaging of our society.

The church has a hope of survival past the Millennial generation if it is willing to molt and become somewhat different than what it has been. This generation is serious about its obligations and is intellectually curious. Formation and education programs are a great way to engage them and will be a gateway to their philanthropy. They have views on spirituality similar to the Greatest and Silent Generations; their practices will be traditional, demonstrated in their willingness, one day, to give to buildings. Our church communities may resurface after two generations of disinclination. This generation is deeply attached to its congregations but not to its diocese or judicatory. They are highly committed to their local parish church—if it is transforming human lives and is a place of sanctuary. They long for solid spiritual practices, love beauty, and long for mystery in an age of technology. The community of connection and spiritual transformation is what makes this generation inclined to invest major gifts into the church and its mission.

On Women as Major Donors

A Barclays Wealth study released in July 2009 showed that women in the United States give to nonprofit agencies, mostly religious institutions, more than twice as much as men do. They control 83 percent of household spending and more than 50 percent of family wealth; of the people with more than $1.5 million, 43 percent are women.

I note recent data showing that the life-expectancy gap between men and women, which used to be quite wide, has recently dropped to slightly less than four years on average. This, however, reminds us that the money left to churches in wills will come from women and will be decided upon by women.

In my experience, women have a deeper peace about issues of life and death. They are often the motivators behind challenging conversations such as writing a will or making a bequest (though some men are willing and able to have these difficult conversations). So I suggest great care when planning for deepening engagement and the resulting request for major and planned gifts and that clergy and lay leaders prioritize their time over the next two decades by creating vision, establishing a worthy fundable mission, and then sitting with the women of your parish, asking them to include their husbands. Men live from a place of power and strength. They find conversations about intimate things such as death (and bequests after death) to be more challenging to embrace than their female counterparts. This is not a value judgment. This is simply borne out of my experience as a church fundraiser. In my vocation as a fundraiser and parish priest, I have helped more than two hundred people talk about their will and the inclusion of their church. Of those conversations, two were initiated by men, and both men were motivated by honoring the wishes of their wives to make bequests through charitable remainder trusts so that the gift could be seen by and honor their wives in their lifetimes.

Men tend to be significantly more passive in church attendance and involvement. Let's face it, without women doing the hard work in our churches, most churches would collapse; women tend to get the work of the parish done. At the same time, however, what we know about philanthropy is that giving follows involvement. The fastest way to increase philanthropy to your church is to track, manage, market, and increase involvement in your programs, liturgies, and leadership. And this is especially true for women.

In short, fundraising is about relationships. It is essential that relationships be given time to form and that the realities of different generations—how they like to be asked for money, how they meet, what they find important—are cared for and carefully honored in conversation. Only leaders good at relationships will be leaders good at fundraising. I have seen too many bullies or leaders with a fear of conflict try to raise money—it will not happen. Only people who love people, respect their boundaries, and have the patience to let a relationship unfold long before a gift is requested—only they will raise money.

Of course, we have a job to do, so the relationship being developed needs to be carefully curated, planned, and managed toward a request to which the donor has the freedom to accede or decline.

In this chapter we have looked at people and relationships. The next chapter looks hard at the planning a church must do to be worthy of the gifts it seeks.

The Rector's Tea, Not Just for Edwardians and Anglophiles Anymore . . .

Your target audience for the next decade or two will be the Silent and Boomer Generations. The Silent Generation and older Baby Boomers will be the last generations to appreciate or engage in hierarchy. The younger Boomers and Generations X and Y will not be as inclined to participate in ecclesial hierarchy, nor will they even engage in it. So, you will find that inviting older members of the congregation to open-house conversations with the rector or bishop, in order to build relationships and hear the ideas and longings of people who have capacity and interest to make major gifts, will serve you very well as long as your interest is in listening and not just in money. People in our society are craving connection more than anything else. These social engagements in small groups will not only offer connection but will also provide leaders with valuable information about their passions and interests, and even their financial capacity. Fundraising is ultimately about relationships.

Try Sending Birthday Cards . . . but First Get Birth Dates

The only way to group your congregation by generation so that you target the messaging and events to suit their needs and preferences is to know their birth dates. Once you have birth dates in some kind of mailing system or even on a simple spreadsheet, then you can begin to tailor the letters and invitations to accommodate their very real and different ways of seeing the world, the church, and their philanthropy. Ask church attendees to write their name and birth date on an index card. It is very important for fundraising in the church to know whom you are talking to. It will take about eight weeks to get to everyone. Every church should have the birth date of each of the congregants in its database. Knowing the ages of your congregation makes you more able to tailor the messages to suit each generation's way of communicating.

Listen to Different Generations

One day, as a special event or an adult-formation session on a Sunday, invite a panel of people to speak—one person from each generation. Let the congregation ask questions about how they see the world, about what they like to do, and about how they like to be asked for money. Ask them what they think of the church, your parish, and the diocese or judicatory and even the larger denomination. Ask them to imagine the future of the church and to tell you what they imagine. And ask them what they think about how to invite people from their generation to join the church and to give to it.

A Bible Study on the Rich Young Ruler (Mark 10:17–22) for Stewardship Leaders

"As Jesus started on his way, a man ran up to him and fell on his knees before him. 'Good teacher,' he asked, 'what must I do to inherit eternal life?' 'Why do you call me good?' Jesus answered. 'No one is good—except God alone. You know the commandments: "You shall not murder, you shall not commit adultery, you shall not steal, you shall not give false testimony, you shall not defraud, honor your father and mother."' 'Teacher,' he declared, 'all these I have kept since I was a boy.' Jesus looked at him and loved him. 'One thing you lack,' he said. 'Go, sell everything you have and give to the poor, and you will have treasure in heaven. Then come, follow me.' At this the man's face fell. He went away sad, because he had great wealth."

This passage from Mark 10 is usually mistranslated. Once Jesus recovers from his exasperation, he softens because he sees the young ruler's desire to be helped. A much better transation of this text is not "Jesus . . . loved him." But rather, "Then Jesus, looking straight at him, warmed to him." Jesus changes his mind and softens his prejudices against the wealthy and so, too, must we if we have any hope of raising money in our churches.

Raising money in the church means raising it especially from those who are rich—from people who have three meals each day and much more besides. Raising money in the church means being compassionate with ourselves (for being annoyed by wealth) and then being compassionate toward the rich, too, who are trying to make meaning of their lives but need help—from us and from Jesus. Financial development in faith-based institutions is a ministry. It is not a chore. Funding Christ's mission through the church is our responsibility in gratitude for all God has given us. To ask requires humility—more humility than is required by giving. Jesus, in this passage, learns an earthbound and human humility toward those trapped by their riches, who still yearn for God.

QUICK-START SUGGESTIONS

Here are a few things you could do to get started so that you can care for the people who are both raising money and giving it.

1. Make a list of all of the people older than fifty who attend your church regularly. Then make a list equal to 10 percent of the first list. This second list should include the names of people with whom you want to have conversations about major gifts that they could make sometime in the future.

2. When you have developed the list of five, twenty, fifty, or whatever number of major-gift prospects (I suggest 10 percent of active, attending congregants), create a file for each one. Into that file place newspaper clippings, certificates, church bulletins, and notes from meetings and telephone conversations. This filing system, antiquated though it may be, is the first step in any major-gifts program. If you are a big church, then you might use a computer system to do this work. But, regardless, never place anything in the file that your donor would not like to see in it. This file will be an archive of a relationship. And major-gifts work is nothing less than the curating of relationships and meaning-making. Nobody can keep all of this information in their head, nor should they. As clergy come and go, these files remain and help the next incumbent.

3. Find a way to learn the birth dates of all in your congregation and place that information in whatever computer system you use. You might even send them a birthday card on their birthdays.

4. Once you have identified who is going to lead your major- and planned-gifts programs, begin a book club and read about effective communication, listening skills, and relationship building.

5. On a Sunday, ask your congregation to stand if they are more than sixty years of age, and remind them that they are the financial future of your church. This might inspire the vestry to begin a spring membership growth campaign to match your fall stewardship campaign.

6. On another Sunday, ask members of the congregation to stand if they are between eighteen and thirty-eight years of age. While they are standing, introduce the seated congregation to the future of the church and remind them that their gifts will make that future possible.

STUDY QUESTIONS

1. How do you feel being asked to be so strategic about raising money in your church? For many, a "write a letter and hope for the best" strategy is more comfortable, even if it is less effective. What will this work require of you? What anxieties will you need to face in yourself and in your parish in order to move forward with courage into a new way of resource development and hosting stewardship conversations?

2. What does leadership in your church think about this more proactive, strategic, and effective way of encouraging stewardship and raising money? What conversations can you host in order to alleviate these fears and anxieties?

3. What teaching and preaching need to happen in order to begin to change the culture of your church from avoidance to engagement? Culture change does not happen by itself. It needs its own plan. What is your plan? Are your church's clergy and leadership ready for this? If not, what is your plan to help them to overcome their anxiety, fears, and resistance?

4. Is everyone on the leadership team excited and ready? Great! But what about the congregation? What do they need in order to drop resistance and engage processes that raise major and planned gifts?

5. Try drafting the annual fundraising letter (three hundred words please . . . short!) and writing two letters. Write one letter to people under fifty-five and a second letter to people over fifty-five. Use what you know of different generational attitudes to craft these two very different letters that seek to accomplish the same result.

6. Are your clergy and lay leaders currently involved in financial development good at relationships? Are they kind, honest, gentle, and patient? Make a list of the people in your parish who are so good at friendship that they will inevitably be good at fundraising. Then recruit them to this work.

PRAYERS

*A Prayer for Those Leading Resource Development
and Stewardship Theology in Churches*

Lord Jesus, they called you Rabbi because you taught them. You walked with people, you taught, and you told stories that illuminated truth. Give us the grace to teach stewardship theology and praxis in our church. Give our leadership strong hearts, full of courage, but gentle hands, full of compassion. Help us to remember how frightened our major donors can sometimes be. Alongside our effectiveness, place within us the discernment we need to know how to teach and lead so that major gifts are given, our mission is funded, and hearts are moved into philanthropy. *Amen.*

A Prayer for Friendship in Fundraising

Gentle Savior, you moved in alongside people, sitting with them where they were. You did not summon people. You went to where they were and accepted them as they were. You loved outcasts and sinners. You listened and then simply invited people to be your friend and to abide with you. When people inquired about your work, you invited them simply to "come and see." Give us grace to live and evangelize as you did—gently, and by listening. Grant us your Holy Spirit to midwife a conversation and to be companions in the breaking of bread long before we would presume to ask for a major gift. And then, help us to ask for that gift as you must have so many times in your ministry. *Amen.*

A GIVING STORY:
JASON—CURATING A MISSION

When I first left the monastery and reentered the workforce as an Episcopal priest, my first job was to help the churches of New Hampshire raise money and people. The title of the position was Canon for Congregational Life. I was rooted in the Church of the Good Shepherd, in Nashua, New Hampshire. I loved Odie, their rector, and I loved that congregation. They gave me a church home, which is a valuable thing for a diocesan priest whose job was to travel the highways and byways of New Hampshire and care for its forty-seven churches.

I lived on a farm called Blackwater Bluff in the foothills of the White Mountains—a farm to which I return to write from time to time. One of my closest friends was the Episcopal priest of a church near Concord, where the diocesan offices were located and where I was the chaplain to the State Senate, opening the sessions weekly with prayer and a meditation. Scott was the church's parish priest, a man of deep integrity and kindness who befriended me immediately on my arrival from the monastery and helped me get settled in my new life. He led a beautiful little church that was quite literally on the other side of the tracks. There was a wealthy church in Concord, perched elegantly on the city green, but down the road and across the tracks lay Scott's little parish, Grace Episcopal Church, East Concord. Only a few months into our friendship, Scott dropped dead of a heart attack after a bicycle ride as he stood at the sink drinking a glass of water. He was in the prime of his life. Something inside me broke that day.

I am a potter. I had a studio in a glade near a pond at Blackwater Bluff. I dealt with my grief by taking seven pounds of rich, white clay and throwing a funeral vase for my friend and colleague.

Months later, a new priest, bright-eyed and kind, was hired to take Scott's place at Grace Church. The Reverend Jason Wells was new at leading a church, though he had been a fine assistant in one of the largest congregations in New Hampshire. He came to my office and asked if I would help them raise money in their little church. It was a small congregation, with people full of faith and joy, though not with great wealth. The church had taken the time to grieve, to process, to discern, and to call this new priest, but they needed to grow, and they needed money for their mission.

Jason and I worked together for four years to discern and establish the mission of the church. We both knew the problem was not fundraising. They had a strong annual pledge campaign. The problem was that the church had been led for decades by clergy who would land and then leave after two years, using the little congregation as a launching pad to higher and more lucrative church posts. Then their beloved priest died. Jason now had the job of trying to convince them that he would not use them, that he would work with them, stay with them, and partner with them into the fullness of their mission. But how?

Jason and I realized that, before the congregation could blossom into God's hope for it, it needed to do the trench work of discerning their mission. Yes, they had a mission to provide a liturgy on Sunday mornings. Yes, the rector would visit the congregation when they were in trouble. But that could not possibly be all they were there to accomplish in that hamlet. This small town just outside Concord was economically depressed. Behind some of the walls of those houses was a lot of pain. If you walked from the church up to the general store (which, I might add, had wonderful doughnuts), you could almost sense a New England version of a ghost town. People were still living there, but just standing in the road you could feel a kind of pain, akin to what one feels getting off a plane in New Orleans. There was despair in the air. On Sundays, many of the kind smiles flashed at me were thin veils over grief.

Jason invited me to lead a vestry retreat. I remember the house, old and cozy, with blue walls and pine floors. We ate good muffins made with New Hampshire blueberries, and I brought blackberries from my farm, along with some heavy cream. As we ate breakfast together, we discussed the need to raise the integrity of the mission of the church so that, when it was time to raise money, there would be something powerful and impactful to give to. We designed a list of questions for the vestry to answer about the mission of the church.

They had so many wonderful ideas that we were almost distracted from the rest of the day's agenda. We began to realize that there were lots of little things these good New Englanders were doing to heal their lives and their parish, as well as the lives of the people in the town. Because the clergy had come and gone so frequently, the church had developed a system that was very nearly underground. They were getting the job done without any real formal structures, much like the house churches of the second century. Our excitement grew, so we made a list of the ministries, and, from the data bank of brains huddled together in that little house by a stream, we applied some questions to each ministry:

- How is this ministry changing the lives of people who benefit from it?
- What members are engaged in this ministry, either as volunteers or as donors? How are their lives affected?
- Who is providing the ministry, and how much is this costing from the budget?
- What more could the church be doing in this area? What unmet needs exist, and what would meeting those needs require, in human and financial terms?
- What do recipients of this ministry say about how they are being ministered to?
- How does this ministry affect the way nonchurched people see our church? What is our reputation and image?

It was wonderful to see the faces of the vestry members light up and their shoulders relax as they began to realize their church had many pearls of great price. They were doing wonderful work, but it was all à la carte and difficult to see. By identifying and ordering the ministries as one might set out ingredients on the kitchen counter before making a dish (the French call it *mise en place*), we were able to see that any major donor would be crazy not to give to any one of these wonderful ministries. What we call in fundraising "a case for support" (the reason the church is worthy of an investment) was developing right before our eyes like gold sparkling in the pan of a Colorado prospector.

After the vestry finished its good work, looking hard at the various ministries of the parish, and then having discussed some other ministries they dreamed about, we set about developing a questionnaire for the congregation that stepped away from individual ministries and looked at the big picture. Here is what we came up with:

- Over this past year, what aspect of our church's life has excited, interested, or motivated you the most?
- In what areas of church life have you noticed the Holy Spirit particularly at work? Where do you sense energy and vitality?
- What requires the attention of your vestry or rector? Of what should they be aware? What would you like to change?
- What task or goal should be a priority for our church over the next three years?
- What is the congregation doing to serve God and the local community?

- What keeps you coming to this church? What might attract newcomers?
- In what ministry would you like to become more involved?
- What could we do to improve communications in the church?
- What could we do to improve stewardship and planned-giving programs in the church?

The congregation met first over a wonderful New England potluck supper. To this day, I can still taste the pot roast rich with wine and vegetables. There was a Shaker sugar pie. Someone made hot rolls. We ate and talked about our answers to the questions. Table after table of newsprint began to fly this way and that. Adult forums held additional meetings between services, and then the questionnaire was also sent to every member of the congregation at their homes. We gathered the data, and the resulting document told the story of the answers and read like a letter worthy to be slipped into the Bible right after Galatians, or perhaps the letter to the Corinthians—the second one.

Jason and I realized we needed to take the analysis to the outside ring of three concentric circles. Circle one, the inner molten core of mission, includes the various ways in which humans pray, worship, love, and care for each other. Circle two includes what the church thinks about all of that. The third circle, at this New Hampshire church, looked closely at the town in which the church sat. What did the people around them, who were not members of the congregation, think of Grace Episcopal Church? What did the people in the town think the church could accomplish to ease suffering and host joy in East Concord?

We developed a questionnaire to use in interviews with the leaders and citizens of East Concord. People love to be asked their opinions. And they often have great insights, because, while not members of the church, they are one step away from it; sometimes, they see more clearly. Here are some reasons that Jason and I came up with to explain the value of these community interviews:

- Community leadership interviews send a message to the congregants that the church's leadership is not managing in an ivory tower but are instead actively seeking data that integrates the mission and ministry of the church with the needs and experiences of the larger community.
- Among community leaders, the interviews dispel notions of exclusivity and mission competition and also communicate that the church seeks to collaborate for good and for economies of scale.
- The interviews also provide valuable insights regarding perceptions

of your church. Some perceptions may be wrong, but that they exist means you need to begin to change them.

- The interviews collect valuable data about changing trends, new growth, shifting demographics, new and planned initiatives, events, potential grants, and more.
- A process like this is usually required for grant applications, especially those based on community impact.
- Simply entering people's offices and homes for conversation helps the church to make friends and connect with its community.

Here are some of the questions the parishioners asked of the community leaders, community members, and area businesspeople in one-on-one interviews:

- What do you know about our church?
- What do you know about the way we work to have an impact on human lives?
- What are your perceptions about how our church eases human suffering in this area?
- What do you see about our church that you think we, as members, might not see?
- What kinds of things do you think the church should be doing in our town that no church is currently doing?
- Do you know any of the people who go to our church or who are members?
- If you inherited lots of money or won a lottery and were thinking about giving a big gift to a church, to what project, known or imagined, would you give? What would you want to make happen in a church with your big gift, and because you felt it needed to be done?
- Do you have any concerns about our church?
- Can you describe our church, its people, and its ministry in your own words?
- While I have you here, would you like to come and join us or least come and see how we live together? You might like our church!

At long last, here is the end of the story. When all of the answers were collated and ordered, a picture began to emerge. The picture was about food. Everyone seemed to agree that some of the children in East Concord were so impoverished that they only ate public-school meals at breakfast and lunch. Many went home to houses where addiction, abuse, job loss, and financial poverty meant empty larders. Many did not eat between Friday night and Monday morning. The community leaders were concerned about the children and wondered if the church could do something.

Grace Episcopal Church in East Concord stepped up. Having looked at all of their ministries, at how the congregation felt about the church, and at what community leaders were saying about their church and about their town, the congregation decided, with singular clarity and courage, that "Grace Church is a place that feeds people."

There was the intentional double entendre in that they knew people were fed by the Eucharist and fed by teaching and preaching and connection. And this little, scrappy church began to physically feed people. They defined their mission and ministry to accommodate people who were local and who were hungry. They bought book bags and knapsacks— the kind kids use to carry their books to and from school—but they filled them with food for the families, so that when the children went home on Fridays they had food to eat for the weekend, without the stigma of being seen on the bus with a brown bag of groceries from the food pantry. The kids would bring their knapsacks back on Mondays, and the church would pick them up and spend the week refilling them.

The church then held a massive pig roast. Interviews with the local butcher revealed he would like to sponsor a pig roast for the whole town. His meaning-making was to provide meat for everyone. The church's meaning-making was to feed people. They partnered on a town pig roast that quickly became the most famous event in the town, annually serving hundreds on the lawns of the church, just down the street from the butcher and the village green.

Village chatter about the church and all the kids they were feeding, all the families with groceries for the weekend and the wonderful pig roast, began to circulate like wildfire. Soon strangers were showing up at church: "So this is the church that feeds people!" Not long after, the church moved from mission status to parish status. The day their church paraded into the diocesan convention with banners and dozens of people singing hymns, I wept like a baby. Jason had done a great job. In his speech to the convention, he told the church's story. We were both so proud.

You can do this, too. Your church can clarify a mission that would make Jesus want to hug you and kiss you on the lips. You can even raise major and planned gifts. To do so, you must, must, must define a mission worthy of philanthropic investment.

●●●

CHAPTER 3

Mission Integrity

The Garden Metaphor

Relationships, especially friendships, feel a lot like gardens to me. In the center of my computer desktop is a document called "My Garden." I open it every morning when I pray. The little tiny square of light will expand into a one-page document where I keep a short list of names—a dozen or so. It is the list of my friends. I call the document "My Garden" because I tend to my friends like I tend to my garden. As my eyes fall on each name, I appreciate them as growing, organic beings whose growth and health is made possible by God's nurturing. As I pray through that list every day, I ask myself:

- What does this relationship need to flourish? How does it need water and food? Do they need a note? Do they need a phone call? Shall I visit them? What have they recently asked for? Is there anything I need to do for them? Is there anything I need them to do for me? How shall I pray for them?
- How is this relationship going? Is it bearing fruit? Does it need to be moved out of my garden? Does it need to be watered or fed, or will it simply not thrive in my garden?
- How shall I celebrate the way this plant feeds me? How shall I give thanks for the way this friend and friendship bears fruit that nourishes me? What kind of fruit do I bear that nourishes them? Am I feeding them as much as they're feeding me?

As I ponder these questions, I am aware of the relationships in my life that reduce my isolation, inspire me, comfort my pain, and bring God to me in the form of human life, love, and friendship—significant ways in which God loves to show up in our lives.

Most any endeavor in our lives—falling in love, building a relationship, seeking to get your dream job—involves a creative process with steps that follow one another to a goal, much like creating a garden. To harvest the vegetables, you have to follow the steps:

1. Mark the plot where you want to create the garden.
2. Set the posts and tie strings to clearly outline the border.
3. Dig up the sod.
4. Till the soil.
5. Remove the rocks.
6. Add manure to the soil, along with some bone meal and peat.
7. Purchase the plants.
8. Plant them.
9. Weed and tend your new garden every day.
10. Water and feed and pay attention to your plants for optimal growth.

There is nothing manipulative about growing a garden, but there are steps to follow to do the job right. Caring for major- and planned-gift donors is similar to caring for the plants in the garden. I often wonder if that's why there are so many gardens in scripture: the garden in the Genesis story of Adam and Eve, the garden of the Song of Songs, the Garden of Gethsemane, the garden of the resurrection, and the gardens of Revelation. These gardens lead us through the Bible.

The steps that it takes to make a friend or to woo a lover or to grow a garden are just steps. They are neither sneaky nor manipulative (unless perhaps they are coming from a manipulative person, in which case I suppose sometimes they can be). This book, like any book that describes a process, can be twisted into something that it is not, simply because of who is reading it. If you see this process of engagement with major and planned donor prospects as manipulative, then perhaps you are simply projecting. We see what we want to see.

Many over the decades have told me they do not like the "cultivation" or "engagement deepening" inherent in major-gift fundraising and that they find fundraising manipulative and, so, do not want to participate. I have never been told this in the YMCA or the museum or the hospitals I help, but the church is full of people who sneer at the work that needs to go into asking for and achieving a major gift. If they do not want to do this work, that's okay. It's not for everyone. There are linens to be ironed and flowers to be arranged. But do not let your lay leaders make excuses for not raising money. And remember . . . somebody needs to raise the money for the flowers and for the linens. And for the irons. And for the water . . .

I have a profound faith in you, my reader. If you are reading this book, then you have courage. I believe there are many good, kind people in our churches like you—clergy and laity alike—who can summon the courage and who want to midwife a future for their church. They want to have great mission, and they want to fund that mission with great gifts. They want to help people give money away. They want to have a ministry that both raises money for their mission and that gently, carefully, honestly helps people to make large gifts to the churches, because they want their churches to thrive, now and long into the future.

This chapter is about deserving the money we seek to raise and then building the relationships essential to the process that leads up to asking for major gifts—a process we will dig into in the next chapter. What I see over and over again, which breaks my heart and inspired me to write this book, is that too many people in too many churches ask too many donors far too quickly. They get nervous both about checking the integrity of their mission and the "case" for it and about developing the relationships around meaning-making so that human beings are investing in the "case" that lights them up with real excitement. We often get anxious about our vulnerability when asking for major gifts. So we jump quickly into asking for the gift. And then we fail to get the gift. We fail to help the donor give the gift away, because the "one ask fits all" methods no longer work (nor did they ever work well for the donor).

Let's try a new metaphor. I've been a potter for thirty years. Being a potter has a process of its own. I have to wedge my clay. I have to order my tools on my potter's wheel. I have to re-wedge my clay on the wheel as it spins and as my hands muddy. I have to draw the clay up and down into a cone, then down into a ball, then up into a cone, then down into a ball, over and over again. Only then can I carefully open the ball of clay with my thumbs, as the wheel spins, and draw the clay into a bowl. Once I cut the bowl off the wheel with a wire tool and lift it onto a board to begin drying, I need to be aware of how slowly and carefully that bowl must dry, lest it crack in the process. Once it is dry, the bowl must be fired in the pottery kiln, again with great care. It is then dipped in glaze and fired a second time. Finally—at long last—a beautiful, sparkly, colorful bowl sits on the center of someone's dining-room table.

Can you see how the bowl could have warped or cracked or have never come into being had I rushed *any* of the steps in making it? Similarly, there is a process one must follow with asking for major gifts, and it takes great care, prayerful consideration, gentle nurturing, honest dealing, and a step-by-step approach, which ultimately leads to the question: "Will you make this major gift to our church and its mission?" The answer may be a yes, or it may be a no; it may also involve some negotiation for something in between. But I can tell you with absolute clarity: if you do not lay a firm foundation for the request of a major gift by carefully following a process of relationship-building, you will not be successful in raising money for your mission. Further, you will not be successful helping people give their money to the meaning-making their heart longs for and in guiding them to the meaning their money can make in the church.

I have written this book because I want you to be successful. I want churches to be fully funded so that they have robust missions. I want churches to raise the major gifts they need for their missions and ministries. More than anything, I want people who have the capacity and interest to give a major gift to their church and to the glory of God. And they will give them, and they will be happy for having given the gifts; and you will be happy by having received the gifts for your mission. If you rush or truncate this process of relationship-building, however, I assure you the result will be a disappointment. Many say that they do not want to do this work of helping people to give their money to a worthy mission. My response is Dr. Phil's: "How is what you are doing now working for you?"

How to Train Your Leadership

Identify the People You Need to Get the Job Done

There are three primary groups of people that need to be considered when managing major and planned gifts.

1. **Leaders**: the people who are not afraid to ask for money. They are usually quite generous themselves, and that generosity qualifies them to lead in the stewardship work of the church—to raise the pledges that fund the annual mission of the church, and to raise pledges of major and planned gifts that fund the future. Leaders have to be carefully chosen, since good choices infuse a major-gifts program with energy and vitality, and poor choices can lead to stagnation, procrastination, or conflict. As church wardens or clergy recruit leaders to do fundraising, especially for major and planned gifts, the leaders they recruit need to be carefully chosen, carefully trained, and carefully cared for.

2. **Annual donors**: the people in our churches who make a pledge once a year and then pay that pledge as an investment in the annual budget. You might ask why annual pledgers are even a topic of discussion in a book about major gifts, since only a few annual donors will have the capacity or interest to give either a major or planned gift. Annual donors are essential to the planned-giving and major-gift work we do, because it is from them that we will find those few names who can

give beyond their annual pledge. Just as national sports teams rely on colleges to provide them with the athletes they need, so major-gifts initiatives rely on annual donors as their lifeblood. This means the best way to ensure that you have a successful major- or planned-gift program is to do great work inspiring the annual pledge donations that fund your day-to-day mission.

3. **Major- and planned-gift prospects**: people who have both the capacity and the interest to give above and beyond what they give annually to fund the mission of the church. Whoever is responsible for leadership for major gifts has, as their primary task, the careful curating and management of this confidential list of people. The combination of anxiety about asking for major gifts, along with the resistance and procrastination this anxiety produces, often inspires us to make a list of people who could give major and planned gifts, only to hide the list in a file—if we dared even to write it down. This is a mistake. Planned and major gifts, most fundamentally, consists of a short list of people and their gentle care and attention by the leadership of the church. I am not suggesting that clergy should take better care of the wealthy in the congregation than the poor. I am saying if you want to raise major gifts in your church you must pay as much attention to that list of people as you pay to the hymns and prayers that populate your liturgy and the tasks that populate your daily lives.

An Intentional Introduction

Many nonprofit agencies have trouble raising major gifts, because it is difficult to get the attention of potential major donors. They get to see them at an annual meeting. They may get to make an appointment with them. The church, on the other hand, has a tremendous advantage when it comes to pledging and major gifts, because the people who give to the church come in and out of its buildings every day, or at least every week. Unlike nonprofits, people allow the church—its leaders, its clergy, and their friends within the congregation—into the deepest parts of their lives without hesitation.

Scripture says that to whom much is given much is expected, and this is true when it comes to major gifts in the church. When discussing major gifts, we are on holy ground. Leaders in the church must be very careful to manage the process of asking for major gifts with the deep awareness of the privilege they have in such ready and deep access to people who are able to make large gifts, indeed, to people who can make gifts of any size.

Raising major gifts is about relationships. It is about the relationship that a person has with their God. It is about the relationship that a person has with their church. It is about the relationship that the person has with the people in their church. And it is about the relationship that person has with themselves: in other words, with the meaning-making that they are holding in their hearts and that they can make real with their money. If it is well done, this is very beautiful work because of the good it provides to the world. And it is beautiful because of the good that it generates inside the heart and soul of the donor.

Anxieties and Persistence

This chapter will help you do something most people in sales and marketing need to do everyday: friend-raising. This chapter will help you manage the steps through which you build relationships for fundraising in your church.

Major-gift donors know they are being cultivated in the same way I know I am being cultivated when I walk into a clothing store. But I walked into that clothing store, stayed, and allowed that clerk to approach me because I was ready to consider a purchase. It is the same in major-gift fundraising. In the clothing store, if they bring me the right clothing and I like it (and I may try on a few different things), then I buy something. Was the store clerk manipulative? Was I manipulated? No to both questions. The store clerk knew I wanted something, or I would have walked out or politely asked them to leave me alone. But I invited the conversation and allowed it to continue, because I thought the clerk was willing and able to help me. The same thing happens when major-gift fundraising is done well in a church. If you gang up on a major donor, or if you manipulate them like the stereotype of a used-car salesman, nobody likes that. Rest assured that most able major donors are well-prepared to sniff out and step away from that kind of sleazy fundraising. Most salespeople are not sleazy; indeed, most are lovely and helpful. Similarly, most fundraising in churches is not sleazy, either; it is also lovely and helpful. In fact, it is even a profound ministry if done patiently.

When you raise money in churches, you are intentionally building a relationship between the project that you want funded and the person who may want to fund it. You are the intermediary—like a midwife. Like the Holy Spirit, you are the third person in this little earthly trinity. It may seem like you do this every day, and indeed you do. But what we know about fundraising is that increasing a potential donor's interest in a project requires careful planning and execution. At any point, the donor may say they are not interested in funding the church or a particular project within the church. That is just fine.

Many people say that fundraising feels awkward, impolite, or socially invasive, and that they want no part of it. That, too, is just fine. I maintain this is truly wonderful work, once you get into it. If you can stick it out the way an athlete sticks it out in endless training—if you can ask for that gift, and they give that gift—you'll be sold on how gorgeous this work is.

The Importance of the Pledge Campaign for Major Gifts

If you are not sure how to manage an effective annual pledge campaign, then you might consider reading my first book, *Fearless Church Fundraising*, and employing the hundreds of model documents and teaching videos at fearlesschurchfundraising.com, a free resource from my thirty years of experience raising money in churches of every size and sort, every denomination and perspective. Until your copy of that book arrives, here are some basic tips for the kind of strong annual pledge campaign that will set you up for success with a major-gifts program.

Recruiting Leadership

If you're just getting started fundraising in your church, then you will want to do a good job planning and managing your annual pledge campaign. It is out of that campaign that you will develop your major donor prospects and planned-giving prospects. Below, in the resources section, is an example of a volunteer job description for a stewardship commission. Also found are descriptions of both the major-gifts advisory committee and the planned-giving committee.

I have focused on people, because people are the beginning, middle, and end of all resource development. If you have the right people in place, you will be successful. If you are attentive to relationships, you will be successful. If you know who the potential major donors are and have identified who can and will remember your church, you will be successful. This work is all about having the right people asking the right people. Attend to that work carefully, and you will find that this is much easier than you think.

The Work

Members of the Stewardship Commission are charged with collaborating with the clergy, vestry, bishop, and lay leaders to ensure the success of the annual pledge campaign, alongside overseeing the five committees whose work contributes to various aspects of resource development for God's mission in our church.

The Hopes

It is hoped that Stewardship Commission members attend regular meetings of the commission. It is the commission's norm to gather over a simple meal that begins and ends in prayer and that manages all aspects of a year-round pledge campaign: planning and implementation, as well as oversight of committees to offer support, creativity, encouragement, and resources.

The Skills

The commission is made up of four to eight leaders from within the congregation, overseen by a commission chair and served by clergy and staff. The commission requires creative design, effective management, kind-hearted encouragement, and measured objectives—all in a context of engaging God's mission for our church.

The Expectations

Stewardship Commission members are asked to be people of prayer in whatever forms that takes in their spiritual practice. They are asked to pledge and to consider planned giving and major gifts, if that philanthropy suits their plans and capacity for giving. The commission members are evangelists for the joys of giving and are invited into a stunningly enjoyable, relational, and rewarding ministry of design and oversight among some of the most gifted and committed leaders in the congregation.

Choosing Leadership in Major Gifts

One of the most frequent and egregious mistakes when churches attempt to recruit leaders for major- and planned-giving initiatives is they choose captains of industry, the tremendously wealthy, lawyers, or corporate executives. It is logical to think these people will have the capacity to give big gifts and are, therefore, the right people to ask for them. That is not always the case.

It is true that wealthy people need to be the ones asking for major gifts, because people being asked for major gifts need to be asked, as a rule, by people giving at the same level. However, the importance of choosing people who are kind, gentle, deeply involved, able to keep confidences, and generally known as trustworthy is even more crucial.

Noticing Passions and Curating Conversations

People are the beginning, the middle, and the end of major-gifts fundraising. It is not about the money, the project, the church, the clergy, the wardens, or elders. Major-gift fundraising is only and always about the donor. The relationship. When a person has decided to take up major gifts as a part of the larger resource development to fund a church's future mission, their most important task is noticing. You may think their top task is asking, but it is not. A person who has decided to lead a major-gifts ministry in a church has, as their most important task, the beautiful work of paying attention to people.

In the story above about Bill and Helen, my job as both minister and fundraiser was to notice what was going on in their lives. I did not need to know anything about their finances, since that is their job or the job of their advisors. I did not need to know anything about their lifestyle. I needed to pay attention to the meaning-making they were trying to express that sunlit afternoon. They were holding hands. They never interrupted each other. They never interrupted me. And I never interrupted them. When there were times for silence, we allowed the silence to hang in the air, like feathers on a breeze. I needed to let them talk. I needed to ask them questions about what was important to them. I needed to ask about their story:

- How did they meet?
- What did they do for work?
- What were their hobbies?
- What did they love about the parish?
- What disappoints them about the parish?
- How long have they been members here?
- Is it their hope to be buried here?
- Where do their children live?
- What do they wish was happening at this church that is not currently happening?
- What would they like to make happen at this church?
- What kind of gift would they like to make? Do they need to make a planned gift so that they have income from the gift, or do they want to retain the income but let the gift pass to the church?

The Role of Vulnerability

God became vulnerable by taking human form, and Jesus became humanly vulnerable by offering his body for torture and death. Clearly, vulnerability is an essential divine and human trait. Vulnerability plays an essential role in raising major gifts. The best clergy, bishops, and fundraisers connect at a very deep level with those who wish to support and fund the church primarily because they are willing to be vulnerable. Vulnerable people tell and listen to stories.

Clergy, bishops, or lay leaders who storm into fundraising without proper preparation, not having carefully involved their major donors on the ground floor of planning, will inevitably fail miserably. I have seen too many stall at about the 25 percent mark, because leaders launched the campaign too early without carefully securing the buy-in and involvement of major donors.

However, I've also seen clergy and bishops lead capital campaigns and major-gift programs in which they generously and vulnerably took their idea (what they wanted to raise money for) in its roughest form in a three-ring loose-leaf binder, while offering potential donors a brand new red pen to make changes. With humility and the willingness to encounter major donors who may disagree with what you plan to build, or simply find that it is not part of their meaning-making, vulnerability can set the stage for meaningful conversations in which the church leader learns a lot and the major donor prospect deepens the relationship. But beware. In order to be successful as a major-gift fundraiser, you must be willing to experience vulnerability and even disagreement.

The beautiful work of major-gifts fundraising in churches requires that the institution and those that lead it maintain a humble stance both articulating their vision and a willingness to see if the vision overlaps with the meaning-making of the donors. By the time you ask the major donors for a gift, they should be long since tired of talking. They should be excited and ready to invest in the project.

It is important for us to have deep compassion for everybody involved in the major-gift solicitation process. It is a tender, holy, and deeply human encounter, much like the early days of dating. There is a relationship, and then there is the work of deepening the relationship with all of its inherent starts and stops, miscues, awkward silences, badly phrased comments, and competing interests.

A good example of this tender and very human vulnerability over issues of wealth, power, and request can be found in the parable of the rich young ruler. In Mark's Gospel (10:17–22), we see two men, Jesus and a wealthy young man seeking advice. Both are vulnerable. Jesus is vulnerable from his annoyance with the wealthy man. The wealthy man is vulnerable because, although he is asking Jesus about the afterlife, he is clearly worried about the life he is living at the moment. Like many wealthy people, his money has not brought him happiness.

Is it possible to have compassion for Jesus whose inner zealot was triggered by the encounter? Is it possible also to have compassion for the rich young man who was confused by Jesus' anger and was trying to get some help living a holy life? In the conversation, Jesus softens. The man's wealth does not trigger Jesus' insecurities. Jesus helps him.

The reality is that many clergy and lay leaders have their insecurities triggered by wealthy people. Clergy and bishops have often left successful careers as lawyers, scientists, writers, and business people. They had taken significant pay cuts and made sacrifices to be clergy. When it comes time to encounter wealthy people and maintain the five or six conversations that will lead to a major-gift request, their patience gets frayed and their egos bruised because a major donor does not like the project, or believes it should be changed. Someone once asked me, "What is the most powerful resource for people raising major gifts?" I said that the greatest resources for fundraising were patience, prayer, humility, and the willingness to listen.

The Sacramentality of Conversation

I believe that when two people are talking about a major gift for the church or the diocese that will ease suffering, spread the gospel, and bring joy to people who need it, something wonderful is happening. Jesus didn't always heal immediately. Jesus sometimes asked, "Do you want to be healed?" When wealthy people give major gifts, something in them heals. The same thing happens when anyone gives something away as a gift. The only way to really tap in to the beauty of humans asking other humans to give gifts is to believe that both the asking and the giving are sacramental acts that emerge from our baptismal vows; they are what we were made for.

People who visit those sick and in the hospital are exercising a healing ministry. I believe with equal ferocity that the people who visit the wealthy are exercising a healing ministry, just as people who give a gift to ease suffering or to create beauty are being healed by their very act of giving.

To help someone give their money away to make healing or beauty possible contributes to peace on earth and assists in unveiling nothing less than the kingdom of God. The work you are doing to build and maintain a major- and planned-gifts program in your church or diocese is great and wonderful work.

The YMCA, museum of fine arts, local hospitals, and schools are very good at helping people give their money to their causes, and that is just great. I also believe that the church has a tremendous role to play in our villages, towns, cities, and that society's need will increase exponentially as technology further separates us. Even today, most of us barely know our neighbors' names. I am thanking you, not just because you are helping donors make meaning, but because you are helping churches become stronger and more resilient as they raise these major gifts over the next few decades. I am thanking you because I know this is emotionally demanding work and that you may be afraid of doing the various things in this book to raise money.

I know that it seems unspiritual and perhaps even undignified to ask people for major gifts, but it is not. Houses of worship have been raising money this way since Zebedee's family back in the first century gave a major gift to a synagogue in Capernaum. Archaeologists found that stone with their names on it. Remember James and John, the sons of Zebedee? They gave a major gift to their synagogue and were thanked with a kind of donor wall, or with a stone in that wall, at least. Oxford University was built with major gifts. Canterbury Cathedral was built with major gifts. The great libraries and hospitals of the world were built with major gifts. The great books were copied by monks and saved from invaders because patrons of those monasteries gave the major gifts to fund the long nights bent over those vellum pages with quill pens and ink and candles. Behind each of those gifts were generous people.

Each gift has people behind it with stories of their own. Some gifts were in memory of loved ones. Some gifts were because of a fascination with the subject. Some gifts were to thank God for something—the birth of a baby, the healing of a loved one, the winning of a new job. But these gifts, and the people behind them, and the missions in front of them, made our world beautiful and interesting. It is my hope that you will summon the courage, take hold of this book, and get this job done. I hope you delight, as I have over these three decades of raising major gifts, in the faces of people who, when they make their major gift, light up with a smile that could compete with the sun for its brightness and joy. And I hope you can see the faces of people whose suffering is reduced because of those gifts.

Mission Integrity

The difficulty inherent in establishing mission authenticity is that there are as many ways to discern and establish an authentic mission as there are churches on the planet. I do not mean to imply that you do not have mission integrity in your church. You may be doing exactly the kind of work Jesus would be thrilled about were you to give him a tour. But, in my experience, many churches from noon or one P.M. on Sunday until breakfast the next, are empty, lifeless, and dull places. The reality in some of our smaller churches is it is all a priest or minister can do to preach a sermon, prepare a Sunday worship service, and visit the sick and the lonely. For many small churches, that is their mission. Jesus was not interested in the maintenance of an institution. Indeed, Jesus was begging for a movement and *not* an institution. It is important to raise money for a worthy mission—one Jesus would recognize at a glance. So do not be tempted to raise money just to keep the lights on and the clergy fed. Raise money that stops suffering and heals pain. It is into that kind of work that the next generations want to invest their philanthropy.

Many churches think that the reason they are not raising major gifts, and the reason they are not receiving as many planned gifts, is that they're not asking for these gifts. That may be true. I hope this book will teach you how to ask for major gifts. Foundational to the major-gift request is this question of mission integrity. Is a major donor making a gift to a chapel of ease, or is the major donor investing in vibrant, exciting, risk-taking, slightly dangerous work to transform suffering into joy for people outside the church walls?

En-Theos

Enthusiasm comes from two Greek words—*en-theos*—that mean entering into the ecstasy and inspiration of God. It is enthusiasm that inspires a major gift. Enthusiasm builds in members of the congregation brought in on the ground floor of an idea—I mean the very ground floor—with that first inkling, expressed as a question like, "I know this sounds crazy, and it would be very difficult, and I have no idea where to get the money, but wouldn't it be tremendously exciting, and wouldn't Jesus just shiver all over, if this church could . . . ?" These are the people who will give major gifts. These are the people who will get involved, roll up their sleeves, and help you get the job done. What often happens is only leaders have that enthusiasm—for their own idea. And they are often so attached to their idea that they're not willing to bring other people, especially wealthy people who can fund the project, into the ground floor of idea-making.

When leaders are willing to bring a tender and vulnerable idea to the people who can fund the idea, and when they are willing to bring the idea to potential donors early, they may find that these major donor prospects are often deeply sensitive to the feelings of the idea generator, even though they may have some suggestions. Of course, sometimes their suggestions are departures, even radical departures, from the original plan, but the issue is that donors, especially major donors, need to feel that their wisdom and experience are welcome. It is interesting that, especially in the church, we are much more excited to ask people for their money than to ask them for their opinions.

A leader's hesitancy can be fueled by questions such as, "What if potential donors have different opinions than I have about this project? What if they change my design? What if their opinions and ideas improve my project so much that it becomes our project instead of my project? What if I lose control? What if they use their money to change what I want to do?" The truth is we do not like vulnerability, and we especially do not like vulnerability in a "father knows best" church. The church has been, for 1,700 years, a hierarchical system based in male authority and power structures, traditionally patriarchal because of how it has presented God. The system is going to have to change as patriarchy crumbles. And leaders are going to have to change because to block influence (so that nobody messes with your idea) is, also, to block funding; if you block funding, then you block input from other people, and the cycle spirals down to an unfunded idea.

Be Whole (Not Perfect)

No church or diocese is going to have a flawless, perfect mission. There are going to be plenty of things you do that nobody has the time, energy, or social capital to shut down, to guide into hospice and ultimate death. It is very important, if a church wants to raise major gifts, that there is a clear focus on what you are going to do and what you are not going to do. As our scriptures say, let your yes be yes, and your no be no. Of course, different churches and denominations have different polities. It may, for example, be harder for a Congregational church to weed out ministries that are not part of that church's mission than it might be for a more hierarchical church in which top-down decisions can weed out ineffective and unproductive ministries.

You do not need to be perfect, but you do need to be whole. Work to create a culture within your church in which everybody knows what your congregation, based on its surroundings and its discernment, has decided it is going to do well. Then do that work. What you will find with this kind of focus is that you will build a reputation, over time, for doing good work in a certain area. The result will be that people in your area will begin to hear about the work you're doing in your church. When Jason's church decided to feed people, and became well-known for feeding people, the local butcher made a big contribution of meat and side dishes to feed hundreds. However, he was not a member of the congregation. He was not even planning to become a member of the congregation, nor did he. He simply wanted to make a contribution to solve a problem in his town. Sometimes, that is how the Holy Spirit shows up—in someone not even connected to your church, but who loves people and has a generous heart.

I recently raised several major gifts for a new organ for our church. One of the major donors, who gave twenty-five thousand dollars, was not a member. He was a member of a different denomination, but he loved organ music, loved beauty, and used to be an organ builder himself. Because the organ was in the cathedral, he wanted to make sure that there was a trumpet stop on the organ console. That was his meaning-making. We wanted a trumpet stop on the organ console. His meaning-making, overlapped with our meaning-making, resulting in a major gift to a church he didn't even attend.

Being Good Ancestors

Take a few minutes and look around your church. Read some of the plaques and see what they say about the donors. Talk to the oldest lady in your church and ask her about some of the major gifts in the past. Notice the kinds of things that people have given over the years, over the decades. In some churches, it may be over the centuries. Who gave the pulpit? Who gave the lectern? Who gave the organ? Who gave the pews? Who gave you some of the rooms? Who made gifts to the endowment?

These are the ancestors of your church. They were men and women who lived during World War II, or World War I, or during the reign of King Edward, Queen Victoria, or perhaps even William and Mary. Some wore corsets. Some may have used quill pens or steel fountain pens to write, with a beautiful script, the checks for their major gifts. The question, as you plan and manage a major-gifts program in your church, is: How are you and your friends going to be great ancestors to the people into whose hands you'll place your church and its mission?

Only you can do this. Nobody else is going to come along and manage a major-gifts program for your church or diocese. You sit on the shoulders of people who made major gifts to your church. You sit in their pews. You drink from their silver chalices. Now it is your turn.

Integrity and Effectiveness

The minister and the chair of the major-gifts committee must take the time to pray, discern, and think through the integrity of mission, institution, leadership, and general financial development in your church. Before raising major gifts, a few things need to be in place, including:

1. **Stability**: A minister who is willing to stay in place for a few years to steward the major gifts you are asking for and receiving.
2. **Leadership**: A good partnership between trustworthy clergy and trusted lay leaders willing to lead major gifts with measurable objectives.
3. **Mission clarity**: A clear focus of mission for the church to exercise and that has been agreed to by all through careful discernment.
4. **A strategic plan:** This shows what the church and its leadership have discerned to be their pathway forward in mission and ministry for the next ten years in general, the next five years in particular detail, and the next year in specific detail.
5. **A gift-acceptance policy:** This document describes the process of accepting a major gift so that there is a way to politely decline something the church does not want to receive or that is not part of its mission.
6. **A strong annual pledge campaign:** This essential element supports the major-gifts and planned-giving programs and supplies a few people who have both the capacity and interest to give joyfully beyond the annual pledge.
7. **Absolute integrity of leadership:** The integrity of the people chosen for leadership in the church, especially the clergy, along with secure confidence in their effective pastoral care are essential. It takes a prophetic voice to call a congregation to do great things. However, before a congregation can hear their ministers and lay leaders as prophetic, they first have to experience them as good and faithful pastors. Any clergy who has failed as a pastor will never be heard as a prophet, and a major-gifts program will be doomed until you choose new leadership.

So you have formed your major-gift advisory committee. You have developed excellent and stable leadership. The church has a very clear and concise mission and ministry, and you're able to communicate it effectively. You've sorted through the membership of your church, and you have identified about 10 percent whom you believe to have both the capacity and the interest to make a major gift, if you're able to manage the engagement phase effectively. You have developed the meaning-making list—a menu of the projects for which you would like to receive major gifts. If you have been able to accomplish these tasks, you are well on your way to success. If you have not yet completed them, then you at least know what you need to do. If you still have some of these things to accomplish, that's okay. The important thing is that you know what you need to do, you know what has been done, and all you have to do is develop a strategic plan with measurable objectives.

The last thing you need to do is expand your meaning-making list. Each of these projects will need some form of expanded case for support, about which I speak in the next section. In putting these projects together, you create a meaning-making menu of major gifts.

A Major-Gifts Case for Support

Many things in my life give me great pleasure. I love dim sum for brunch. I love Paris in February and coffee with bread and cheese. I love having my friends close to me on a movie night. I love walking my dog on a cool Denver night, and I love to watch movies with big explosions or gorgeous costumes in a theater with popcorn slathered in butter and salt. I love making a meal for close friends and then watching the candles burn all the way down as we take six hours to eat the meal together. I love stationery. And beautiful pens.

For all of the things I love, there are tools of the trade. For a dim sum brunch, I need chopsticks, chili oil, and jasmine tea. For a walk in February in Paris, there should be a great scarf and a good book in my pocket for the frequent stops for coffee. Walking my dog means I need bags for poo. At the movies, I need plenty of napkins. For dinner with friends, I need tall beeswax candles—tall ivory tapers with brass followers, so the wax does not drip all over the dining-room table. For letters, I need stationery, and for my pens I need good ink—cobalt blue, sepia brown, or turquoise. These are the tools for the things I love. I also love asking for major gifts, or at least helping others to ask. The tool for asking for a major gift is neither chili oil, a long scarf, nor candles. The three tools of the trade for major gifts include time, a living room, and a case for support.

A case for support is a document, a video, a speech, or a brochure— any form of storytelling tool—that tells why you want to raise money. It communicates both emotion and data to show the prospective donor how important and vital your project is. When you get a brochure in the mail, explaining how wonderful the Girl Scouts are and why they're asking for a donation, that is a case for support. When you get a letter from the rector explaining why they need your pledge, that, too, is a case for support (though not usually a very effective one). When asked to give to a capital campaign and someone hands you a beautiful brochure, that is a case for support. When someone sits you down in front of a video that takes you on a virtual tour of the new wing of the museum, shows interviews with leaders, and explains why it is the right time for the museum to expand, that is a case for support. The meaning-making menu, of which I spoke earlier, consists of thumbnail sketches outlining cases for support. Each of these little paragraphs can be developed into a larger case for support.

It is important to match the right tool with the right situation. When asking for major gift, a video case for support is valuable with a group or when you want to convey significant emotion or visual impact. Unless you are able to get the video donated (and many churches can these days, with easily available videography and editing software), this can be an expensive route. On the other hand, "it takes money to make money" is definitely a truism in fundraising. Most churches will need to dedicate up to 8 percent of money that is raised to the budget needed to raise the money. I have seen church campaigns spend 80 percent (not 8 percent) of what they raised on campaign counsel, staffing, and resources, which is unconscionable. So it is very important for the integrity of your campaign never to spend more than 8 to 10 percent of the money you will raise when trying to raise it.

Regardless of how you are going to use your case for support, you will generally want to create the case in video format due to video's prominence on the Internet and in social media. Older members of congregations who are not using online video can easily watch a DVD delivered by the clergy or one of the leaders of the major-gifts program. Many churches develop pamphlets and brochures that explain their cases for support.

Spiritual Underpinnings of Leadership

Often the most challenging part of fundraising in the church is making countless visits to inform and include people in advance of the actual request of the major gift. It can be a dark place—and I mean dark. It can even be menacing. I actually believe in powers and principalities that upset goodness and frighten gentle, good people. I have seen churches floating along like a gentle river with a docile minister unwilling to make any waves. And then comes a major-gifts program and, quite literally, all hell breaks loose. I do not know who or what Satan is. I suppose as an aged priest I should know. I suppose I should also know what *heaven* means and perhaps even *hell*. I can spout doctrine about them with the best of my peers, but we are all unsure of the facts. We have faith, not certainty.

One thing I have seen from my experience is that when the devil (or Lucifer or Satan or evil) notices we are beginning to make waves, raise money, build our church, and strengthen it for its mission, Satan shows up in no uncertain terms. Usually in the form of something like resistance. Whenever the Holy Spirit is moving and shaking and pushing the church into a profound and deep mission, you can bet that Satan is going to be nearby in some form.

For this reason, I end this chapter on relationships by writing about the most important relationship of all: our relationship with God. If you're reading this book, I assume you are in some way a leader in your church, charged with raising major gifts, or at least charged with leading the process. I've spent these last many pages talking about the relationship that has to be built and nurtured between people raising major gifts and the major donors. Would it not be the height of irony, if we did not discuss the spirituality involved in the relationship between the church fundraiser and God?

The most important decision of a church fundraiser today, with all the fear and resistance they will face, is not a decision about the stewardship plan for annual pledges, nor about campaign or program or vestry leadership. The most important decision is not about the church's strategic plan, or its major-gifts plan, or even the content and form of the case to support. The single most important decision that any person raising money in the church needs to take seriously is the decision they make about their spiritual life.

Raising money in churches is a spiritual endeavor that has logistical implications, not a logistical endeavor with spiritual implications. Please do not move into such a demanding, vulnerable role as stewardship or fundraising leadership in a church without first "girding your loins," as our scripture says. If you're not a person who prays, then learn how to pray. If you are a church leader who doesn't often go to church, learn to go to church regularly. If you are a church leader who makes choices like a corporate executive rather than prayerfully discerning from the Holy Spirit like a spiritual leader, then learn the ancient and great art of discernment before you take up leadership in the church. If you live a scattered, frenetic, overstimulated, overcaffeinated, emotionally unintelligent life, learn how to be centered, rested, calm, and wise before you take up leadership in the church.

I do not mean to sound harsh or judgmental, but I do mean to be very, very clear. Disaster will follow leaders who are not spiritually grounded, but simply rich or powerful. I do not care if you have an expensive car, a large house, a large cross on your chest, or a purple shirt. You will be dangerous to good and kind people if you try to lead without doing so in a centered, well, sober, and prayerful manner.

The single most important thing to do when you're trying to raise major gifts in a church is this: practice your Christianity in an intentional, solitary, and measurable way before you take up church leadership. We already have too many corporate executives leading our churches. We need more humble, kind, honest, and prayerful people in leadership. I am grateful for the wisdom and experience of corporate and governmental executives, but only when that wisdom is grounded in a spiritual life. And by spiritual life, I do not mean the idea. I mean the practice.

Job Description—
Stewardship Commission

The mission of the Stewardship Commission is to create, plan, and build a ministry of giving that transforms our approach to resource development in ways that foster and strengthen our collective desire to fund the collective discernment of our mission, as well as to invite new visitors to our church for membership discernment. The commission oversees the raising of pledges in the fall, people in the spring, and philanthropy and hospitality year-round. In addition to campaign design, evaluation, and oversight, the commission will encourage and support the missions of the five stewardship committees—planned giving, invitation, major gifts, art of hosting meaningful conversation (participatory leadership), and hospitality—to provide the necessary resources to support our church's mission.

Job Description—
Major-Gift Committee Charters

The mission of the Planned-Giving Committee is to educate around the need and importance of planned giving, to encourage participation in planned giving, and to ensure good stewardship is demonstrated through planned gifts to the ongoing and future mission of the church.

The mission of the Major-Gifts Advisory Committee is to manage the process by which church members consider, discern, and make major gifts to the mission of the church. The committee, in coordination with the Planned-Giving Committee, will identify members who can make such gifts and oversee the process by which major donors are informed, encouraged, and invited to make investments in the mission of the church now and into the future.

Wow Cards

Keep index cards in the pews of your church. If you are able, have them printed at an online postcard service with a beautiful image of your church on one side and blank on the other except for the question, "What ideas do you have for ministry of this church that would make Jesus say, 'Wow! That is exactly what I was hoping you would do'?" Across the bottom of the card, ask for contact information and instruct the writer to place the card in the offering plate. If you can't afford such a card to be printed, then simply use index cards and make announcements about what to do with them. Every once in a while, someone will offer a great idea—and they may even have a major gift to back it up. This work contributes to deep mission integrity since it both raises ideas and reminds the congregation that it is *their* church, their mission, and so must be funded by their major gifts. This culture change will help immeasurably to raise major gifts.

A Case-Development Exercise for Confidence and Joy

Working with your stewardship leaders or church leadership, take an oversized piece of paper and with a marker write a headline across the top, much like one you would see on the front page of a newspaper. Imagine a positive headline about your church or diocese resulting from a successful major-gifts program that raised ten times your annual budget ten years from now. Then write the story underneath the headline explaining how the money will change lives. This is a good exercise to do with a vestry, a major-gift leadership team, and even a small group of major donors. Playfully imagining a great future in fundraising might be all you need to move past fear and into your success.

The Community Interview

1. Community leadership interviews send a message to the congregants that the church's leadership is not managing in an ivory tower, but is actively seeking data that integrate the mission and ministry of the church with the needs and experiences in the larger community.
2. Among community leaders, the interviews dispel notions of exclusivity and mission competition, and send a message that the church seeks to collaborate for good and for economies of scale.
3. The interviews also provide valuable insights regarding the perceptions of your church. Some perceptions may be wrong, but that they exist means you need to begin to change them.
4. The interviews collect valuable data about changing trends, new growth, shifting demographics, new and planned initiatives and events, potential grants, and more.
5. Such a process is usually required for grant applications, especially those based on community impact.
6. Simply entering people's offices and homes for conversation helps the church make friends and connect with its community.

Summary of Discernment Tools

1. **Ignatian discernment**: There are many books about Saint Ignatius of Loyola, whose groundbreaking work created what we now know as discernment. The Reverend James Martin, S.J., has written extensively and creatively about the kind of prayer in which Saint Ignatius was involved. Discernment is not only something one can study, but it is also one of the spiritual gifts—what the church often calls "charism." Look for people in your church who have this gift. They are people of prayer, and they have a particular gift for hearing God speak, without boasting about it.

2. **The right leaders**: Choose your leaders carefully. We tend to do in our churches what corporations do. We look around for the richest, most financially and professionally successful people, and we put them in high places such as vestries, boards, elders, and diocesan commissions and committees. There is no problem as long as the people you elect are people of deep prayer and daily spiritual practice, and are also known for their honesty and integrity. Electing the right leaders will set you on the path of discerning the right mission.

3. **Prayer, and silence in worship**: The most powerful tools your church has at its disposal are not the powerful executives on your board, nor your famous rector. The most powerful tool your church has to form great mission that your major donors will fund is your willingness to pray and remain silent together during corporate worship. When I travel and speak, I am often asked, "What can our church do to raise more money and form great mission?" My response is always the same. "Insert a three-minute-long period of silent meditation into the beginning of your worship, about halfway through your worship, and again a few minutes before the end." When I suggest this set of three long periods of silence in worship, most leaders look at me as if I just took off my clothes. They are shocked. They are confused. But a little bit of silence during worship—so that the Holy Spirit gets a chance to say something, and to be heard—is the best way to ensure that a church is able to hear God, when God calls them to mission rather than just to gathering. And it is mission to which major donors will give.

4. **The Art of Hosting Conversations That Matter** is technology for leadership that I employ with great success when I'm helping churches discern their mission. I was taught by three of its greatest leaders: Chris Corrigan, Caitlin Frost, and Tenneson Woolf. They took me under their wing, on a crisp fall day on an island off the coast of British Columbia, and they lovingly taught me tools and techniques that have helped me live my life and lead in the church. For more information on this technology for hosting the kinds of conversations in your church that lead to clarity of mission, go to artofhosting.org.

RESOURCE

A Ministry-Effectiveness Survey

1. How is this ministry changing the lives of people who benefit from it?
2. What members are engaged in this ministry, either as volunteers or as donors? How are their lives affected?
3. Who is providing the ministry, and how much is this costing from the budget?
4. What more could the church be doing in this area?
5. What unmet needs exist, and what would meeting those needs require, in human and financial terms?
6. What do recipients of this ministry say about how they are being ministered to?
7. How does this ministry affect the way nonchurched people see our church? How does it affect our reputation and image?

Member Questionnaire

These questions may be posed in a series of adult forums, with a leader posted at each table to take notes. They may also be circulated by mail or e-mail and returned to the church leadership.

1. Over this past year, what aspect of our church's life has excited, interested, or motivated you the most?
2. In what areas of church life have you noticed the Holy Spirit particularly at work? Where do you sense energy and vitality?
3. What requires the attention of your vestry or rector? Of what should they be aware? What would you like to change?
4. What task or goal should be a priority for our church over the next three years? What is the congregation doing to serve God and the local community?
5. What keeps you coming to this church? What might attract newcomers?
6. In what ministry would you like to become more involved?
7. What could we do to improve communications in the church?
8. What could we do to improve stewardship and planned-giving programs in the church?

The Art
of Hosting Meaningful Conversation—
Method for Leveled Engagement

> Conversation is a sacred art. It illuminates the spaces between us and gives voice to the longings that Spirit inspires within us. Becoming skillful practitioners of conversational leadership helps build engaged communities, address strategic issues in organizations, and strengthen families.
>
> —Tenneson Woolf, consultant in the Art of Hosting

The Art of Hosting Conversations That Matter is the core material of training in participatory leadership. Practiced worldwide and developed in the for-profit sector to reduce siloing in corporations, this material will introduce you to the profound practices of hosting, and harvesting, powerful conversations.

Through Christ, God hosted conversations that mattered to humans and met them as human. Face to face and person to person in conversation. Jesus wandered, meeting people along the way, inviting them to come and see what he was about. He reoriented God's relationship to humanity as one in which friends meet, eat, and converse on equal terms (John 15:15). Jesus sought real, equal connection with royal leaders, the financially destitute, and the spiritually destitute. He asked that we love one another, not manage one another. We are made in that kind, humble, loving image; now we must try to live that way together as the body of Christ—the church—and even within our families.

In these times of change and challenge, no one person has the answers we need, but there is a vast collective intelligence that simply needs to be released and harvested. We need to increase our capacity to be in shared, participatory leadership, and we need to be in meaningful, effective, connected, inspiring, and even challenging conversations. We need to address our own ecclesial and even personal anxiety and increase our emotional intelligence so that conversations do not slip into top-down, power-based control.

The Art of Hosting, in which we learn new ways to host conversations, is an extraordinary experience for personal transformation around facing limiting beliefs, gaining listening skills, leading peaceful communications, and hosting conversation. For more information on the work of facing limiting beliefs, go to thework.com/thework.php. Practiced worldwide, and within my parish these past few years, this learning experience will introduce you to the simple, yet profound, practices of hosting and harvesting powerful conversations. The technique involves several practices, including:

- methods of hosting meaningful conversations useful for large groups and one-on-one conversations (Circle practice, World Cafe, Open Space Technology).
- inquiry, resilience, and presence-making that allow you to accept challenges of leadership. The techniques help make sense of the complexity we face and emphasize the imperative for dialogue as a way of moving forward together.
- the art of creating powerful questions and a narrative arc that can help take groups to deeper levels of conversation, strategy, and sustainability. The practice results in the ability to discern mission from the ground up, rather from the rector's chair and the bishop's throne down. This process will engage your congregation and help them to feel that their opinion matters and is clearly heard both by powerful people and by the rest of the congregation. You will walk away with the experience and tools, frameworks, and worldviews that will enable you to navigate challenges and opportunities in your work, community, and personal life.

I have been training and leading churches in this work for more than a decade, and I am never disappointed by what I see unfolding in front of me. In the church in which I serve as canon steward, we have been using the Art of Hosting Conversations That Matter to change the culture of our church. It was hard at first. Cultures do not naturally like to be changed. Indeed, they are cultures, usually, for a reason, and exist usually to serve the purposes of someone or something. But the more our congregation was trained to trust the willingness of leadership to let them speak freely, the more freely they spoke. And the more freely they spoke, the more they heard each other saying things that began to resemble a vision of hope.

Often our congregation holds what we call Dream Together Conferences. Most of our active congregation joins together on Saturdays, sitting in a circle around a low tablescape covered in beautiful things: candles, icons, orchids, mementos. Then we form groups of four around small cocktail tables and move conversations around the room, like speed dating, while a cartoonist draws our conversations on a wall of cardboard the height and length of a large university whiteboard. It is wonderful to see our conversations emerge as images in bright colors. It is even more exciting to see the people watch their own words turning to playful images before their eyes. This way of creating an artifact is so different from typing up the minutes of a meeting.

This is the future of our church. Meaningful conversation. Equality and creativity win out and prevent megaphone voices from dominating or the wallflower voices from receding and being dominated. It is my fervent belief that the only way to raise major gifts in a church is to change the way we have our conversations, such that everyone feels involved and heard, and everyone participates in the discernment of the mission. When that happens, major gifts will flow like, as scriptures say, honey from the rock. Not only will there be financial bounty, but there will be relational bounty as well. And it is to that mission that we are all called.

A Sample Letter
Asking for the First Visit

Dear Sarah,

Many exciting things are happening in our church. Jennifer, our minister, and our leadership team/vestry are excited about her leadership and the ministry she is helping to unfold and uncover in our church. Our budget is balanced, our mission is clear and focused, and our Sunday attendance is growing by leaps and bounds. We are running out of space. Last week I saw the youth group meeting in the stairwell, because all the rooms were spoken for.

I am one among a small group of people imagining how to host a larger conversation about our church's future. Demographics from the town say we are growing, so we need to prepare. We would like to expand our building. May I stop by your house, or might we meet for coffee to chat about this growth and its implications? I want to hear what you are thinking as an established member of our congregation. I know you have ideas that will help us.

If I may, I'll call you over the next few days to ask if I may stop by. I would be grateful for your time.

(a live blue-ink signature . . . always)

Johnathan Menninger

A Sample
Donor-Engagement Continuum

Mrs. Johnson's engagement continuum (last year and this year) toward a request for twenty-five thousand dollars to help renovate the church kitchen. Leadership gift. ($110,000 goal)

June 3	met with minister to make friends
July 6	met with senior warden of the church to ask opinions
September 7	gave increased annual gift from $500 (past seventeen years) to $1,000
November 26	thanked personally (after immediate handwritten note and letters)
December 10	invited to help cook a Christmas dinner in the old kitchen
January 30	invited to see the list of major-gifts needs (twenty-eight) of the church
March 12	discussed the list of twenty-eight needs, mentions interest in kitchen
April 4	gives special gift to fund kitchen evaluation
June 1	taken on a tour of the kitchen with evaluator, shown report
September 3	invited to lead kitchen campaign, accepts chair position
October 7	invited to focus-group conversation about kitchen
December 19	invited to help cook a Christmas dinner in the old kitchen
January 9	leads annual-meeting discussion on new kitchen
March 15	leads special parish meeting to review plans for new kitchen
April 18	designs major-gifts campaign to raise seven major gifts for 90 percent

Next step

May 1	asked by minister and senior warden for the leadership gift

As you can see from Mrs. Johnson's engagement continuum, she was never manipulated and only invited into a discernment process into which she herself expressed initial interest in renovating the church kitchen. She was tired of the state kitchen inspectors constantly condemning the stove and the ventilation system and shutting the kitchen down for weeks at a time. She remembers seeing an infestation of cockroaches one morning when she flipped on the lights to make coffee for a church retreat. Mrs. Johnson loved to cook. She came from a large Greek family and was famous for her spanakopita. With six children, she had cooked thousands of meals and was never happier than when she was in the church kitchen with six other cooks, chatting and laughing and sharing recipes while they prepared a meal for the parish. She hated seeing the many bills that paid for repairs when in fact they should have been paying for replacements.

Mrs. Johnson had a dream. Her next two daughters were engaged and had expressed their desire to be married in the church. They both wanted a big reception in the parish hall with all their church friends. Mrs. Johnson wanted that seventy-year-old kitchen with the avocado-colored refrigerator and mustard-green stove upgraded. So she told the church that her meaning-making was to make a gift, one day, for the kitchen. In fact, she was a little annoyed that the church, which has always avoided asking for major gifts, had never bothered to do much more than eke out an existence by keeping the lights on and the minister employed. She was thrilled that the new leadership had shown her a list of twenty-eight things for which major gifts were needed at that church: a new sound system, a new lighting plan for the sanctuary, the renovation of the bell tower, a handicapped-accessibility ramp, a new kitchen, an endowment to expand the capacity of mission beyond pledges, and an addition so that the new kitchen can be used to serve the homeless.

As you look over the above example of an engagement continuum, you can see the planning. At any point along the way, the donor can say, "Stop talking to me about a major gift, I do not want to give one"; or, "Hey, you are talking to me about the wrong major gift. I don't want to give to the new kitchen. I want to give to the learning garden"; or, "I am sorry, but I have had a change in my finances, and I cannot make a major gift." Then the planning can shift. After every engagement with a major donor, the plan for the next event in their life (a visit, a tour, a chance to edit a document, meet with a planner, tour a facility, or chat with a previous donor) is decided upon based on the information they offer. Donors will tell you what they are interested in funding, but not without engagement, and not quickly.

Example: Moves-Management or Engagement Continuum
A Donor-Engagement Plan for Mr. and Mrs. Smith

Congregant who may be willing to make a major gift to your church	The first event toward discerning a possible major gift to your church	The second event toward discerning a possible major gift to your church	The third event toward discerning a possible major gift to your church	The fourth event toward discerning a possible major gift to your church	The fifth event toward discerning a possible major gift to your church	The sixth event toward discerning a possible major gift to your church	The request for the gift
	Month 1	**Month 3**	**Month 5**	**Month 11**	**Month 13**	**Month 14**	**Month 15**
Mr. & Mrs. Smith jands@expedia.com 34 Poplar Lane Waynstown, Ohio 24871 592-457-9726 (c. Sarah) 714-817-3347 (c. John) 720-346-2817 (home) Annual pledge: $1,200 Last major gift: $8,000 for a new stove in 1989	Invite John and Sarah to a parish dinner, during which a "Meaning-Making Major-Gifts List" of possible gifts is discussed. Get input on the list. Make sure they sit with William and Emily, who have been their best friends in the parish for decades.	The minister visits John and Sarah to discuss their impressions of the event and of the meaning-making menu of major gifts the church seeks. She asks John and Sarah what they are interested in giving to, were they interested in giving a major gift. Asks if they are missing anything.	The minister and Harold Williams, chair of major gifts, returns to the Smith home with a revised list that takes into account the Smiths' suggestions, agreed to by the vestry. They express interest in the new industrial kitchen the church is planning. They ask for more information.	The minister returns with the lay leader who leads ministry to the homeless. John and Sarah express interest in donating to a kitchen that will make meals for the church and homeless possible. They both have volunteered for years in the old kitchen.	John and Sarah attend a luncheon at another local church that has just renovated its kitchen and that provides meals to the homeless. They meet with that church's major-gifts committee to hear about their renovation. The kitchen consultant from the Smiths' church also attends.	A few weeks later, revised plans for the new kitchen are developed. The Smiths go to the church to see how the renovation will proceed. The Smiths, who have served hundreds of meals there, make suggestions that slightly change the plans. They see floor and tile samples.	The minister, along with William and Emily (the Smiths' close friends), set an appointment, asking if they may come to request a major gift for the new kitchen. The Smiths welcome the visit. Emily, who has given $15,000 to the new kitchen, asks John and Sarah if they also will give $15,000.
Mr. Symington	need plan						
Mr. & Mrs. Williams	need plan						
Mrs. White	need plan						

A Sample Parish
Meaning-Making List

Air-conditioning system: The parish church and buildings can reach ninety degrees in mid-summer without air conditioning. The old system is beginning to deteriorate, and it is necessary to provide a new heating and cooling system for the entire parish in order to maintain the building as a place for meeting and worship. $45,000

Window repair: The windows of the parish have been evaluated by Johnson and Sons. Both the glass and the lead in the two main windows over the altar and in the west door of the church need repair. Without these repairs, water will leak in, and the windows will become increasingly unstable. $18,000

Sound system: The church sound system is currently twenty-seven years old, and it is in need of replacement. Sound is distorted past the fifth pew and is nearly inaudible after the ninth pew. This means that visitors, who tend to sit at the back of the church for the first few visits, are unable to hear. $13,000

Fenced playground: As the church begins to attract young families, we need to have a secure fenced area in which children can play. Plans have been developed, and funds are needed to accomplish this goal. $9,000

New church plant: As the church begins to discern the possibility of a new church plant, a feasibility study will be needed in order to determine the best location on the north side of the city. $27,000

Godly Play materials: As the number of young families increases in our parish, we have decided to establish a new Godly Play program and need new materials to make this possible. $15,000

Parishioner Emergency Assistance Program: The parish is seeking major and planned gifts to fund a new assistance program for parishioners who lose jobs or who need medical expenses that are threatening their financial well-being. $2,000,000

Endowed pledges: Please remember to endow your pledge in your estate plan. We receive $200,000 in pledges, and so we need an endowment of $4,000,000 or more to be established from the bequests left to the church by congregation members at their death.

This major-gifts meaning-making menu is just a start. If, as you read and pray about these opportunities to make major gifts to our church, you see anything here that piques your interest and to which you would like to make a major gift, please contact _____, our minister, at _____ (phone) or at _____ (e-mail) in order to receive a proposal letter, a full case for support, or a visit to discuss this project in more detail. If you would like to give to something you do not see here, call and ask about the project you have in mind! We would love to talk to you.

Also, as part of your meaning-making list of options for major gifts, always remember to include endowed pledges as a reminder of that form of major gift.

QUICK-START SUGGESTIONS

Note: This chapter is about preparation . . . so the list of tasks is considerable. Take them one at a time.

Here are a few ways to get started in discernment and clarification, focusing and communicating, prospect identification and donor engagement:

1. Go to the Art of Hosting Conversations That Matter website (artofhosting.org). Watch the videos and try to envision how this could play out in your own church.
2. Host one Dream Together Conference per year. Gather your congregation on a Saturday and have an open conversation about your church's mission.
3. Interview community leaders using some of the questions above, communicating your church's mission and learning about your town's needs. Then look to see where they might overlap.
4. Interview the top-three major donor prospects—people who could give a gift equal to 1 percent of your church's annual budget. Ask them what they think about your church's mission. Then compare that perception to reality. In most nonprofit agencies, including the church, most people in the organization have a perception that is ten years old.
5. See if you can define your mission in three words. When Grace Episcopal Church defined its mission, they said "we feed people." How would you define yours?
6. Once you have defined your mission, draft a one-page communication plan, so that, over one year, you are clear and relentless about communicating that mission. If the mission is compelling, the major gifts will follow.
7. With a trio of deeply trusted, honest people who have been in the church for a long time and who know just about everyone, set up enough meetings for this small group to discuss each adult name in your church in order to come up with that essential list—the names of people who could give a major gift.
8. Go back to that list of names and keep reducing it until you remove *all* the "suspects" (people with high philanthropic capacity and low interest in your mission, or people with high interest in your mission and low philanthropic capacity) and are left with only the real "prospects." With that list you can focus your time and energy.

9. Create a spreadsheet for "moves management," such that the names of your prospects run down the left margin. After each name are eight blocks into which you place ways you plan to engage that donor prospect. This could be a visit, a note, a tour, a conversation with another major donor, and so on. For each event in engaging that donor, there should be a date, a task, and the name of the person doing the task. This will provide accountability and forward movement.

10. The one person in charge of making sure that major gifts are cultivated and asked for in your church needs to be measuring monthly (and, in large churches, weekly) progress. One person needs to own this process and oversee it as well as reports on progress to the church leadership. This person asks at the end of the week or, at least, at the end of the month and must answer these questions:

   a. What specific things have we done this week to deepen the engagement of our major donor prospects in the project for which we one day hope to ask for a major gift?

   b. How many conversations were held in the living rooms of our major donor prospects?

   c. What is the written next step in deepening the engagement of these prospects?

   d. Who is ready to be asked for a major gift next month, and what is that plan?

   e. How many people were asked for a major gift this month, and what was the result of that meeting?

11. When your vestry or board of directors meets on monthly basis, one of the agenda items, along with a written report, should be "progress on major gifts." The whole group does not need to see the names of the people from whom you're asking major gifts or with whom you're in the process of cultivation. But they should be hearing a report that shows how many visits were made in the major-gifts program that month, because, if you're making visits, then you will raise major gifts. If you're not making visits, you will not raise major gifts. It is that simple.

12. Study the Art of Hosting (artofhosting.org) and host your own Dream Together Conference. Use the tools and techniques to host a meaningful conversation (see the website for models) and let the mission your people long for emerge.

13. What is the one thing your congregation says it wants to be known for in your area? Do you know what it is? If not, pass out index cards

and ask your congregation to write down that one thing they think the church should be known for in your area. From what do people suffer? What is your church doing about that suffering?

14. Host a town meeting and ask the community what they think your church should be doing to meet basic human needs in your area. This is a vulnerable move, because they may suggest something you are not doing—perhaps even something you do not have the means to accomplish. But asking the non-church-attending community what they think is a great step toward evangelism and self-awareness as an institution. One way to accomplish this is with a community dinner. But be sure you invite people. Invite everyone, but be sure to get leaders there, too.

15. Establish a questionnaire with a dozen questions about what community leaders think of your church and of the overlap between your ministry and the town's needs. Mobilize a few of your leaders to interview community leaders so you find out what they think you might do to improve the life of the community around your church.

STUDY QUESTIONS

1. What questions would we ask if we were to ask local civic leaders what they think our mission should be in this town or city?
2. It is easy to be distracted by many things, spreading our ministry out over a wide plain with shallow waters. If we had to choose one thing, just one, that our church would be well-known for having accomplished, what would that one thing be?
3. Looking back over history at leaders and groups with a clear mission, who were they? How did they stick to that mission? What was it about that mission and their work that makes it easy for us to see that they had a clear focus?
4. Find a moment in the Bible in which a leader had a clear mission and was able to articulate it. Discuss how they discerned the mission, and why that mission is so clearly evident to us today.
5. Imagine that a major donor is sitting across from you. How would you articulate your church's mission so it was clear and inspired enthusiasm? What is the "why" of your request? If what you were raising money for did not exist, who would miss it? What would happen? Why is this thing for which you are raising money important to humans and in sync with what Jesus spoke of in the Gospels?

PRAYERS

A Prayer for Mission

Giver of all good gifts, we offer up to you those people who have the capacity to give a major gift to this church. We know from scripture that you gave gifts even unto the cross, and then gave the gift of life by rising from the dead. Place your loving hand on all those who could give gifts to the mission of this church. Inspire them, through your Holy Spirit, to let go of their fears and to access that gratitude for all of life's gifts that inspire giving to others. When the church is too pushy, protect them. When the church offers them good opportunities for major gifts, inspire them. And when they have made their major and planned gifts, grant them peace and guide the church in the good stewardship of those gifts, now and to the end of the ages. *Amen.*

A Prayer for Faith and Courage

Help us to help our community of faith to see the great potential of our mission. Help us to so inspire them that they will be willing to invest in it with major and planned gifts. We will sometimes be afraid to do this fundraising; when we are afraid, give us courage and encourage our hearts. When we doubt our ability to ask for gifts, remind us that we are helping people to make meaning with their money. When we feel rejected, comfort us the way angels comforted your son Jesus Christ in the wilderness after the temptations, for you, O Lord, are the lover of our souls. *Amen.*

A Prayer for Mission Discernment

Lord Christ, from your baptism in the river Jordan you were propelled into the wilderness, where you were tested. You were clear about your mission, imbedded as it was in the love and word of God. Remind us of what you named as important. Help us to define our mission and then live to see it through with singular devotion and focus, so that people will see our good works and glorify you by giving gifts, just as the women who followed you funded your mission on Earth. *Amen.*

A Prayer for Mission Integrity

God of all mercies, we your servants seek to follow your way, but there are so many paths, and some lead us astray. We know that the Evil One lurks, not tempting us to do evil as much as tempting us to do so much good that we become unfocused, exhausted, and lost. Gather us together under the banner of your love so that we do that one thing, just as you asked Mary of Bethany to focus on one thing. We want to know what one thing you are calling us to do and on which you hope we have an impact. Help us to see it and then help us to do it, by the mercy of your love. *Amen.*

A GIVING STORY:
CAROLINE—THE UNEXPECTED DONOR

Sitting in Caroline's beautiful living room, I balanced what seemed to be a very expensive teacup in my left hand, grounded firmly on my left leg. I did not want to break that teacup. I recognized it as a rose medallion pattern, and holding it made it hard for me to breathe. She had always seemed a bit stern to me. I did not want to be on her bad side. Caroline had inherited the cup, along with a bunch of other beautiful things, but she lived very simply. Had I not helped with major donor fundraising dinners in the president's house at the College of William and Mary, I would never have recognized the china. Indeed, I probably would never have become interested in fundraising to begin with.

Caroline's inheritance had come from a distant aunt who died suddenly and left her assets to her niece. It was not massive wealth, but she had some pretty things, and she had enough money to live on, with some to give away each year to things about which she cared deeply. Her simple lifestyle was one she had adopted on her librarian's salary at a middle school in Iowa. She lived in a small World War II bungalow with one bedroom and a study with a Murphy bed. Now in her seventies, Caroline ate simple, healthy food, had her house cleaned every other week, and drove a fifteen-year-old Honda Civic with the confidence of a race-car driver. Very well-read and wildly curious, Caroline gave her money away carefully and intentionally—the way some people make an investment in a corporation—for a return. Looking at her, one would never know she was anything other than a retired librarian on a pension. And she liked it that way. Indeed, she had a few million dollars invested here and there by her nephew. She gave all her money away before the end of her life. Every major gift she gave was anonymous, and most of the nonprofits who received her gifts thought they came from her nephew. Needless to say, her nephew received a lot of mail, e-mails, and phone calls asking for money.

Caroline had approached me because I was a priest at her church. She was afraid of death, as many of us are near the end of life. Actually, she was not afraid of death; she was afraid of dying. I went over to talk to her from time to time about her life, my life, and, mostly, about Jesus. One day she looked at me and said, "Charles, what kinds of things does the church need?"

I asked her to clarify the question. Did she mean the parish church, the diocese of the bishop, the international Episcopal Church, or the American Christian church? I'm glad that I asked that question. I thought she was thinking about our little parish church, but my question inclined me to think about the other levels of church for a few minutes. I did not rush her. I let her think, drank my tea, and ate one of her lemon squares. Maybe two of them.

After a few moments, she said simply, "Our little church."

I had not, at the time, been ordained for long. There had been a few years of seminary between my fundraising career and my new vocation as a priest. I did not have ready a "meaning-making menu" (a church wish list for major gift donations) like the one I have suggested all clergy have ready in the event that someone asks this question on your way to a third lemon square. I remember being rather panicked. "Am I a fundraiser, or am I a priest?" I was asking myself as I sat in her living room. Did I not leave "filthy lucre" behind when I became a minister, or was that just a reprisal of dualism? "Weren't these hands for Bibles and goblets, and not money?" I thought.

She looked at me and burst out laughing. "Eat that damned lemon square before you get that white powdered sugar all over your black clothes," she said. I obliged.

Even as I sheepishly ate the lemon square, that moment began a change in my life. In that moment, I realized that if I had made vows to help people—in divorce, betrayal, grief, loss, joy, celebration, birth, death, the use and stewardship of their time and their gifts—then how could I place their money, and their work to figure out what to do with their money, into a special category that let me out of the responsibility of helping people figure out that part of their lives out as well? In my many earlier visits to Caroline's house, we had discussed many things. We talked about her love of books. She had admitted that she had felt abused as a child by the abandonment of her mother. We had talked about the lump the doctors found on her breast, and I sat in the hospital with her after she had it removed. We had discussed politics when she was angry and church affairs when she had questions. We had even discussed our favorite flavors, which is why she always had lemon bars when I arrived. Now she wanted to discuss her money. What was I do to? Would I somehow be dirtied if I spoke of such worldly concerns? Or, by avoiding the discussion, was I both abandoning her need to give and my own responsibility to help her do so (. . . not to mention my responsibility to raise resources for the parish for mission)?

I explained that, based on my conversations with the rector and meetings I had attended with the vestry, I knew some of the major-gifts needs of our little parish, and I listed a few. She nodded as I spoke, then rolled her eyes and blurted out, "Oh, Charles, painting the church is not a project! It is a regular part of life with a building! Why was a maintenance reserve account not established for annual savings since we know full well we will need to paint the place every few years?"

I drank my tea and remembered the years in which I was the vice-president of the YMCA in Richmond—we saved 18 percent of our budget to maintain the buildings. I made a mental note to ask churches why they did not contribute annually to a maintenance reserve fund for regular repairs and replacements.

As we talked about the various needs of our little church, she kept coming back to the parish library and the parish archives. After all, she had spent her life teaching and caring for school libraries. She wanted books to be available and cared for. She invited me to make a typed list of all the major projects that could not be funded by the budget. I did so, and we went over the list in two subsequent meetings, in one of which she asked that the rector be present so that she might ask him questions. She explained that she was thinking of making a major gift, and I remember his shock. She lived so frugally that it had never occurred to him that she was capable of such a large gift. He learned a valuable lesson that day. On the way home, he kept saying, "Charles, Charles, I had no idea. No idea."

Over time, we took Caroline to the church and showed her the blueprints for a new library. We explained that we would like to move it, establish an archive with acid-free paper and locked manuscript drawers, and wanted also to create a reading room. She smiled. She looked back at the blueprints and suggested we change the configuration, flipping the reading room and the library, since one room had massive windows and the other did not. We had not noticed that. We had the plans immediately redrawn.

Caroline gave a small annual pledge, about two hundred dollars. She had not increased it in her forty years at the parish, because nobody had ever asked her to do so. We brought the architect to her home to discuss the project and took her to meet the builder. Our church librarian and archivist went with us on one visit, and she and Caroline became fast friends, even exchanging lemon-square recipes.

Two years later, the plans changed again. A skylight was added; she loved natural light. She also donated a stained-glass window she had picked up on a trip to Europe (nobody knew she traveled to Europe). It was an image of a monk bent over a desk, copying a manuscript. Perfect.

Caroline gave a major gift to that library. She then gave other gifts to the garden, the sacristy, and the food pantry (she bought all new shelving and added two refrigerators and freezers). Each time I visited to discuss her desire to make a gift, we decided what would happen next—meetings, dinners, viewings of architectural plans, introductions to lay leaders involved in that ministry—so that she could take the time she needed to discern. Sometimes she aborted projects in favor of new ones. Bigger ones.

We became fast friends, she and I. We did not always agree, and sometimes we got into arguments, but we loved and respected each other. She helped me to get over my anxiety about talking about major gifts.

On her deathbed, I left the monastery to visit her. She took my hand and said, "You helped me to give it away. It made me happy. Have you seen the new reading room?" Even as she lay dying, her tired eyes sparkled.

"I am glad you gave that money, Caroline," I said, fighting back tears.

"I am glad you asked," she said softly.

I did not see her again after that meeting. Sometimes I go to that reading room, pull a cookbook off the shelf, and look up her recipe for lemon squares, just for fun.

CHAPTER 4

· ·

Asking for a Major Gift

Jesus Is the Word Made Flesh

In this book, as in others I write about fundraising in churches, I often repeat how important it is to see fundraising as a ministry that heals people—the people giving money away. Many of us, especially clergy, hold deep resistance and sometimes even passive aggression toward people with money, because we wish we had their money. Perhaps we think we deserve that money. Like Jesus' encounter with the rich young ruler, sometimes sparks can fly.

If you are like me, you don't even understand why you should have to ask. Shouldn't they just give that money to the church? Why do we keep having to ask for it? Why do we have to go to countless meetings, inform them of giving options, show them building plans, and ask their opinions? Wasn't it better in the old days when the priests went up to an old matriarch and explained to her that she was going to be giving a new baptismal font? This book argues "no."

Jesus comes as the Word made flesh. God gives God's self to us as a gift. God must have cared for the things of this world in order to become so vulnerable as to become part of it. There is nothing unholy about flesh. There is nothing unholy about dirt. And there is nothing unholy about money, or about asking for it. In fact, to help someone give their money away is a great gift to both the person asking and the person giving. You are midwifing meaning-making.

When clergy have to design an important worship service, there must be planning. Months in advance, we sit around a table and walk through planning the liturgy. Indeed, we begin by planning the plan. We chart out the plan, and then we take the plans step by step until we get to that wonderful moment, on that wonderful day, when we attend the beautiful worship service for which we planned for so long. But there is very little vulnerability in planning a worship service. Nothing talks back to us. We are in complete control. Asking for a major gift is a vulnerable thing. We do not know what to expect from people. What if we make a mistake? What if we say the wrong thing? There is often pomp and circumstance in our church liturgies. This book argues for matching the pomp with rather more circumstance.

Planning the steps in building a relationship, which moves toward the successful request for a major gift, is like planning a big meal or a worship service. There are steps. One step follows the next. If you get them out of order, you will not be successful. It is important to remember that when raising major gifts *you are not trying to "get the gift."* The gift is a side benefit. What you're *trying* to do, instead, is to help a person, a real human being with feelings, to make a very important decision that, if made well, over time and with the help of people from the church they love, will make that donor very happy. This chapter will help you see how tremendously important vulnerability is in this process.

On the Beauty of Presence-Making

When Jesus was hanging on the cross, Mary and John stood at his feet. They were presence-making. They did not lobby the guards to take Jesus down. They did not make speeches about how wrong it was. They did not try to make changes in the laws, nor did they try to climb the cross to bring Jesus food and water. They did not tell Jesus it was going to be okay. They just stood there. Unlike the other disciples, they were present. They were presence-making while Jesus was meaning-making.

The most beautiful time spent with a major donor is in the silence you both keep together—presence-making. It may be a pause in conversation. It may simply be time for both of you to think. It may be time in which the donor is processing their decision. In those presence-making moments, you are doing great ministry. This chapter will slow you down, stop you from asking for a gift too quickly, and encourage you to practice the beautiful art of presence-making.

On Listening

The cornerstone of building relationships is storytelling. We humans were designed to tell stories and to listen to them. Part of our genetic makeup for survival is that our bodies will be rewarded with chemicals, such as oxytocin, when we tell or listen to a story from beginning to end. You will find, over time, that much of major-gift fundraising is simply a matter of sitting with someone in their living room and telling or listening to stories. Jesus did that with the people among whom he walked. Most major-gift fundraising is that simple and that beautiful. This chapter will provide a step-by-step process of good listening.

On Co-creativity, Ideas, and Vision-Casting

In this chapter, I'll discuss how important it is to have major-gift conversations in an organic, equal, relationship-based way, setting aside hierarchy and the occasional ego-based building initiatives that bishops and clergy will try to force on their parishioners in a desperate attempt to "leave a legacy" (which sometimes actually means "build the résumé for the next job climb.") Generation X will have none of this. Clergy careerism is about to end. Centuries ago, the church raised the major gifts through intimidation, guilt, or shame. Even as late as the turn of the twentieth century, major gifts were given to churches by wealthy magnates, and it was expected that they would do so. At the beginning of the twenty-first century, major gifts to churches are now a matter of co-creativity. No longer does "father knows best" work very well, even when "father" is a religious title. Perhaps especially when it is a religious title.

Today we need to learn how to involve a donor from the inception of an idea. They need to be in on the ground floor, and they need to be involved at every turn of the project. I have seen many projects crash and burn simply because the leader had an idea, developed the plans, and then sent them out expecting major donors (and, in the cases of bishops, their parishes) to pledge as an act of loyalty. The problem is that nowadays loyalty is earned, not demanded, and so money is no longer raised through ecclesial intimidation. In fact, donors are generally aware of and annoyed by a truncated process that destroys confidence in the leadership in question. Co-creativity is as important between leaders in the church and their donors as is it is between humanity and God. Major donors often have very good ideas that can improve the original plan. Sometimes, the major donors themselves cast the original vision. It takes great humility for a clergy leader to allow this to happen. However, it is often best for the church if the leader can access the required humility. Clergy come and clergy go. The congregation stays. Respect the congregation. Let them chart their course, and they will fund it.

Capacity and Interest: Making Your Prospect List

Perhaps *prospect* is a term that makes you cringe. It is a fundraising term. Perhaps you have a prejudice against fundraising (as so many in the church do), and you see it more like selling used cars and less like ministry. You can use a different word if you need to, but I am afraid that one possibility is that you soften your judgment on fundraisers and on fundraising in church.

Here is a metaphor that may help explain what I mean about fundraising and stewardship. Imagine that you need to fill a position in your church—let's say, a new leader for the altar guild. It is a specific job that requires a certain skill set. The same skill set and temperament would not be found in the chair of the finance committee and the chair of the evangelism committee. They are different kinds of jobs, and they require different kinds of people. Similarly, when you want to find the right person to lead the altar guild, you first need to come up with a list—a list of people who might be right who have the skills and temperament for this special job. There are requirements for the job: available time, flexible work hours, attention to detail, ability to work well on and to manage a team, a calling to hospitality . . . the list goes on. You would not want the Wicked Witch of the West in that job. You would want a kind and effective leader more like Dorothy. Or her mother.

So when searching for the chair of an altar guild, you need a "prospect list" of good candidates to lead the altar guild. You then can speak to the people on that short list to see if they have interest. And then you choose someone. This is just like the process involved in searching for prospects for major and planned gifts. The work of defining *suspects* (people who can't give or won't give a major gift) and qualifying *prospects* (people who are both able financially *and* interested enough in the church to give a major gift) is similar: develop a list, strike through the names of good people who don't fit the parameters, and contact those who do, in order to set up a specific conversation. There is nothing manipulative about this process, unless you project manipulation onto it, in which case you will, of course, see what you want to see.

Just as the altar guild went through a list of names, conversation about them, and some discernment in order to define a "prospect list" to lead the guild, the major-gifts committee needs to discern the difference between prospects (have capacity *and* interest) and suspects (have capacity or interest or neither, but *not* capacity *and* interest). The process is important because, if you get this right, then you have what you need to raise major gifts in your church. What do you need to begin a major-gifts program? You need a list of names equal to 10 percent or more of your attending families, that is, names of people with capacity to give a major gift and interest in doing so. Then you need this book to begin cultivation and making requests. And you're off and running.

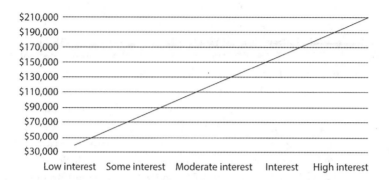

$210,000				
$190,000				
$170,000				
$150,000				
$130,000				
$110,000				
$90,000				
$70,000				
$50,000				
$30,000				
Low interest	Some interest	Moderate interest	Interest	High interest

As capacity and interest/engagement increase, so too does the potential gift.

Imagine a graph with the vertical line descending to meet a horizontal line. The vertical line represents a person's capacity to give a major gift. The horizontal line shows the person's interest in the church.

In the grid above, you see a line that slowly rises across the grid. It shows that gift sizes increase with increased capacity (the financial ability of the donor) and interest of the donor in making the project a reality.

Let's say that this donor has very high interest and that they are very involved in the life of the church. They go to church a lot. Their family and friends are involved in the church. They are on a couple of committees. Maybe they grew up there. Now they are raising their family in the church. If this person is wealthy, they show a large gift potential because both their interest and the wealth are high.

What if the donor has high involvement in your church, but they are putting three children through college? They are wonderful people, and their interest is high, but their capacity is low, which means, though they are generous and kind, they simply do not have the financial capacity to make a major gift.

Finally, let's say that the donor has low interest because, perhaps, they left the church or were hurt by a leader there. They may have a high capacity to give (wealth), but their interest is low. They will not be making a major gift and so will not appear on the major-gifts prospect list, because they are a "suspect." The likelihood of a major gift from a member of your congregation relies both on high *interest* in your church and high *capacity* to give a large gift. This is not a value judgment on anyone's character. I'm sure that all the people in your church are lovely and kind, and I am not encouraging classism—just strategy and planning. I am sure that they all have big hearts and, upon hearing that you're sick, would be over in a flash with a casserole, ginger ale, and sherbet. I also know that it is considered impolite to even think about, let alone talk about and certainly not write down, what a person would give to the church. But if you want to raise major gifts, then you have to talk about these things. If you think it is unpleasant or impolite for a committee of two or three to discuss these things, then you will not get the job done, and you will not raise the money. And worse still, you will deny the donor the opportunity to find the meaning-making they seek with their philanthropy. So I encourage you to summon the courage to do this work.

It amazes me when clergy say they do not want to know what people give or pledge. Clergy are willing to hear about their parishioner's sins, but they're not willing to hear how much money people give. It doesn't make any sense. I have heard clergy say, "If I know what someone's giving, then I might treat them differently." Although I can understand how someone might feel that way, I suggest they might need to find a different job. If you treat me differently because you know what I give or do not give, then how can I be confident you will not treat me differently when you know the sins I have committed? If a clergyperson is going to lead a congregation effectively, then they must know what people give, both their annual pledge and their major and planned giving.

Part of being a good steward is the careful stewarding of one's time and resources, and, like any other spiritual discipline, we sometimes need our clergy and leaders to help us make these good choices. The strategic discussion, in a small, carefully selected committee of major-gift donor advisers, about the capacity and interest of potential major donors, is stewarding our time carefully as leaders. And it is the first step of a major-gifts program in any church, large or small. It is also, I would argue, a ministry to the donors. We help people give their money to good mission. The gift is a side benefit.

Prospects and Suspects

The three components of a major gift are linkage, ability, and interest.

- *Linkage* means that the person asked for a major gift is linked to the church by real attendance and by personal involvement.
- *Ability* means that a person is able to make a large gift without in any way jeopardizing their well-being or their annual pledge.
- *Interest* means that a prospect has a vision, inspiration, and personal involvement, and they are so invested in a project's success that they desire to make a major gift in order to make a vision into a reality.

A prospect is someone linked to the parish (church), able to give, and interested in giving in advance of asking for a major gift. A suspect may have some linkage, may have financial ability to give a large gift, but has not been personally engaged and inspired to make a pledge or a gift that results in a major gift. Too often, a parish will simply assume that the person whose family owns the department store and most of the town will make the leadership gift when, in fact, they have only been to church a few times and are not personally known by any of the vestry, stewardship team, or clergy. Or, they are not even church-affiliated. Just because a person is wealthy does *not* mean they will give to a major-gifts program.

The first attempt to make a list of potential major donors will not be perfect. Some people on your list will be able to give major gifts because, as we've said, they have high interest and high capacity. These are real prospects. On the other hand, some people are not going to be able to give. Even if they are wealthy, they may not be interested in your church. They may not be members of your church. They gave to the library and the local theater, because they love the library and the theater. They don't love your church. They are suspects.

I realize it is uncomfortable placing labels on people. It's as uncomfortable as reading scripture that talks about the sheep and goats, or the saints and the sinners. Labeling is unpleasant. But, when it comes to major-gifts work, you want your list to contain prospects, not suspects—so what you are doing is defining and discerning . . . not labeling. It is tempting to put the wealthy person at the top of your list of major donor prospects. You could put Bill Gates on your list, or Donald Trump, or Brad Pitt, because one member congregation knows him or saw him once at a coffee shop. But they are not prospects for your major-gifts program. Their name on your list may make you feel better, but, the truth is, it is better to have a short list of the real prospects than a long list full of suspects.

Living-Room Visits: Test the Vision and Listen Carefully

Once you have your list of major-gift prospects, you are ready to start making visits. Living-room visits are the heart and soul of relationship building, which is, in turn, the molten core of major-gifts work. Call the people on your list, ask for an appointment, sit in their living room, and listen to what they say about your church. If you're new to this work, this might sound daunting. But, as our Buddhist friends say, "Start from where you are."

I remember arriving in my current position as a priest at a church in Denver. I sat in my office on a cool fall day, looking at the snowcapped mountains to the southwest. In my hand was a major-gifts list. It was a short list of names. They were people who had given to the last capital campaign, so I knew that they were major-gift prospects. One of the names I recognized because I had seen it on our church's largest building. She was a successful businesswoman with degrees in architecture, accounting, and law. She was much smarter than I am. And I was intimidated. Who was I to call her? She didn't even know me. Even if she did know who I was, she knew I was both her priest and the church fundraiser. She would never take my call. (If there's one thing I'm good at, it is catastrophizing.) I convinced myself I was going to fail even speaking to her, let alone ever asking her for a gift to the church.

Fast-forward three years. She had heard me preach many times. She and many of her friends had received pastoral care from me. She read my blog, *The Daily Sip*, about domestic spirituality (how we live our best lives), and she knew a lot about me, my dog, Kai, and how much I love Jesus. I remember making the first phone call to her. I was nervous. She was kind. She immediately set up an appointment and called the day before to find out what kind of sandwich I liked. Over time, she began to trust me. Over time, I began to trust her. Today we are friends. I have asked her for many major gifts, and she has given many of them. Some she gave because they were exactly what she wanted to do with her philanthropy. Some gifts she gave because she loved the people involved, even though she didn't much like the project. She gave because she loved the people and she loved her church. Listening to her and answering her questions about me were some of the best times I have spent in this church. She is among those to whom I dedicated this book. We humans are designed to tell and listen to stories. As I look back, I remember how nervous I was making that first phone call to a wealthy woman I didn't know. But she and I go to church together every single week. The people who raise money at the YMCA cannot say that about their major donors; I know this because I was a development officer in a YMCA, and I was jealous of how easily the church could raise money. The people who raise money at the museum do not see their major donors at the museum every week. And the people who raise money for the SPCA or the children's hospital or the local university do not see their major donors every day in their buildings.

The church is unique in philanthropy, with a privileged position in the lives of the members who can give major gifts. I remember a fundraiser friend at the Red Cross saying, "Charles, if my major donors came in and out of my building and had their lives changed the way your major donors do in your church every week, I would be able to raise a lot more money than I do." Then, after another sip of her Cosmopolitan, she winked at me and said, "If you do not raise a lot of money for that wonderful church of yours, I must assume you're as dumb as a rock." I love her, and she loves me. I knew she was just joking. Well, I think she was just joking.

The bottom line is she was right. The church has an extraordinary privilege of position and connection in the lives of those who give money—a reality that means we must take great care in the way in which we raise money so as not to abuse this intimate trust. Remember that people pledging in our churches are *not* giving their major gifts to the church—they are giving their major gifts to God *through* the church. That is both a great opportunity and a great responsibility. Church fundraisers mediate a conversation, they do not just host it.

Ask for a Donor's Opinion before Asking for a Donor's Money

I remember my nervous energy as a child as I prepared to run through a chilly sprinkler on a hot day. I saw the sprinkler going back and forth and knew the water from the hose would be cold. "Do I, or don't I?" I thought to myself. And then came the shock of the cold water on my hot skin, reminding my six-year-old self that this game had pros and cons.

Similarly, when raising major gifts in church, we tend to run into the living room of a person who can give a major gift the same way I ran into that chilly sprinkler water, hoping to get out as soon as possible, without taking much care to look where we are going. Over and over, I see clergy and lay leaders run into the living rooms of people to ask for major gifts. Or send a quick e-mail message. That approach is not only wildly ineffective, but it can also damage the relationship between the church and the donor.

We do well not to go from the first date to marriage simply because we don't want to be alone. For most people, a courtship is necessary. We need time to get to know each other. We need time to see if we're compatible. We need long conversations about what is important in life and what is not. We have to meet each other's friends and check each other out before making such a big decision. The kind people from whom you're raising major gifts take time and care, research and consideration, before spending five hundred dollars on a lawn mower. Why would we think these same people, whose care and intelligence are often the source of their wealth, would make a quick decision about a major gift?

We need to spend time in people's living rooms. We need to give major donors time to think about what they want to make happen with their money. They deserve that consideration. You may believe so strongly in the church and the mission of Jesus through the church, that you expect, with a certain self-righteousness, that the major donors should simply give to whatever you tell them to. There may be little as invigorating as self-righteous indignation, but it will not help you raise major gifts. The better idea is to sit down with a pencil and paper and plan. If you do not like to sit with your members chatting long and slow over an hour or two, then I assure you, you will not enjoy major-gifts fundraising. It requires patience and humility. If you have these two great characteristics, then you have what it takes to lead, and you have what it takes to raise money in a church or, indeed, in any nonprofit.

It's Like Hosting a Friend

Perhaps you have done this when friends come to town for a visit. Your goal is to give them a great experience of your town. You want to delight them. You want them to have a good experience during the week. So, you create a schedule:

Monday: Pick them up at the airport; take them to your favorite restaurant.

Tuesday: Host a luncheon with your closest friends so that your out-of-town guests can meet them. Then you take them on a tour to see what they react to with enjoyment and questions. That will give you a better sense of what they would enjoy doing, because what *they* would like to do with *their* day may be different from what you would like to do. After all, they are your guests—*it's all about them and their needs*.

Wednesday: Yesterday, while on the tour and while chatting, you noticed that they have a real interest in the natural world. They kept asking about gardens, botanical gardens, and parks, remarking on their beauty. They noticed signs pointing to a national park for which your town is famous. So, you take your guests to the botanical gardens in the morning. Sure, it's not really your thing; you would prefer to go to see the new da Vinci exhibit at the local art museum. But your guests have a real interest in gardens. So you go to the botanical gardens, get some meats and cheeses, bread and wine from a local Italian grocery and trundle off to the gardens, for a picnic. It's not exactly how you would have spent your day if you had been alone. But this day was about noticing the interests of, and creating enjoyment for, these friends from out-of-town. It was a great success. They loved every second of it.

Thursday: Now that you know they are interested in nature, parks, and gardens, you take them to some of the great parks in your area to hike.

Friday: Your friends would like to plant some plants in your garden pots (currently empty, due to your disinterest in gardening), and so you spend the day shopping for the right plants and soils. This is a gift your guests want to leave with you.

Saturday: Take friends to the airport.

In this metaphor for deepening engagement around major gifts, perhaps you can see what happened between the host and guest: the host determined the guest's interest and then tailored the trip to meet them where their interest lay. This is exactly how major-gift fundraising works. In the past, we raised money by simply making a list and telling the donor to give, much the way one might make a list of sights and tell the guest what they will be seeing. But when you shift from major-gifts campaigns to major-gifts programs (as I suggest in this book), you are now letting the visitor build the list of sightseeing venues by watching and listening *to their interest over time*. In this metaphor, the visitor builds their own experience, and the host simply curates their interests along the way. This is how we create and manage a program to raise major gifts. The people seeking to raise major gifts take the prospect through groups and experiences that expose their interests, and then the church sees the overlap between the needs of the church and the interests of the donor. The trip would have been a failure if you had spent the entire week in museums (which you, the host, like very much) as your poor guest kept trying to steal peeks of the lovely surrounding parks.

The Individual-Engagement Process

If you are considering a major-gifts program, you must have a plan. Like the analogy with the out-of-town guests, there is a step-by-step plan. This plan can take a donor from a lack of interest, to excitement about giving, to a major gift. This does not happen quickly in most cases, though there are some exceptions (the foreword to this book represents one such example).

Just as a goblet at home can become a chalice, or a table can become an altar once we have blessed it for that purpose, secular terminology around fundraising can be useful. Church leaders get anxious about fundraising jargon. We convince ourselves that the church is different and special. The fundraising name for the process we've been speaking of—moving a major donor from disinterest to passionate interest in making a major gift—is *donor cultivation*. In church fundraising, I prefer the term *donor engagement*.

If you are unwilling to develop a donor-engagement plan for each of your major-gift prospects, then you are unwilling to do major-gifts fundraising.

Why Is the Work of This Chapter Important?

The ancient practice of *Lectio Divina* is a well-known tool for prayer and meditation. In *Lectio Divina*, the person praying or seeking an encounter with the living God chooses a passage from scripture, reads and rereads the passage, then uses their imagination to engage the scripture so as to place themselves in the moment. They imagine the scene with their mind's eye—the land, the people, the birds, and the sunlight. Church tradition says that the Holy Spirit informs our imaginations as a means to encounter God.

In the eighth chapter of Luke's Gospel, Jesus changes the lives of some of the women following him.

> Soon afterwards he went on through cities and villages, proclaiming and bringing the good news of the kingdom of God. The twelve were with him, as well as some women who had been cured of evil spirits and infirmities: Mary, called Magdalene, from whom seven demons had gone out, and Joanna, the wife of Herod's steward Chuza, and Susanna, and many others, who provided for them out of their resources. (Luke 8:1–3)

Luke is clear that Jesus changes their lives before they give their money to support his mission and ministry. But Luke is equally clear that the women indeed do support Jesus' ministry financially. The story teaches us that mission breeds financial support, not the other way around. The implication of Luke's Gospel is that these women funded Jesus' ministry at high levels. Much of church tradition inclines us to believe that Mary of Magdala was a woman of substantial wealth, which may be a reason for the strange and rare decision of the Gospel writers to name her. However, in Luke's passage about the women philanthropists, notice that Mary; Joanna, wife of Chula (Herod's business manager); and Susanna all contributed "out of their own resources." They were major-gift donors to Jesus' ministry, and they were recognized in the Gospel. The Gospel says that Jesus "took his twelve disciples along with some women." We know that Jesus was particular about who followed him. Many he sent home. But Jesus was clearly building relationships with these women, and it was the women, say our scriptures, not the men (disciples), who funded Jesus' ministry.

One of the most compelling reasons to ask for major gifts for the funding of our mission and ministry is because Jesus did the same work—made the same effort—and took the same relational risks. Regardless of whether he sat down with these women face-to-face (which is highly likely), he asked them for support simply by engaging in great mission, both in their lives and in the lives of the people they saw being changed around them. That is how major gifts were raised two thousand years ago by an itinerant preacher, who was also the Son of God. And that is how major gifts are raised today by clergy and lay leaders who have the integrity of mission and the personal resources of courage, patience, humility, and determination that it takes to ask for major gifts. I am writing to encourage you to be like Jesus and to ask for what you need from the people around you who have the capacity to give. Help them to make meaning and fund your mission along the way.

It amazes me that we in the church spend so much time doing things that Jesus would not even recognize, nor consider important. But some of the very things Jesus did while walking on this planet—including asking for major gifts from the people who followed him and whose lives he had changed—we church bureaucrats often avoid like the plague. We procrastinate. We improperly prioritize. We delegate the wrong tasks—often major-gift solicitations—to people who have neither the capacity nor the courage to do the work. Rarely will we roll up our sleeves and engage in major-gift fundraising, even though we know that Jesus himself did this work. Jesus and his followers were wanderers. They needed places to sleep, food to eat, and rooms in which to gather. How did they pay those bills? Jesus asked for the money.

As you consider this chapter about asking for the actual gift, consider using *Lectio Divina* to reduce your fears and anxieties while, at the same time, increasing your courage and determination. Spend time on passages in which Jesus is engaging people, asking for money, or discussing it (such as the text about the rich young ruler or the time spent with these female philanthropists). The Holy Spirit will indeed show up to fan the passion in you for this work if such passion emerges, in part, from the study of scripture. Also make time for prayer. Sit with a candle in the dark and imagine Jesus with his followers. Imagine the disciples, and imagine some of these women. What were they wearing? What were the land and the light like? What did they look like? How did their voices sound? What might Jesus have said to them? When meditating, were you able to listen in when Jesus asked them for the money he needed for his mission?

This meditation could be valuable for a committee or vestry beginning the planning for major-gift solicitation and also for preaching on stewardship and giving. The Holy Spirit could transform your fears and anxieties about this work into passion and joy. Is not one of the great results of prayer courage in Christian community? Christian ministry is for the courageous and the determined. So be courageous and determined, but do not try to do that on your own. Christian ministry was designed to be done in community so we can lend each other courage. And Christian ministry was designed to be done in prayer so God can lend us courage.

I admit that the most important chapter in this book was chapter three on relationship building. That is what the church most easily gets wrong when it comes to major gifts. However, this chapter, though perhaps not the most important, is definitely the most dramatic and, in my view, the most fun.

If you make many visits, deepen the donors' engagement with your mission, and do everything right on the engagement continuum, but make a hash of the actual ask, then you have wasted a lot of time and failed to help someone make the right gift, not to mention having failed to raise the money you need for your mission. This chapter is important, because asking for a major gift is essentially an act of hospitality.

One thing we know about *hospitality* is that its root is *hostility*. This means that, etymologically, *hospitality* necessarily involves vulnerability. Anyone who's throwing a dinner party knows this to be true. You can cook the right food, dress in the right clothes, and create the right atmosphere, but it is always possible that a guest could misbehave, or at least be quite dull. It is the same in major-gifts fundraising. We have to do all of the things that create and maintain the relationship, but the actual request for the gift necessarily includes vulnerability and hospitality. Regardless of where the event takes place, you, the person who is asking for the gift, are the host. They, the people being asked for the gift, are your guests. Like you, they are vulnerable in this moment. Your request needs to be curated carefully because people, and their feelings, are tender.

This chapter is important because it is your mission to help people give their money away. Raising money for your mission is just a side benefit. For many, fundraising is work that frightens them, so I hope this chapter will give you the knowledge, courage, spiritual awareness, and confidence that will reduce your fears. Finally, if you do this work well, you will be a good ancestor to the future of your church. Many men and women in the history of the church were good ancestors and left us an important inheritance. The mantle has come to us now. It is time for you and me to be good ancestors to the future generations, especially in these days in which our church is molting into something new.

How to Do This Work

You will notice we have spent a considerable amount of time on the introductory work that precedes the actual "how-to." I have talked about what you will accomplish, how the major-gift request affects the life of the donor, and why this work is so important. My emphasis is intentional, in part because the how-to of this chapter is quite brief and simple. The actual request for the major gift is generally less than forty-five minutes. It is a simple conversation, but it follows the preparation and often five to eight two-hour living-room visits. Look back through this book for a moment to all I have said about moving past our fears, identifying the right people, identifying the mission, connecting the people to the mission, engaging the major donor prospects on the continuum of connection to mission, and the many hours of living-room time in which you will get to know your prospects without even asking for the gift. These hundreds of hours contribute to the little meeting in which the major gift is requested.

After all of the time and effort that goes into caring for the relationship with the donor and the mission of the church, when the request for the major gift is brief, simple, genuine, authentic, and joyful, it will be a relief to a donor who has long been ready to make this gift. However, if those previous steps are truncated or skipped in any way, then the actual request can be long, unpleasant, frustrating, and disappointing for both sides. Or very, very short!

Let's take the request of a major gift step by step, and then I'll provide a handy template that you can use when planning to ask for a major gift of your own.

The Premature-Request Double Checklist

Let's say you have done all of the careful rating and engagement, and it is now time to call a prospect and ask for an appointment to request a major gift. I know you think you're ready to make the request, but it has been my experience that it is still wise to review the following checklist in order to be absolutely sure the request is not premature. If the request feels in anyway premature, that's great. You can see if there are other ways that you can deepen the engagement continuum and better prepare you and the prospect for a successful request. It is better to listen to what your gut is saying. It is also, of course, a wonderful time for prayer. Any leaders in a worthy church's major-gifts program should be involved in silent, meditative prayer—waiting for God—in their meetings and in their work. The Holy Spirit will help you, but you must pray in order to discern. If prayer and listening are not a part of this process, then you are not discerning; you are simply choosing. Local nonprofits are busy choosing at their schools, agencies, and museums around your church. They are busy asking your donors for gifts to their institutions. You are part of a church. And those in churches discern, they do not simply choose.

Discern if you are ready to make the request, and, even more important, discern if the person you are visiting is ready for you to ask for the gift. If you feel more should happen to deepen their engagement, then come back to the request in a few months when you feel the donor is ready to receive your request and respond with a gift worthy of the donor's love of their church and the project.

I have heard many church leaders say, "I would love to just get this over with, burst in and ask for the gift, let the cards fall where they may." And you can do that. I advise against it, because that may harm all the good work you have done to deepen relationships with projects and mission, and you will inevitably disrupt, and perhaps harm, the confidence of the donor. Remember, you are probably not the first person they have had in their living room asking for a gift. Most major donors have done it before and with people who are very good at what they do. In 2010, there were 1.3 million nonprofits raising almost three hundred billion dollars, which is still only 2 percent of after-tax disposable income for average families making gifts. Natural disasters since the 1960s have tripled, and armed conflicts have doubled. One in six are fighting hunger, and 1 percent of Americans are homeless. People who make major gifts to churches are making meaning, not just making gifts. They are often giving *through* our churches, not *to* churches. We need to be humbly and deeply aware that many others, in the very towns in which our churches sit, are asking for major gifts. We believe that giving to the church is paramount, because we weight the receipt of gifts with God's glory. And that may be the case. However, the other area nonprofits, your "competition," as it were, often have very compelling "cases for support." Other local nonprofits are full of good Christians, too, and are raising money to preserve beauty (museums), to ease suffering (care for those experiencing homelessness), to heal (hospitals), and to educate (schools). These are all initiatives Jesus would recognize and that Jesus promoted, whereas Jesus never promoted worship. So it behooves us to be aware that other nonprofits have fundraising budgets that are creating beautiful and effective communications, major-gifts officers skilled in cultivation and engagement, marketing staff skilled in crafting cases, and powerful boards able to manage with effectiveness. If churches want to raise major and planned gifts, they will need to let go of old fears and anxieties, roll up their sleeves, and get to work, because the structures and cases that drive other nonprofits to ask for major and planned gifts are often profoundly compelling. Younger generations are, as the years pass, less and less likely to make gifts to the church. So expediency is crucial.

Okay. So you have your list of prospects. You have weeded out the suspects. You have worked hard on the engagement continuum to deepen the prospects' connection to, involvement in, and input into your church's mission.

Your major- and planned-gift prospects love your mission, trust your clergy and bishop or judicatory, are engaged in your daily life as a parish, and are ready, even longing, to make a major gift. How do you know you are ready to request a specific gift or will inclusion? This is important, because a premature request will fail and will place that donor back at square one, mired in distrust.

Are You Ready to Make the Major-Gift Request?

You need to be able to answer an emphatic "yes" to each of these questions before setting the appointment for the request in their living room:

1. Is this gift a part of the written, published, and approved major-gifts menu, for which the vestry or board or leadership has established a gifts policy, and been declared a need of the church for its agreed-upon mission? (Leadership must never ask for a gift in secret or in solitude. Money for pet projects outside the mission should never be solicited, especially gifts for departing clergy.)
2. Was the prospective donor included on the ground floor of the project for which money is being raised through major gifts?
3. Have they been listened to, deeply, by the clergy and one member of the vestry or church leadership, so that they feel well-known?
4. Does the clergy (one of them, if you have multiple clergy) know them immediately by sight and by name?
5. Has the prospect been guided through a series of presentations to get to know the project?
6. Has there been an opportunity for the prospect to mark on the plans, such that they feel that they had a role in the project's planning?
7. Have they met one-on-one, for more than an hour, with one other staff person or lay leader, during which they felt heard and felt real friendship was established?
8. Do they feel like a representative of the project for which you are raising money, rather than simply a person with money to make it happen?
9. Has someone sat in the prospect's living room or office for more than forty-five minutes prior to the meeting in which a request is being made?
10. Is the person asking for the gift a senior clergyperson with a warm and real relationship with the donor and someone who has given at the same level as that gift for which they are asking? If two people visit to ask for the gift, is the second person someone who has also, at some time, made a gift of the size for which you are asking, either to the church or to an organization whose mission is beloved of the prospect?

11. Are you fully prepared for the actual visit with a proposal letter in your pocket (in case one is requested by the donor as you depart), plenty of time in your schedule on either side of the visit, cell phone turned off (not on vibrate), and aware of what roles each person will play in the conversation and in what order? Has every step in this donor's engagement continuum been considered, and does each visitor have a copy of that list?

12. Have those going to ask for the gift been praying for this prospect daily for at least seven days? (Not for the gift, but for the joy and well-being of the prospect and for the Holy Spirit to encircle the meeting and bring from it what is God's hope, regardless of the outcome.)

13. Do the leaders in deciding about timing truly believe that this is the right time and project for the donor, or is this meeting an attempt to satisfy some campaign deadline?

14. Does it seem that the donor is so ready to make the gift after so much involvement that they are frustrated at not having been asked yet? If they seem frustrated that nobody has asked them for a gift they have clearly indicated they would like to make, then they are ready to be asked.

15. Have you asked permission from the donor to ask for the gift?

If you are able to say yes with confidence to each of the above questions, then you may be ready to ask for the major gift. Generally speaking, if a prospect for a major gift has had five or six to as many as eight interactions specifically designed to involve and engage the donor, and, if after those experiences, the donor prospect is clearly interested in making the project a success, then you are ready to set the appointment and to do the work preparatory to its culmination.

Setting the Appointment

In my experience, the actual visit often goes quite well; however, setting the appointment often does not. It is essential that the top leadership actually making the visit, and not someone else, contact the donor about a visit in which a major gift will be asked for. This call should never be delegated to a secretary, an inexperienced or well-meaning layperson, or any other member of the church staff or stewardship committee. The telephone call—and by now you should be such good friends that you can easily make a telephone call, and have it received—should be made by the clergyperson or lay leader who will sit across from this donor and ask for the gift.

Furthermore, the caller must make clear that the visit is to discuss a gift to this project. If the donor prospect is not quite sure which project you speak of, then clearly the request is premature. Similarly, if they are surprised or reticent to make the appointment, then you have misjudged the donor's readiness and should make an alternate visit to deepen engagement rather than to ask for the gift.

If you're absolutely sure that it is time to ask for the gift, and if the donor accepts the phone call and energetically sets the appointment, then there are some things to know about the appointment itself. Donors over sixty years old would prefer to meet in their home. Donors younger than sixty generally prefer to meet either in their place of business or in a local public establishment, such as a coffee house or restaurant. The ideal place for a major-gift request is in the living room of the donor, because they are less likely to be interrupted by servers asking for orders or inquiring about the quality of the meal, or by friends popping over because they recognize one of you and would like to say hello. The request of a major gift is an intimate act best surrounded in silence, if for no other reason than silence lends itself to discernment and consideration. A donor feels safe in their own home. They can control how long the meeting lasts, and they feel confidence from familiar surroundings. It is true that there could be minor interruptions from family members, but if the donor knows what the meeting is about, they will ask family for the privacy that the meeting requires.

You will never be asking a donor for a major gift without their spouse. Unless the donor is single, a widow or widower, a major gift is always asked for of a couple. If a wife is deeply involved in your mission, but a husband does not go to church, you still want to ask both the husband *and* the wife together unless illness (especially dementia) prevents it. So when you make the appointment, you will need to be sure both are present. If the person from whom the gift is being asked is in any way infirm due to illness or age, it is essential that the entire process on the engagement continuum, leading up to and including the request of the gift, be done in the presence of a second or third generation, such as children over twenty-one or adult grandchildren in the event of deceased children. In a request from an elderly, confused, or ill donor, I suggest you ask that the donor involve their legal counsel. However, in general, work to avoid asking anyone for a major gift if you are not positive of their mental competence to decide.

If the donor would like to meet you in public, such as in a restaurant or other place of hospitality, I suggest that you try to redirect the meeting to their home. If they insist on a restaurant, I suggest that you set the time at mid-morning or mid-afternoon, to reduce the likelihood of interruptions and to avoid a meal. Throughout the engagement continuum with this major donor, there may have been many opportunities to meet in restaurants and enjoy wonderful meals. The requesting meeting is not one of those situations. The request for a major gift is a quiet, brief, Spirit-led event that should not be vulnerable to interruptions, distractions, or public gaze.

If the meeting is being set, as is preferable, in the potential donor's home, that meeting should also be set at mid-morning, avoiding meals and, indeed, any hospitality at all. If a major donor is bustling around trying to serve you food and drink, it will be hard for them to settle down, get quiet, and listen to what you're saying so they can discern a choice that is right for their meaning-making.

Many people asked for major gifts are more than sixty-five years old. It is important to remember that older people take longer to get up and to get ready for the day than those who are younger. Unless a donor requests an early meeting, I suggest one at mid-morning. Similarly, meetings after lunch or in mid-afternoon can be difficult since the human metabolism can inspire fatigue. If an afternoon meeting is essential, schedule it for late afternoon, prior to dinner, but nowhere close to the dinner hour.

Remember when you are calling to ask for a meeting in which you will be asking for a major gift, you will actually be asking for permission to make the request. The donor may deny permission to ask for the gift, which is in no way a failure as long as you honor their decision and realize that what you're now asking for is one or more engagement meetings prior to the ultimate request for a gift. The donor will tell you when they are ready to be asked for the gift. If, when you are calling to make this appointment, they hint or even tell you outright that they're not ready to make a gift, then fall back and respect that you were premature in requesting a solicitation visit. The donor is always right. The worst thing you can do is argue over the phone, especially if you're trying to get a gift by a certain deadline or in a certain order among requests of the other donors. The gift is about the donor, not about the institution asking for the gift. The meaning-making is the donor's and so, too, is the timing and discernment.

When you're making the appointment, have been clear it is going to involve asking for a gift, and the donor has granted the appointment, I suggest that you tell the donor what will happen. Here are some things to make clear:

1. Tell the donor who, other than you, will be coming on the visit.
2. Tell the donor that you plan to spend about forty-five minutes together.
3. Ask the donor if they have any questions.
4. Confirm the exact time and address for the meeting.
5. Confirm that their spouse will be present, if you're speaking to one or the other of a married or partnered couple.

6. Leave your telephone number, in case they have any questions prior to the meeting.
7. Thank them for the time that they're giving to this conversation.
8. Ask if they have any questions.
9. Close by reminding them of the date and time of the visit.
10. If possible, send a handwritten note immediately upon ending the conversation in which you confirm the date, time, and place of the visit. Mail the note if you believe it can arrive safely days before the meeting you have set. If time is short, send an e-mail and call to confirm the night before the visit (before 7:00 P.M.)

Preparing for the Request of a Major Gift

Prayer

In the days preceding the visit, you will want to pray for the person that you're visiting. You're not praying that God will give you the gift, and you're not praying that God will incline the donor to give you the gift. You are praying for the well-being of the donor. You may also want to pray that God would incline all hearts to what is best. Indeed, do pray for the funding of the mission of your church and, perhaps, even for the funding of this project, but do not pray that God would incline the donor to make the gift. Simply pray that the Holy Spirit will be present and that you will be obedient to whatever She whispers, even if that includes not receiving the gift you had hoped to receive. God is not Santa Claus. God does not make major gifts happen that way. You and God are working together to fund a mission, and there will be successes and failures even in your major-gifts solicitations. God's ways are not our ways.

In the church, we practice prayer as a part of discernment. Asking for money in a church, without prayer on the part of all involved, is like planning a meal but forgetting to bring the food. Prayer is our tool, and discernment is the result of its use. Remember that there are egos at play throughout the meeting, not to mention normal human fears and anxieties. It is important to make room for these. You are human beings in relationship, and that can get complicated. Be gentle with yourself, and be gentle with your donor. Everyone has fears and often many deep anxieties bubbling just beneath the surface.

Useful Details

It is important that the people visiting are absolutely clear about the location, time, and date of the visit. I suggest, if more than one person is going (a clergyperson and a lay leader, for example), the two of you meet at the church or at one of your homes (again, clearly established) and briefly pray together about the meeting with the major donor. It is important that those making the visit clear the calendar for the hour prior to and the two hours after the visit in case there is traffic or confusion on the way, or in case the meeting requires more time than you had expected, at the request of the donor. Take notes for the donor's file immediately after the meeting, remembering of course only to mark down those things that you know your donors would be pleased and comfortable to see in their file, such as who said what and what steps there may be for follow up. Do not have pen or paper on your lap during the meeting and definitely never take your cell phone out of your pocket. If you need to know the time, then you did not allow enough time—the meeting should tell the donor that you have nothing more important than time with them. Checking your cell phone often tells people that you are not fully present.

If two of you are visiting, you may want to meet together a few days prior to the donor meeting to plan precisely what is to be said, by whom, and in what order, in which case this itinerary should be memorized since you will not hold papers on your lap. If the visit is from one person, such as a clergyperson or a donor who has given at that level and is a close friend of the prospect, that person will need to do the work of writing out, in advance, precisely what they're going to say and in what order. What follows is an outline for the solicitation itself.

The Request for the Gift: An Outline

The solicitation should take about twenty to forty minutes but could take longer if the donor invites a longer stay; however, the ask should happen within the first forty-five minutes. Do not procrastinate the actual request. Stalling indicates that you are unsure about what you are doing and what you are asking for, so do not take too long to ask for the gift in this meeting.

Below is a brief outline of the various components of a major-gift request, along with estimated times. Of course, any topic could take considerably longer than what is outlined; however, I suggest you try to keep to this outline and its time suggestions. I've seen situations in which the introduction and the preliminary remarks took a long time, because the person asking for the gift was nervous and filling the silence with noise. Be brief. If more than one of you are asking for the gift, one should be designated as the timekeeper and charged with moving the conversation along if it seems to drag. If, however, the donor is delaying the conversation by asking further questions, you may find that your request is premature and that you need to allow your meeting to be part of the engagement continuum and not the actual gift request. Usually, this is not the case since you have asked for the meeting with a clear request for permission to ask for the major gift.

What follows are six steps in the major-gift request conversation. Each step is examined and explained in detail, including who speaks, what is said, and what expectations you might have for each step. This is just an outline. Thus, your reality might be different, but this outline shows how an ideal request is made, its parts, the progression, and what roles are played and by whom. Videos showing role-playing and explaining templates and documents in the major-gifts request may be downloaded at fearlesschurchfundraising.com.

The basic steps are as follows and are outlined in more detail in pages to follow:

1. The introduction (two minutes): establishing common ground
2. Setting up the request (eight minutes): reviewing the case for support
3. The request (two minutes): requesting the gift in a specific amount
4. The conversation (four minutes): conversing about the gift
5. Negotiation (two minutes): discussing a gift's payment and designation
6. The ending conversation (two minutes): thanking the donor for time and consideration

STEP 1: The Introduction (Two Minutes)

Why are you here?

After thanking the donor for their time, this first minute is an opportunity to mention the project for which money is being raised and for which you hope to ask for a major gift. For example:

> _____, you have been involved in the planning for our church's new kitchen over the last many months, and we're grateful for the time you have given to this leadership. We are raising the leadership gifts, and we are here to ask you to make one of those gifts.

What is your common ground?

In the second minute, remind them of a project about which you have been speaking together these last many months. You would not be in their living room asking for this particular gift if the money you are raising were not for a project of common interest and even passion (for example: you both like to cook, and you are raising money for the kitchen). So this is a good time for that conversation as well: *"We have all eaten many meals together at our church. Remember that fiasco when the stove caught fire? Our church loves to eat together! We need this kitchen."*

STEP 2: Setting Up the Request (Eight Minutes)

Prior to asking for the major gift, you will want to reengage the memory of the donor with the details of the project. This is an important part of the meeting, because it is like a guided tour back across the engagement continuum through which you have walked these last many months or years. Of course, you all know what has happened—how many meetings you have had, how many plans have been drawn and redrawn, how much money has already been raised, what major successes you had along the way. However, it is important briefly to run through the time line to remind the donor prospect how carefully you're prepared for this day and for this project. It is also important to place this particular project into the larger context of the mission of your church.

Review the case.

In this first two minutes, remind the donor why the project is essential to the life and mission of your church. Refer to your community interviews to demonstrate why people think the project is important. Mention the mission and strategic plan of your church and how the project is essential to that plan. Mention how lives will be changed when the project is funded. At the risk of sounding flip, if you cannot make this case by explaining why this project is essential to human life and to the mission of your church, then you should not be raising the money, and you should not be in their living room. The review might sound like this:

> You will remember that our church has established that we are a place that feeds people. We took many months to clarify our vision and mission, and we were in part responding to the town, which has been saying that many of our people are physically hungry. Our church, located so close to schools and the village common, is just the right location for an industrial kitchen that could serve the poor and the marginalized. And, of course, you have cooked too many meals in this kitchen not to know how important it is that we cook good meals for our own congregation as well. We are a congregation that loves to eat together. We feel that without this kitchen our mission and ministry could be compromised. And Jesus said, "Take this bread." Our liturgy is based on a meal. We want to be a church that feeds people. We need this kitchen to do that work.

If the donor gets bored, ask questions to let them state the case.

As you're asking for the gift, pay attention to body language. You will be able to tell if the donor is bored. Nervous hand and leg movement, lots of eye contact, crossed arms, tented fingers, a hand positioned across one's mouth, or the ringing of hands are all indicators of boredom or frustration, as is checking a cell phone. Respond to those signals by asking questions. Adults have an attention span of about eight minutes; this means that, every eight minutes or so, it is best to ask a question that engages and refocuses them.

- Do you have any questions about the kitchen we hope to build?
- What are your hopes for mission and ministry we will be able to accomplish once we get this kitchen built?
- You have seen the plans for our kitchen. What most excites you about them?

Ask if you have been understood.

You never know what kind of day the prospect is having—how their day has unfolded, what their body is doing, what pains or worries they may have, or what may be distracting them. Remember that a major-gift visit is a pastoral event with logistical implications, not a logistical event with pastoral implications. Prospects may be anxious because they may not know how much money they're being asked for, or they may feel anxious about disappointing you once you make the request. Slow things down a bit just prior to the request. You may ask if you have been understood, or you may simply choose to remain silent for about the time it takes to inhale and exhale once. (Biology note: breathing deeply is a valuable tool to slightly over-oxygenate the blood, reduce your heart rate, and reduce your tension. And, in doing so, you allow everybody else to do the same.)

STEP 3: The Request (Two Minutes)

It is important that the person asking for the major gift is clearly named in advance so there is not more than one person making the actual request. If you have carefully outlined and planned your meeting, and you know precisely who is taking what parts, you will know who is asking for the gift. If a clergyperson and a layperson are making the request together, and the layperson has given a gift of approximately this same size, then the layperson is the one to actually ask for the gift. Peers ask peers.

It is important that you who are asking for the gift are also mindful of your own body language. Sit facing the donor and, if possible, without furniture between you. Do not sit side-by-side on the couch. Sit across from each other in individual chairs. If you are on the couch, shift your body so you are facing the major donor. Keep your hands open and on your lap. Be mindful of your caffeine intake prior to the meeting so that you are neither jittery nor aggressive in your conversation. A long night's sleep the night before will stop the tendency to yawn better than caffeine. If possible, sit upright, with your body slightly away from the back of your chair. And remember to smile. You may naturally be nervous, and we lose our smile when we are nervous, which disconnects us from the people with whom we are speaking.

Prior to entering the house, make sure you have turned off your cell phone. Let me be clear here. I am not suggesting that you simply turn off the ringer or the vibration notifications; I am saying to turn off the phone so that you are not tempted to reach for it during this conversation. If your phone is vibrating in your pocket, you will be distracted from the conversation at hand. If you cannot turn off your cell phone, leave it in your car prior to entering the house. You can always use paper and pencil to take any notes. Do not schedule any meetings near the anticipated end of your conversation so you will not feel pressed for time.

After you have spent a few minutes reviewing the engagement of the prospect, and after you have reminded yourself and them why this particular project is essential now, by this church, in this place, at this time, you are ready to ask for the gift.

I find it helps to check my body in that moment. Are my feet on the floor? Are my hands on my lap? Have I taken two deep breaths? Am I looking the prospect directly in the eyes? Have I said a tiny prayer asking for God's presence and quiet confidence?

The prayer I use when asking for a major gift is the same prayer I use as I mount the pulpit: *"Lord, I am merely the glove—tattered, burnt, soiled. Be the hand in my glove, Lord God. So fill me that it is your hand that signs love to these people. Amen."* Unless it is your church's custom, I suggest not praying with the donor. Simply make this prayer internally. If you pray out loud with the donor, you run the risk of communicating the dangerous notion that God wants the donor to make the gift.

The prayer I shared above may be too long and perhaps better said on the front steps. It was inspired by watching a person signing to a deaf audience while wearing white gloves. In no way do I mean to say that the people with whom I'm speaking are deaf, but I love the silence of God. In the incarnation, God chose to use flesh to interpret love to God's people. I love that God fills us the way a warm hand fills a cold glove. Though we all sometimes feel ripped and torn, burnt and marred, it is through the holes in the glove of our lives that God's warm hand shows. The sign for "love" is the open hand with the middle two fingers between the pinkie and first finger closed down over the palm, leaving the pinkie, thumb, and finger next to the thumb open. It reminds me both of the crucifixion's three crosses as well as our tendency to cover our soft palm as a symbol of self-protection. Find a prayer that is right to pray at this moment, even if it is one word such as "love" or "faith" or "courage."

Once you have said your brief prayer, it is time to ask for a specific amount of money. The amount should have been established in advance. I don't recommended changing the amount in the middle of this conversation. What we know about discernment is that we do not make decisions in the midst of turbulent waves; we make discernment decisions on peaceful waters. All of those meetings, in which you have been managing the process of deepening engagement and discussing how much money you were going to ask for in this solicitation, were carefully planned. Do not change the amount in this meeting. Do not increase the number because you feel optimistic and do not decrease the number because you sense danger or failure. A thought is just a thought. Decide if the thought is true. Stay with your plan. If the amount you have asked for is too high or too low, the donor will gently and kindly guide you to the number they are able and willing to give. Remember that you are friends. You became friends through the many engagement-deepening experiences you have had over the past months. Trust those experiences and trust the friendship. Trust the care you took when you looked at their giving past, examined their pledge history, reviewed their largest gifts, and discussed with the major-gifts advisory committee what you felt was the right amount of money to ask for this project and from this donor. Do not, on a whim, reconsider all of that good work. Instead, remember that you were careful about deciding what you would ask for and maintain the plan.

After the request: silence

When I ask for a major gift, I add this sentence immediately after I mention the specific amount, and then I am absolutely silent and do not break the silence until the donor speaks.

> _____, on behalf of Saint James' Church, we are asking you to prayerfully consider a pledge to the renovation of our kitchen, in the amount of _____. I have made a pledge of that size myself. This leadership gift from you will set the pace for a successful campaign. It may be less than you were considering for your gift, or it may be more than you were considering. But we are asking you to make a pledge of _____, paid over the next three years.

We Americans do not like silence. It makes us uncomfortable. However, it is within that silence that the Holy Spirit speaks. It is important that you not interrupt the Holy Spirit while the Spirit is speaking with the donor. Let them sit with your request. Do not be tempted to wiggle out of the anxiety in the room by blurting out something that will be a distraction. You may feel anxious, but I doubt that the donor does. Do not be tempted to project your anxiety onto the donor. You be you. Let them be them.

Once you have asked for the gift and the donor breaks the silence, you have moved into the conversation section of the request. Remember it is a conversation, not a debate. If the donor says the amount is too high, nod peacefully and smile. If the donor says it's too low, nod peacefully and smile. At this point, the donor must make their decision. If you have done a good job working through the previous chapters, then you probably have asked for the right amount. If the donor says the request was more than they were thinking, smile and thank them. If they say that the request was less than they were thinking, remain equally as calm and listen.

It is essential to remember that, although you may be in their home or office, you are, in a strange way, the host. You asked for the meeting, you led the conversation, and you asked for a large amount of money. Stay loose. Do not get caught up in the drama of the moment. You have a responsibility to hold the space in the same way the liturgist presiding at the Eucharist holds the space during the eucharistic prayer. Although your hands may be in your lap, your heart needs to be in the praise position, often called by clergy "the orans position." (In my church tradition, this is when the hands are lifted while saying the prayers over bread and wine—a bodily attitude toward prayer and of holding space.) This is a very tender moment, and the most important thing is not the amount of the gift, but the feelings and experience of the donor. The donors and their feelings are your top priority. Be a good host to their tenderness in the moment after the request and the conversation that will inevitably follow. Your top priority is not getting the gift but retaining the connection you have with these good members of your church community. If you are in any way disappointed, do not show it in your face or body. Equally, if the donor makes a pledge larger than you were planning on, also try not to show your response in your face or body language. Keep the whole setting quiet and respectful of the work being done by the Holy Spirit in that moment and in the conversation to follow. Everything is always and only about the donor and God. Always. Only.

It may be that, if you are asking a couple, they will begin to talk between themselves, or they may even ask to be excused (though this is rare) to chat in a separate room. If you are speaking to an older parishioner and their son or daughter, or perhaps an advisor, you may need to let them chat together about the request. Do not interrupt their conversation unless you are asked a clarifying question.

You will be tempted, perhaps, to rush an answer about the amount they have decided. Let the silence hang gently while they do their discernment, and do not let your anxiety interrupt that internal work. They will give you an answer when they are able and ready. The answer may not even be in this meeting. A quick answer might be, "No, not at this time . . . ," though that should be rare if you have done all the advance work on the engagement continuum, and they were ready to be asked. By the time you get to this request, you will have done so much in their lives and they will know you are coming to ask, so they will not usually decline unless you got your wires crossed and asked prematurely. More likely will be their very real and reasonable need to speak to accountants or financial advisors or to look at their philanthropy budget over the next months or years. These donors are wealthy for a reason. They are careful with their money, so they may need to delay a quick "yes" in order to discuss assets, cash flow, investments, and other philanthropy budgeting. Remember that many people wealthy enough to give the largest major gifts often have family foundation boards to which they must go with this request. Perhaps they manage their own philanthropy but need to account for other philanthropy asked for by other nonprofits in previous years and on which they are still making payments. Many major donors plan five to ten years out when planning their philanthropy.

It is rare that a major donor makes and informs you of a decision right there in the request conversation. More likely is that a conversation follows and that confirmation of a major gift is made a few days later. A quick "yes" might even mean that you did not ask for a large enough gift, which is something to note for asks in later years.

STEP 4: The Conversation (Four Minutes)

After the request is made and the silence has been broken, the conversation will be directed back to you as the one asking for the gift. This conversation is to clarify the request. The kinds of things a donor may want to know include:

- How and over what period of time will the pledge be paid?
- Who else has made pledges to this project?
- Whom do you plan to ask for major gifts after we have this conversation?
- How does this major gift dovetail with my annual pledge?
- If we make this pledge, will you want me to participate in future major-gifts requests?

■ Can this pledge be paid through planned giving in my estate?[1]

Within this conversation, the donor may wish to discuss, in more detail, the project being funded by their gift. Discuss the program or project as best you can, but do not answer any questions for which you do not have clear answers. If you do not know an answer, be honest about that. In the heat of the moment, I have seen church leaders give answers they think the donor wants to hear in hopes that they will get the gift they seek. That is a terrible plan. The best thing to do is remain calm and honest.

Given that the gift hangs in the balance, the donor may have some changes they would like to make. This is not the time to have that conversation. If the donor wants to make changes to the project and appears to be using their pledge as leverage, do not engage in the conversation. Remind the donor that church decisions are made in community. Welcome their suggestions, note their concerns, but agree to nothing in order to get this gift. I've seen too many clergy triangulated between a major donor who wants a red carpet and is willing to give it, and the vestry that wants a blue carpet. The brief moment in which you're asking for and negotiating a gift is not the time to make changes to the project for which you are raising money. The conversation, at this point, is about the gift, not about the project. Stay focused on the gift and the donor.

Holding space—a holy work

Remember, as you have this conversation in the middle of this request, that solicitation meetings can be tense. It may be that, briefly (and it should be only briefly), the donor will change the topic. It is okay to take the pressure off for a moment or two. Let the conversation wander and then carefully guide it back to the question of the gift.

If the donor says they would like to have time to consider the pledge, or if you inquire about donor recognition, such as plaques, donor walls, or named-gift opportunities, then you are moving out of the conversation and into negotiation. Don't move there too quickly. Stay in conversation about the actual gift with an emphasis on transforming lives with this project. Do not manipulate the donor with guilt or flattery. Simply state and restate how

---

1. The answer to this question is there are many planned-giving tools available, but those plans should be made with the donor's financial advisors. Do not advise the donor, no matter how much you may know or think you know about planned giving. A simple irrevocable trust made by donors of great age is the most common way that major gifts are paid though estates, but most donors pay major gifts out of assets, annual pledges out of income, and then leave planned gifts to general endowment funds. This is what I suggest for most churches.

the project is going to change real human lives, how it will infuse the church's mission with integrity and effectiveness, and how Jesus would recognize the work as powerful mission. If the money you seek is well-deserved and is worthy of the kinds of things Jesus asked us to accomplish in his name, then you have every right to encourage the donor to make the gift because it is an opportunity for meaning-making. You are helping them to make meaning with their philanthropy. You are not manipulating them. You are not managing them. You are not guilting them or bullying them. You are hosting a conversation to help them do something they may wish to do and may find difficult to do. They accepted your invitation. You were not randomly ringing doorbells and bursting into homes with speeches. You were invited. The conversation is a dance; it is a chance for the donor to get the information they need to make a decision in discernment. Sometimes it takes time for them to decide, and, in truth, the conversation gives them time to think and pray and imagine possibilities both for the church's mission and for their own finances, philanthropy, and meaning-making discernment. Present in the conversation is the Holy Spirit. The silences may be for her to speak.

I have been in many conversations immediately after a request for a major gift. Sometimes it feels like the conversation slows down and even becomes a bit light with side stories and side comments. That is normal. The donor is stalling a bit, and that is just fine. They may need time to process the request but do not want to leave their own living room, plunging you into deeper and solitary silence. They are trying to be two things to you in this moment: they are trying to be a good member of your congregation by thinking about this request, and they are also trying to be a good host as you sit in their living room. Be patient. Try to guide the conversation not so much back to the gift and the decision, but to the human or spiritual or ecclesial needs funding the project will accomplish. You are not trying to get them to say yes to the gift or to the amount you have proposed. You are presenting them with a proposal in the form of a conversation. (And, hopefully, you have a proposal letter in your pocket with this same request, in one page, with your signature, in case they need the letter to think about or discuss with advisors).

Pray in the silence and the space. Do not pray, *"God, please incline* _____ *to make the gift I want so that I can win the confidence of my vestry and get on to my next task."* Instead, hold the donor tenderly in your mind. Imagine their fears (use yours as a touchstone) and realize that your role is as midwife to their meaning-making.

The role of clergy

There is a massive power differential between clergy and members of the congregation. Clergy must be particularly aware of boundaries, which is why I usually suggest that lay leaders (who are active donors at the same level as the prospect, or who are deeply loved, respected, and trusted) ask for the gift and manage the conversation that immediately follows. From the turn of the last century and through the 1950s, clergy asked for the gift, often in their study and over a massive mahogany desk. That may have worked with the parents (the Great Generation, born 1902–1924) and grandparents (the Lost Generation, born 1883–1900) of our modern donors, but it will not work today. That is not the way for clergy to use their power—and they often have a lot of power, especially if they are good preachers and pastors. Clergy can make the appointment, go along on the trip, and even remind the donor of the engagement continuum, but I suggest, if possible, that a lay leader manage the actual request and the follow-up conversation. Either the clergyperson or the lay leader can manage the negotiation phase of the conversation, since it is about the logistics of the gift.

There is concern among some clergy that fundraising is somehow "secular" and that "stewardship" is somehow spiritual and theological. Though there is some merit in the distinction, it can marginalize fundraising as a way to sneak out of actually having to do it. *Stewardship* is what we do when we try to figure out how to curate our bounty in different forms. *Fundraising* is what organizations, including churches, do when they use specific tools to help provide containers for conversations that encourage discernment about stewardship. A pledge card is a fundraising tool that encourages and facilitates the donor in discerning stewardship. Without stewardship, the work is simply a purchase of goodwill. Without effective fundraising strategies and tools (special events, strategic plans, sales of items, pledge campaigns, thank-you letters, articles, videos for case development), we have theology and spirituality about the idea of giving without the tools to make the gifts reality. I do not want to imply that clergy should abandon major-gift solicitation, or any other aspect of fundraising, to a professional fundraiser or a lay leader. That would be an abdication of responsibility and an abandonment of the wonderful ministry of helping people with their stewardship. The mental and emotional construct that a priest or minister has hands for "chalices and not calluses" is a revolting twist of the gospel ministry begun by a God who became human and worked with his hands on wood and with his feet in sandals. Jesus had calluses. Lots of them. He did not sit in a study reading about theology and liturgy. He walked with people and helped them with all aspects of their lives. So should clergy. When I was an idealistic young priest and my clergy shirts were still dark black, I wanted a "study" as my office so that I would look smart and well-read. I wanted a living-room atmosphere with lovely things and walls of books, beautiful mood lighting, and symbols everywhere of my piety, like icons and rosary beads. Fifteen years later, with clergy shirts that have faded to Charleston green after too many tumbles in the washing machine of life, my office is simple. I have a computer screen and, immediately above it, an image of Jesus. The rest of the room is bare. I do not meet people in my office. I meet them in their living rooms, or in our small room of comfy chairs by the kitchen, where we make tea together and weep a bit or laugh some.

This conversation immediately after the request for the major gift is beautiful ministry. Do not let your fears, anxiety, insecurities, or addiction to busyness distract you from how beautiful the ministry of sitting with people really is. You are there. Jesus is there. Your lay leader is there. Your wonderful prospective donor is there. The Holy Spirit is there. Enjoy the time. This ten minutes will be, when you look back on your life, some of your best time on this planet. You are not a fundraiser; you are a midwife. There are pledge cards and proposal letters. There are campaign plans and budgets that need funding. There are major gifts and tax letters. But what you are holding in this moment, as you ask for a major gift from your parishioner, is none of those things. What you are holding is the prayer and hope you brought into that room, just as a midwife holds a bowl of hot water and a towel. You are doing fundraising, and you are encouraging stewardship, but you are also doing midwifery. And it is wonderful work that changes lives.

Ending the conversation phase

Remain within conversation to make sure that all your donor's questions are asked and answered. Some of the things that may be discussed include:

- **The remaining time frame of the campaign within its strategic plan.** Your donor may want to know where they stand in relation to the lineup of other major-gift requests. They want to know the context of the request being made. They also want to know whether the campaign is well-organized. Many people with wealth are planners. They often own businesses. They want to know that they are investing in something successful. Your donors are practicing discernment and philanthropy at the same time. Discerning what to do with our wealth is stewardship, while giving our wealth to support and ease the suffering of human beings is philanthropy. A gift to any institution that moves the institution forward is as much an investment in the church or nonprofit as it is a gift. The work of a major donor is to discern gifts to worthy causes that meet their meaning-making criteria, but it is our job to receive their gifts into extremely effective, proven, excellent management systems. Donors are looking to see if their gift will be an investment in the church's mission-building, or if they are simply making possible one leader's empire-building or résumé-building. They will give the investment, but if they sniff the other objectives, then the church will, and should, lose the gift.

- **The goals of the campaign.** Most major donors, asked frequently for major gifts, have created simple mathematical formulas that calculate what percentage of a campaign goal their gift will fulfill. For some donors, the calculation changes depending on the organization that is asking and the nature of the project for which money is being raised. I have one friend who says that she will generally not give more than 10 percent of a church campaign goal, not more than 5 percent of an art-museum campaign goal, and not more than 3 percent of a social-service campaign goal. This tells me her top three priorities are church mission, art, and easing human suffering for the poor. It also tells me into what level of leadership she is willing to step up. Philanthropists wealthier than her might have a policy that includes larger percentages. I have another friend who never gives more than 2 percent of a campaign goal. When you tell a major-gift donor prospect the campaign goal, they will calculate their potential gift based on their personal percentage policy. They may change that policy from time to time if they're deeply passionate about the project. But, in general, you will need to work hard to change their policy and percentage formula. Most major-gift books show an image of a pyramid. Each brick of the pyramid, embedded in layers that descend from top givers to the smallest givers, will show you larger but fewer gifts at the top and smaller but more numerous gifts at the bottom. I suggest you do not cram your major-gifts program rigorously into that pyramid, because these days we are dealing less with campaigns and more with rolling programs that support general giving. I see many churches and nonprofits that plug a prospect's name into a brick at a particular level, because they have already decided what that prospect might give. And that's fine, but it means they probably won't ask for much more than that. And here's the problem: the giving pyramid is usually created early in a campaign to ease leaders' anxiety and lift their confidence about raising the money. You will need to go back and adjust that pyramid, because early conversations with prospects are fluid and require constant discernment and reevaluation. Let your giving pyramid prove that you have prospects, but do not imprison your prospects into the bricks on that pyramid. God is fluid and organic. Your major-gifts program should be the same.

- **Construction time frames (if this is for new construction or renovation).** At this point in the conversation, donors often want more information about the project being considered. When you are raising major gifts for a specific program, the kitchen renovation, for example, you should travel with the "Kitchen Project Travel File" at all times. It should contain the basic documents you have produced in planning, including some of the following: blueprints; a table or pyramid showing you have the prospects to make the campaign a success (no names); a time line for the campaign; a time line for executing the project once it has been funded; a list of project planners and leaders (note that the people who plan may not be and are usually not the people who raise the money); the church's annual budget and strategic plan showing that this project is essential to mission; statements from civic leaders testifying to the value of the project; and a similar letter from your bishop or leader.

- **Pledges from the vestry or church leadership.** This is a tricky one, but one that you want to get right. While it is absolutely true the vestry is not filled with major donors simply because they are major donors or corporate executives (at least I hope that's not what you're doing), it remains true that the vestry or church leadership should pledge first in a major-gifts program for one of the projects on your meaning-making menu. Staying with the kitchen project, it is just one of a dozen projects on the meaning-making menu. What you want to be able to tell your major-gift donor is not necessarily that every one of your staff and leadership have made a gift to the kitchen, but that every one of them has made a gift or a pledge to one of the major-gift projects on the list. This way, you are remaining true to the idea central to modern major-gifts fundraising, which is that different donors give to different things, all contributing to the mission of your church in real and tangible ways and within your written strategic plan but form their own meaning-making. If your church does not have a written strategic plan in some detail for the next year, a second plan in brief detail for the next three years, and a brief bulleted plan for seven years, you should not be raising major gifts. Donors discern stewardship, but they also invest in a plan. To see and download sample strategic-plan templates, go to fearlesschurchfundraising.com.

- **Questions about other projects in which the donor may also be interested.** You are asking for a major gift to one specific project because you believe that, over the engagement continuum, your prospect has settled on that project as a priority for their giving. If it were not so, you would not be sitting in their living room having this conversation. However, your donor may also be curious about one or more of the other major-gift opportunities on your church's list. They may, for example, provide a smaller gift than you anticipated or hoped for in the project at hand because there is another project on the menu to which they want to make an additional pledge. I once asked a person for a major gift of twenty thousand dollars to fund a new learning garden. The donor was thrilled to give, but she divided that gift between the learning garden and equipment needed for teaching in our parish hall. The two things she cared most about were gardens and teaching, so she wanted her gift divided when she real-ized that both the garden and the teaching equipment were listed on the meaning-making menu of our church. I was trying to raise money for the learning garden first and was hoping she would give her entire gift to it, but she had two passions, and they were both on the list of things we needed. Because major-gifts fundraising is donor-based, it was important that she feel free to divide her gift and maintain the integrity of her interests.

STEP 5: Negotiation (Two Minutes)

This segment of the conversation signals that it is near an end. Negotiation follows a donor's decision to give or to think about it for a while. Either way, the meeting is coming to a close, and there may be negotiation about the terms of the gift or the receipt of the gift. Topics may include:

- **How and when will payments be made?** There are no hard-and-fast rules about pledge payments in major giving. Various realities will influence the donor's payment including taxes, the payment of other pledges to other agencies, the use of stock or other noncash assets, the expectations of a salary bonus, and the intricacies of inheritance. The list goes on. It is not the work of the church to suggest how a major donor pays their pledge. Every time you ask for a major gift, you should have a pledge card that the donor can fill out and sign if they wish to make an immediate pledge. I suggest that this pledge certificate be both effective and beautiful. Given that you are receiving a major gift, the certificate on which the pledge is made should be on heavy paper and beautiful. Microsoft Word can create a certificate, with images, to print on heavy stationery. Such a document speaks both to the value of the project and the gift. Or, you may find a sample on my website. Generally speaking, auditing agencies accept a three- to five-year payout for a major gift. I suggest a three-year payout for any gift under fifteen thousand dollars. A five-year payment plan is also possible; however, the sooner the gift is made and paid, the sooner it is possible to begin new conversations about new gifts. It may be that the major donor makes a gift only to find that it was much easier to pay than they thought.

- There is a mythology in the church that a major gift will reduce or negatively affect an annual gift; however, quite the opposite is true. The best way to increase annual giving is to increase emphasis on major gifts. Similarly, the best way to prepare for a major-gifts program is to manage an effective and productive annual giving campaign with significant growth over three consecutive years. When you're asking for a major gift, it is essential that you remind the donor that you would like them to maintain and slightly but steadily increase their annual pledging, and that their major or planned gift is being requested to be over and above that annual pledge. You do not want a major donor to cannibalize their annual pledge by making a major gift. Here's an example script:

  _____, you have pledged two thousand dollars annually for the last few years, and we are grateful for the way you support the mission of our parish. I am asking you to maintain and even slightly increase that pledge so that we may maintain our current ministry, and to add to that annual pledge a gift of twelve thousand dollars to provide the new walk-in refrigerator needed in our new kitchen. The gift would be paid over three years and it would make it possible for us to buy bulk food at a greatly reduced cost, while at the same time eradicating the waste which we currently experience as we throw out food that won't fit into the refrigerators at the end of our meals. We could also receive free food in bulk from local grocery stores and store it, thus allowing bulk availability to guide our menus.

- **What kind of donor recognition will be involved?** These days, many donors do not want donor recognition, though some might. The helpful thing about a plaque, a donor wall, or a major-gift memorial book (in which names of major-gifts donors are written chronologically upon the receipt of a pledge) is that the other members of your congregation will see the names and remember that they, too, could give a major gift, or leave one in their estate. I remember standing next to someone who was staring at the planned-giving donor wall in our church. We stripped down all of the massive brass plaques, making the room bright and open, and then we placed a shallow cabinet with doors in which posters listed all who remember the church in their wills. On the edges of the cabinetry were beautifully painted illustrations of the history of our church and its engagement with the poor in spirit. She saw the name of a friend and exclaimed, "My goodness! James and Allison are just like me. I thought this was for rich people. I should remember the church in my will." I agreed. The next week her name was on the poster at her request. Her gift will not be big, but it will be the biggest financial gift she will have ever given. It will be her only major gift to our church, and she was so proud, in hospice years later, that she had changed her will. The major gift she left was about eighteen thousand dollars. It was what was left after funeral expenses. And she gave it because she saw a friend's name on our donor wall and remembered she did not have to be wealthy to give a major gift to her church.

- **How might this donor, once they have made their pledge, be involved in the major-gifts program to raise money for this project?** This is truly a wonderful question in the negotiation phase. The donor realizes that, by making their major gift, they are in a new position to help ask others. Their first gift may be financial, but out of that gift they are able to make other gifts of time, based in the integrity of their having given already. Major donors may give ten thousand dollars, which is wonderful, but that means they can get involved and ask three other people for the same amount. That forty thousand dollars is also wonderful.

STEP 6: The Ending Conversation (Two Minutes)

Once you have answered the donor's questions about the request for a major gift, and once you have had a chance to talk about details regarding that gift, it is time to end the conversation. If there are two people visiting the major donor and one of them is clergy, and the other has just spent the last few minutes speaking about the gift and the negotiation, I would suggest that the clergy lead the ending conversation.

Restate the case summary.

You may or may not want to restate the case summary. Remember, in fundraising terms, *case* refers to "the reason or reasons why the project is essential or, at least, important to the mission and ministry of your church, and why it is worthy of being funded." If your donor is deeply involved (and they will be, because for many months they have been engaged along a continuum), then the case summary is as brief as a sentence or two. If, on the other hand, you feel that the donor would benefit in their discernment by hearing, one more time, why the project and their gift are important, then this is the time to make that case. You could use language similar to:

> _____ (donor prospect name), this new kitchen for our church will become the hub of everything we do—similar to the way a family and their friends tend to gather in a kitchen at a party. I've been to some wonderful parties in your house, and we both know that everyone at your parties hangs out in your kitchen. You both have been involved at the church for so long, and I think you can see how much life will come from our church members enjoying food we cook for ourselves and food we cook for others. Our congregation has clearly stated in the Art of Hosting Conversations that it senses a calling to feed the poor and the marginalized. People are hungry on many levels. This new kitchen will feed us and others on many levels. You were on that first visioning commission. I'm so grateful that your leadership and gifts have brought you and others to this place.

Restate the request.

Once you have restated the case for support, restate the request *only* if the donor has not yet decided about giving the gift. If you have asked for fifteen thousand dollars and the donor has agreed, hand them the pledge certificate you brought with you. They do not need to fill it out at that moment, though that would be ideal. If the donor does not fill out the pledge card, suggest a date and time you would be willing to pick it up. It needs to be filled out, and it needs to be signed. I realize the pledge card can be an anxiety-producing tool, perhaps giving the impression that there is no trust in the verbal agreement. But a pledge card is an essential tool required by auditors and is a valuable contract to clarify an agreement. You may be anxious about asking the donor to sign the pledge card, but I assure you the donor is not anxious about receiving or signing one.

Whether the donor has or has not decided about the gift, you might wish to leave behind the proposal letter and pledge certificate in a personalized envelope (which you have been keeping in your breast pocket and which has this day's date on it). Explain that you would be happy to follow up with them after they have had some time to think and pray about the gift. The proposal letter should be outlined precisely as this request visit has been outlined: date, inside address, reminder of the deepening engagement that has brought you to this place, summary of why this project is important, request for certain amount of money, expression of gratitude for the discernment and prayer, reminder of why the project is important, a specific day after which you would like to have a conversation about this gift, a closing salutation, and your signature. Do not give them the proposal letter unless they ask for one, or they have not yet decided on a pledge. In the latter case, ask if they would like you to leave a letter behind for their discernment.

If the donor has declined to make a gift of any kind, you have misjudged the situation in making the request or you have gotten new information about the donor's interest or capacity or both. If this is the case, then there's no need to restate the request or leave the proposal letter. In the rare event of being declined when asking for a major gift, use the end of the conversation to ask the donor a series of questions that will better help you understand why. If you are in a living room asking for a major gift, you thought they had both capacity and interest. If they do not have one or the other, then ask to what they have interest in giving. You may say something like this:

> _____, you have been kind to let us into your home and to listen to what we have to say. I understand the kitchen is not a priority for you. Is there a project on this meaning-making list [remember to bring the list in your traveling file] that does interest you? We have many needs in our church and are wondering if any of these other projects are of interest.

If the donor has declined because of capacity (they cannot afford to give a major gift), then the conversation changes considerably. I suggest that you stay focused on the meaning-making list of projects but shift the conversation to involvement and away from major-gift solicitation. Ask them what they are interested in and what they might like to get involved in, and then try to engage them in whatever they mention as an interest. When you get home, call a member of your congregation interested in that same thing and ask them to invite the person the next time people gather around that project. It is essential you remember your role as the host of the conversation, even though you are a guest in their home. As a host, you have a lot of power. If this donor declines to make a gift to your project, or gives a very small gift as a way of declining, then your job is to work so that they do not feel uncomfortable or that they have disappointed you, even if that is the case. Do not drop your shoulders, heave heavy sighs, roll your eyes, and get sullen, sad, curt, frustrated, or angry—or, if you do get frustrated, be sure not to show it. Remember "no" is always "no, not now" or "no, not for this." Many times I have walked out of the home of a person who has declined a gift only to get a call the next day asking for another visit to further discuss the gift, or to discuss a different gift to a different project.

Establish the next step.

As you get up to leave, the last bit of conversation is to establish the next step. And there is always a next step. The next step may be any one of the following:

1. May we stop by in a few days to pick up the pledge certificate?
2. Is there any further information you would like us to deliver or send?
3. Would you allow your name to be used when asking others for major gifts?
4. If the agreed gift is different from the one in the proposal letter: Would you like me to revise the proposal letter with the new information and drop it off in a day or two?

Immediately after asking for the gift

When you leave the home or office of a major donor, it is important not to race into the rest of your day. Most major gifts are asked for by one, two, or three people. It is important not to bring a crowd. You do not want to outnumber the people from whom you are making the request. If you're visiting a couple, for example, then you may bring one, two, or possibly three people, but I would suggest two, as a group of three can be unstable. Regardless, the team that made the visit should stop for a cup of coffee, some pie, and a brief conversation about how it went. Do not pledge that you will get together later in the week, because that will never happen. Every time you plan to make a major-gift request, build in an hour of discussion after the visit. Make that your norm.

A Final Word Regarding the Major-Gifts Request

Fundraising is an art, a ministry, and a science. It is an art because you are dealing with human beings, soft with feelings, hopeful with faith, and quite often afraid. Your major donors—no matter how powerful or wealthy they may appear—are still flesh-and-blood humans with all the same hurts and fears as you. Sometimes more. You are also human, endowed with vulnerabilities and fears. Gentleness and kindness are the words of the day. Be prepared. Know the answers to the questions. Pay attention to details. Do not be greedy. Be absolutely sure you need to raise this money and be able to explain why it is essential for the project at hand. Be prepared to tell why someone would miss it if it wasn't there. That question applies to your church as well. Who would miss it if it wasn't there?

It is easy to second-guess yourself, especially when you are frightened or nervous. But after three decades of raising money in churches and non-profits, nobody has ever been insulted by my asking for too much money. Nobody has ever been annoyed by being asked for too much money. Nobody has ever become angry for having been asked for too much money. I have seen people angry because they were asked for too little money. I've also experienced the anger of major donors asked for a gift to the wrong project. I know one minister who had rather an overzealous attachment to beautiful things. I've never seen anyone able to spend as much money on vestments, books for his library, crosses, and church decorations as quickly as he could. If the leadership of the church had not been paying attention, he would have drained its assets with his love of beautiful things. He wanted six of the most beautiful vestments and five sets of them. The plan would have cost hundreds of thousands of dollars. He decided to make a major-gift call on one of his wealthiest donors, who had just joined this priest's church. The major-gifts prospect had moved to this new church after decades in an evangelical church, where he was a generous benefactor to the library, the music collection, and the ministry that filmed and broadcast the services each Sunday. But now he was in a new church, and the rector asked him to fund his new vestment plan. The donor was able to give large gifts, but he was not from a liturgical tradition, and he had a passion for the written and spoken word. Why in the world would the rector ask him for vestments? The clergyperson asked because he was more focused on winning a gift for his new-vestment idea than in meaning-making for the donor.

So, although it is rare that a major donor is angered by being asked for too much money, it is not uncommon for the donor to be frustrated by being asked to give a major gift to something which is not of interest to them and is seen as even, perhaps, unnecessary. It is a valuable exercise to close your eyes and imagine telling Jesus about the project for which you are raising major gifts. Tell him why you need the money. Tell him who will benefit from the gifts. Tell him how lives will be changed by the gift. And then imagine his face. That exercise will keep you from asking for the wrong gifts. New vestments may be needed. But ask the person who loves liturgical beauty for that gift, not an ex-Baptist who loves the idea that Jesus came to us as "the Word made flesh." Ask him for Bibles, for money for classes, for new teaching technology, for anything having to do with the Word. But do not ask him for vestments—not vestments the value of which could feed a small nation of starving children.

Never be afraid of asking for too much money. If you ask for too much money in a major-gift visit, the donor will say you have asked for too much. Be careful to ask for the right gift from the right person so that they hear the message that you have been paying attention to what they feel is important.

On the other hand, when you ask for too much money, be off by "the correct zero." I had a friend who was working for a local museum director. The two of them were in an elevator heading to the apartment of a woman they were to ask for fifty thousand dollars. Everything had been done well. The engagement continuum had brought this woman from the edge of the museum directly into the center of its leadership. Over time, she had become committed to the museum's mission and dedicated to its new campaign to add a small wing for nineteenth-century engravings. She collected engravings and loved them, so she was even donating some of her collection. On the way up the elevator, the director asked the director of development for the proposal letter, opened the envelope, added a zero, in his pen's blue ink, to the end of the "$50,000" on the page, suddenly making the request five hundred thousand dollars. When he asked for the five hundred thousand, she saw the blue-inked change in the proposal and invited them both to leave, immediately. If you ever place the needs and wants of your church before the feelings of your donors, you will not meet with success on any level. Be prayerful, not impulsive.

Example—How to Identify
Your Major-Gifts Prospect List

If you are first looking at the list of your members to determine who might be able to give a major gift, then what you're doing is called "identification."

If, say, you have a congregation of a hundred families, then gather a small advisory committee of three, look at the list of your hundred families, and decide together which has a high interest in your church. Let's say eighty have high interest because you haven't seen twenty of them a while, and nobody remembers who they are. You start with eighty families who might be able to give a major gift simply because they are deeply involved and show high interest.

Then, looking closer at that list of eighty, you have to ask a harder question: How many have assets such that it might make it easy for them to give a major gift five to ten times their annual pledge? Your committee will look at each family individually. Let's say that there are ten families who are not only very interested, but also have the financial wherewithal to make a large gift to the church. Then your church has a major gifts prospect list of ten families. With that list in hand, and the two or three people willing to lead major gifts in your church, you have the beginnings of a major-gifts program. Congratulations.

Making the list took courage, I know. It feels creepy to talk about people and about how much money they have. But here is the thing: the YMCA has those people on their lists. The art museum has those people on their lists. The Society for the Protection of Cruelty to Animals (SPCA) has those people on their lists. Colleges and universities and private schools all have those people on their lists. And those agencies will be visiting the same people on your major donor prospect lists. They will call and visit them again and again and begin to talk to them about making gifts to their institutions. Because those nonprofits are busy talking to them and asking for major gifts, your congregants are *giving* their money *to them*. Why are members of your congregation with capacity and interest to give major gifts not giving them to your church? Because you are not placing the option before them. You are not asking them for the gifts.

A Sample Preparation Outline

Use this resource to outline your major-gifts request (in fundraising, often called "the ask") to a specific person for a specific gift. Use it for preparatory role play and ask for peer critiques; use it with those who have made their major gift already and with those willing to help you imagine how the conversation might play out. Once you have refined it, the outline will be the map by which you make your way through the living-room request of a major gift. I suggest you place this outline on a computer, so that you can use it as a template for every visit you make in which a major gift is requested.

The solicitation should take about twenty to forty minutes.

1. The introduction (two minutes)
   a. Why are you here?
   b. What is your common ground?

2. The preliminary to the ask (eight minutes)
   a. Review the case.
   b. If the donor gets bored, ask questions in which the donor states the case.
   c. Ask if you have been understood.

3. The ask (two minutes)
   a. A specific amount is asked for, and silence follows.
   b. Conversation and negotiation (six minutes) (imagine possible negative responses and how you would face them)

4. The ending conversation (two minutes)
   a. Restate the case.
   b. Restate the "ask."
   c. Establish the next step.

A Sample Phone Script
to Ask for the First Visit

1. Be sensitive to the generation of the person with whom you wish to speak. If they are a young person, call in the morning. If they are in the Silent Generation or older (sixty years plus), call in early evening between 5 and 7 P.M. And, of course, most of these calls will mean leaving a message.

2. Introduce yourself and try to help them register who you are. "I'm a lector, and I often make coffee. My name is Sally and my husband is John, who helps with the youth. We have two boys and have been going to Grace Church for the past three years."

3. Try something like this: "I am part of a small group helping our church to imagine our future. We are thinking of some changes to our building [or adding a new ministry], and I am calling to ask if I might speak with you in person to get your input on some of our early thinking and planning. I do not need more than forty minutes of your time. May we schedule that at your convenience?" (Or, in a message: "May I call back to schedule that visit, unless, of course, you are willing to kindly call me back at 555-1212?")

4. Close the call by restating your name, phone number, and e-mail in case they want to e-mail a response. Reiterate that you will call them back if you do not hear from them in a few days, since you know they have many demands on their time.

5. End by thanking them in advance for their time and remind them of how wonderful the church is and how excited you are to be chatting with them about the future.

How to Plan for a Good Living-Room Visit— A Summary

1. Call the person you want to visit.
2. If you do not know them very well, write a short letter saying you're going to call.
3. If you leave a message, tell them you are going to be calling back in a few days, unless they can give you a call at their convenience.
4. When they say that they would be willing to speak with you, tell them you would like to visit them at their home. If this major donor happens to be younger than forty, make the first visit in a diner or coffee shop. The rest of the visits should be at their home.
5. When you are setting the date for the visit, do not squeeze it into a busy schedule. There's nothing worse than being late to visit with a prospective major donor. Well, with anyone really. Make sure you set it in your calendar so that you have plenty of time to get there, to get slightly lost on the way, and to have a good fifteen minutes in your car before the visit, to pray and collect your thoughts. Do not fiddle with your cell phone or check your e-mail. In fact, turn off your cell phone and leave it in your car so you are not tempted to check it and so that it does not ring while you are talking to your prospect.

Make sure, when you get back to your car and before you turn on the engine, to make some notes from the visit. Don't write anything salacious; everything you write in a donor's file should be something you would be pleased for them to read. Do record what you learned about their life, about their capacity to make a major gift, and most especially about what they're interested in and who their close friends are in the church.

Sample Schedule
for a Major-Gift Visit

9:00 A.M.

1. Make sure the backup file of case and support materials is in the lead car.
2. Make sure the proposal letter is absolutely correct, and do not second-guess the amount being requested.
3. Make sure there is a pledge certificate (ideally, with the donor's name and address already on it) inside the envelope with the proposal letter. You may need to separate the certificate from the proposal. Both should be on your person.
4. Double-check the location of the home, the distance it takes to travel (with traffic variabilities), and get a map or use GPS to be sure you do not get lost.

9:30 A.M.

The team meets at the church to discuss the visit and determine who will say what.

Use the sample preparation outline above and write what you will say and exactly who will say it.

10:00 A.M.

Pray together about the visit, inviting the Holy Spirit to move within the visit.

10:10 A.M.

Depart with a plan to get there ten to fifteen minutes early, and stay in the car until it is time to ring the doorbell. It will give you more time for prayer and more time to review your notes and the materials in the case file so that you can readily answer questions. Turn off your cell phone and place it in the glove compartment of the car. Do not take your phone into the meeting. (Clergy on-call are exceptions, but I suggest getting someone else to take emergency pastoral calls when you are making a major-gifts visit.)

10:30 A.M.

Ring the doorbell exactly on time.

11:15 A.M.

Depart exactly on time, unless conversation warrants a longer stay.

11:30 A.M.

Meet at a local coffee shop for coffee and pie, ask yourselves how the visit went, and consider what you would do differently the next time you visit a new donor. Also review what needs to happen as follow-up to this visit with these donors.

12:15 P.M.

Write notes from the visit to go into the major donor's file at church. If you have a computer system that takes data like this, then fine. But I suggest keeping red-colored files on each of your major donors, with records of visits and pledge cards, newspaper articles, and other notifications. Files are red so that if you see one mistakenly lying about you can quickly put it away.

12:30 P.M.

Hand-write a thank-you note and drop it in surface mail. People love to get real notes with real ink. Do not send an e-mail.

1:00 P.M.

Write a formal letter thanking them and, if they made a verbal or written pledge, mentioning the results of the negotiation. If the pledge was verbal, enclose a pledge card for their use with a return envelope marked "private and confidential." It will be returned to the clergyperson or to whomever leads the next visit.

The Next Day

Call the donor and thank them for the visit. Ask if they have any follow-up questions.

QUICK-START SUGGESTIONS

1. Gather the people you believe will do a good job of asking for major gifts. Host a training retreat with plenty of time for role-playing, conversation about fear and resistance, and the how-to of the work. Then make this a small group that gathers regularly for meals to discuss how things are going.
2. Check to be sure that you have one major-gift and one planned-gift sermon in the liturgical year.
3. Write your meaning-making menu now. Do not delay. Write the top ten to twenty things you need as major-gift contributions, and get that list out to your congregation. Be sure it is printed and set out on tables, given out at meetings, inserted into Sunday bulletins (perhaps one item per week for twenty weeks).
4. Make sure that you invite your congregation at least monthly in letters, bulletin announcements, and verbal announcements to endow their pledges. When we die, our pledge dies with us unless we have set aside enough money in our planned giving to endow our pledge. If you pledge one thousand dollars, then endow that pledge in your will with a gift at your death of twenty thousand dollars. The earnings from the twenty thousand dollars will provide the one thousand dollars forever after you have died. This is essential for a church whose members are aging and whose deaths will cripple the parish budget.

STUDY QUESTIONS

1. What bothers or frightens you about talking about the people in your church to determine if they are major-gifts prospects? In order to discuss prospects and suspects, it is necessary to talk about people and to discuss income, assets, philanthropy to other agencies, and interests in particular projects. If approached the wrong way, the process can feel manipulative, but if approached as a ministry of helping people give their money away, then this discussion is no different from those we hold when recruiting for leadership. If you have fears, what are they?

2. From time to time we sit with students, asking questions to help them make a good college choice. Similarly, we talk sometimes to our parents to help them make good end-of-life choices. When talking with athletes, it's necessary to discuss training regimens to reach a goal. How do you feel about sitting with people considering making a major gift? Are you willing to help them?

3. For what do you hope to raise major gifts? What is the "case development" of your project—the motivating statement that explains why you believe this is an important project? List the things you would be passionate about raising money for and describe why you would be so passionate.

4. There is, built into this process of relationship engagement, inherent vulnerability. What does it feel like to be vulnerable in this process? If someone says "no" to a major gift while you are trying to build the relationship, and before you even ask for the gift, how will this make you feel? If the process causes tension, where would you find that tension in your body? What would you need to do to shake off the anxiety of such a rejection? How could you accept the "no" from this prospect without taking it personally?

5. What are your fears about asking for a major gift? Imagine yourself sitting in the living room of someone who has capacity and interest (one of your major donors) and imagine your thoughts, hopes, and fears, soon to ask for a major gift. What fears do you hold within? How might you let them go?

6. Why is it important to manage an effective engagement continuum that moves a major donor through a sequence of awareness and involvement? If you think the review audit of the engagement continuum is manipulative, then discuss why. If you see that this process

simply helps people make the right choice, regardless if it is "yes" or "no," can you articulate that to those who feel anxious about donor engagement?

7. Choose a person from whom you would like to ask a major gift and outline the thirty to forty-five minutes using the preparation resource above. What would you say? Who would you bring? Who is the person you are asking? For what would you ask? Why is what you are asking for essential and deserving? What would that thirty to forty-five minutes look like on paper?

8. Try writing a proposal letter—the essential tool that we always bring, in our pockets, in case the donor would like to retain in writing what we just said and as part of their discernment. Imagine a major donor and gift request, then write a sample major-gift proposal letter. You may use the model proposal letter on fearlesschurchfundraising.com if that helps.

9. Write a list of the fears you may have about doing this work. Then write the reasons that you need not really be afraid, using theological and relational awarenesses of peace and hope. Burn this page outside on sand or rocks, with prayers asking God to support you in this ministry.

PRAYERS

A Prayer for the Engagement Continuum (Deepening Involvement)

Jesus Christ, lover of our souls, you built relationships in your brief ministry on this earth. In that last meal together in the upper room, you feasted not only on bread and wine, but also on the relationships you had been developing, nurturing, feeding, and sometimes even challenging. We know that you came to be a friend and that you want us to love each other, ourselves, and our God. May your Holy Spirit weave us together the way a maker of cloth weaves so many threads into a tapestry—knotted and tied, full of diverse colors. Build a relationship with us through your Holy Spirit, so that we have the energy and courage to risk the vulnerability of relationship with each other. Soften our hearts so that we can see that finding major donors for projects that need funding is holy, life-giving work. *Amen.*

A Prayer for Those Getting Tired of Managing the Engagement Continuum

Jesus Christ, source of all vocation, you do not tire of moving us along in life, all the while inserting yourself to create the life that will bring you glory and offer us peace. You are constantly moving us from this experience to that experience, teaching us what we need to know. You do not manipulate us; you move and manage the process by which you encourage us and form us. Defend us from our fears that we are manipulating people and remind us that you have us on an engagement continuum of your own design, constructed to deepen our relationship with you and with each other. As you defend us, also encourage us to manage this process in the lives of major donors so that their joy is complete in their giving, and our mission is complete in the receipt of that gift. This we pray in the awareness of your body, a major gift of God. *Amen.*

A Prayer for a Person Raising Major Gifts

Lord God, giver of all good things, grant, we pray, strength and courage to anyone considering a ministry in major gifts. Inspire in us courage, patience, and deep kindness. When we get frustrated in this work, draw us into deep compassion for the fears that torment those of us who worry about money. Help those of us who work in major gifts to feel your presence and to remember that you did this work as a part of your mission and ministry. When we are successful and receive a major gift, help us to rejoice in your power and glory, so you are the source of all success. And when we ask for a major gift only to find that the donor declines, move in with your angels, comfort and encourage, and remind us that a "no" is the beginning of a new conversation, not just the end of an old one. Call us to center ourselves only in you. *Amen.*

A Prayer of the "Askers" Waiting in an Idling Car before Making the Request

Lord, here we sit in this car, in front of the home of a person from whom we are soon to ask a major gift for the mission of our church. We have some fear because this is a vulnerable act. Yet you remind us over and over again not to be afraid. Send your Holy Spirit to dwell within me and the others in this meeting. So fill this living room with light and joy that your will be done, regardless of the outcome. Grant us all peace so that we might be friends as we struggle to fund the work of your body, the church. Inspire authenticity in us, who are asking, and discernment in those from whom we ask. This we pray in the name of the One Who Is. *Amen.*

A Prayer for the Donor Being Asked for a Gift

God of our Fathers and Mothers, you asked our ancestors—the women who followed you to fund your mission—for major gifts. They also funded your work because of the fruit they could see coming from the work you were doing. In Luke's Gospel, we are told that these women gave out of their resources. Help us to do good fundraising, and help those we ask to do good stewardship. This work must be done, and there is no other way to do it than by tried-and-true methods. Indwell those whom we ask for major gifts. Give them discerning hearts. Help them to decline the invitation to give, if it is not the right gift for them. And incline their hearts to give if it is the right gift to give at the right time and for the right work of your church. And in the end, when we all lay down our hearts, grant us your peace. *Amen.*

A GIVING STORY: KENTON

Kenton was a long and wiry man. He had long arms, long fingers, a long torso, and legs that only stopped because there was a floor. He moved more like an octopus than a human, graceful and fluid. He had piercing eyes and an equally piercing intelligence. He looked straight into your eyes, as though he were evaluating whether or not you were speaking the truth. I have tried very hard in my life to care for two specific ways of being: truthfulness and kindness. I fail from time to time, like any mere mortal, but I work hard at truthfulness and kindness, which provides confidence when faced with an evaluating stare like Kenton's.

My first meeting with him was after a difficult phone call. Our organist and choirmaster suggested I call Kenton as we were working to meet a campaign goal for a new antiphonal organ. We had several major gifts in hand, but there was still a ways to go, and we were beginning to run out of prospects for whom, we felt, contributing to a pipe organ would be part of their meaning-making. There are not many people left who get excited about making major philanthropic gifts for a pipe organ. Some of our donors had shown interest in a new kitchen. One was interested in renovating the bell tower. A couple of people thought that a new sound system would be valuable, but there were not many left in the congregation who had the capacity to give a major gift and also *wanted* to give for a new organ. Kenton was one, and the next story you will read, about Chuck and Janet's planned gift, also concerns this same antiphonal organ.

When the choirmaster mentioned Kenton's name, and that he might be interested in giving to a new organ, I sat up straight and listened intently. I asked him to tell me more about Kenton, and he answered in a vague and uncomfortable way, giving me the impression that Kenton was not a prospect, but a suspect. Then the hammer dropped: Kenton was a member of a different parish—of a different denomination. My heart sank, but I promised to call him, and so I did.

It was a difficult call. He was gruff and a bit grumpy. He started asking me detailed questions about pipe organs that made me a bit rough and grumpy, given that I have never liked the insecurity of feeling stupid. I was a priest and a fundraiser, not an organist. How could I possibly know what an *en chamade* was, let alone a "hooded tuba"? Something in me stayed with the conversation. Not the fundraiser in me, but the pastor. He was angry and frustrated. I wanted to stay with him beyond that stage.

Against my better judgment, I invited him to meet. Given that he knew the choirmaster, I invited the choirmaster along, too. As the three of us talked, it became clear that Kenton had been in conversation with my church about the organ campaign for a very long time—years, in fact. I was trying to reach the fundraising goal of an organ campaign that had begun many years before, and then had stalled for a few more years. I was trying to close it out so that we could build the new organ before the price went up, due to an increase in the cost of steel.

Tension arose as the choirmaster and Kenton discussed the nomenclature of the trumpet rank in the organ. Suddenly, I realized what was going on. Kenton had not only been an organist, but an organ builder. He had been part of the original planning committee for this very antiphonal organ, but had moved away from the conversation in frustration because the organ did not have the kind of trumpets he felt necessary.

Years had passed. Here we were, back at the table again. Our second meeting was just Kenton and me. I needed to let him vent his frustration. He needed a chance to rant about the organ-design plans, in his view, not being correct. It took a whole session for him to get that out of his system. I let him talk and talk until he stopped himself and laughed out loud. It was the first break in the dark clouds that seemed to hover over his head. As he finished laughing, he looked at me and said, "Oh, my! I am so sorry. I had no idea all that frustration was inside me. Thank you for listening."

On our third visit, we looked over the plans in detail with explanations from the organ builder as to why the organ was not being built the way Kenton felt it should be. It had to do with the size and shape of the church as well as the design of the organ, which was more English than French. Once the organ builder was able to convince Kenton about the different pipes and their different names, and still get the particular trumpet sound Kenton thought was appropriate, he softened. He even smiled.

Our fourth visit was more social than anything else. We just wanted to connect with each other and chat. He wanted to tell me about a new friend in his life, and only toward the very end of the conversation did he ask about the organ. Were we still building it? Did we have all the donors we needed? I told him we needed more donors to give about one hundred thousand dollars. I explained we had a fifty-thousand-dollar donor who used to play the organ and was a member of the congregation. Kenton knew him and liked him. There was a long silence. I asked Kenton if he was willing to allow for one more visit about the organ. He folded his long fingers across his lap and smiled. "You're going to ask me for a gift, aren't you?"

I said that I would like to.

He closed his eyes and nodded slowly. "Let's meet again, then."

A few weeks later, we did. I was ready to ask for his major gift, fully aware that he was a Presbyterian and from a different church in our city. I had been stunned that he wanted to make this gift to a church he did not even attend. What was very clear from the beginning was that this man's meaning-making had to do with beautiful music, and not just any music—organ music.

The new antiphonal organ would complete the original design after more than eighty years of sitting in blueprints. The original organ had been built just before World War II. They had then put off the antiphonal organ until after the war, thinking it would be a better project once things settled down. But the steel necessary for the war effort contributed to the closing of the organ-building shop, and the plans sat in a drawer. Our hero of a choirmaster found an antiphonal organ that matched the plans almost exactly. It was for sale by a church that no longer needed its antiphonal organ. A minor miracle. Some might say a major one. By purchasing and installing this antiphonal organ, our church would have a musical instrument designed for the building, making the completed organ one of the most stunning in the nation. Kenton had been in on the ground floor of this possibility. Two other major donors had given well over half the cost of the project, making it a possibility for church. We just needed a few last gifts.

Kenton had made one gift of twelve thousand dollars when the original planning had begun years before. I asked him for a major gift and said, "I hope you will add to the $12,000." He had been to countless organ committee meetings a decade before. He had watched major donors come forward in the last few months, making the organ possible. He knew we had a narrow window in which to make this purchase before the price would go up. He and I had met to discuss the possibilities over and over again. He had vented frustrations, pored over plans, talked to our organ builders, met with other donors, and now he had invited me to ask for a major gift.

I began by recounting the long and wonderful story of our conversations. We laughed at some points. He smiled when I mentioned how grumpy he was at first.

"I was, wasn't I?" he exclaimed with almost a giggle. "I still don't like the name of the trumpet, but I want to make a gift that would name that pipe— the biggest in the whole organ," he said, like a child describing the biggest tree in a forest. "It makes such a big sound that it's almost inaudible. You can feel it in your body—in the walls."

It was wonderful to see him enjoying the idea of making that part of the organ possible. He was excited. Giddy.

I reviewed the major gifts that had moved us to within range of meeting our goal and said that I hoped he would name the tuba with a gift of twenty-five thousand dollars. He hemmed and hawed, crossed and uncrossed his legs. He furrowed and unfurrowed his brow. He then said that he was thinking along the lines of doubling his original gift. I thanked him. He was pleased. He said he had some money set aside for the gift and was happy to make it.

When we met again, I thanked Kenton for the original pledge of twelve thousand dollars and then asked if there was any way we could name the great tuba pipe after him with a gift of twenty-five thousand. He said, "I want those pipes built. I want that organ built. I want to hear it play, and I do not want a delay to cause the loss of the contract. So yes. I would like to make the twenty-five-thousand-dollar pledge."

After some conversation and many thanks I showed him out of the church. I remembered when he and I had first met and his frustration with the organ design. I remembered our many conversations, meetings, and near-arguments. I remembered how he had intimidated me, at first, with all his knowledge. But here we were, walking to the door having agreed to a twenty-five-thousand-dollar pledge when he had originally given twelve thousand so many years before.

As the organ was installed, I invited Kenton to see the progress. Finally, on the night we inaugurated the organ, I placed him and his partner at the center of the church so that the sound would be perfect. Then I positioned myself so that I could both hear the organ and see his face when he did. As the guest organist began the first fugue, Kenton's face changed. His smile broadened. His eyebrows arched. He sat up as straight as an arrow and moved to the edge of his seat, beaming.

He had made the moment possible. This was his meaning-making. He had left his mark on the planet by making this gift. Even though it was not his own church, it was a gift to the city in which he lived, and a gift to the music he loved and wanted to live beyond him. His gift was his meaning-making. He was not a wealthy man, but he wanted that organ, in that church, and he helped make it happen. The Kenton Longrith Hooded Tuba thundered above us as the organ pushed out astounding music, and my life was lit up from the inside just seeing his face. I, a fundraiser and a priest, had helped Kenton make meaning with money he was able and willing to invest in something he wanted to exist: that new organ.

A few months later, it was time to bless the antiphonal organ and install the donor wall. Raising donor walls can be very expensive. There are hundreds of companies around the nation who design and create massive walls of brass plaques that take up valuable space, take massive amounts of money from fundraising, and end up flat and dull. You have seen them everywhere—in hospitals, in university lobbies, and at the YMCA. I was determined not to take that route.

So I called the organ company and asked if they had an old organ pipe sitting around in their warehouse. They had many, it turned out, and they gave us a beautiful five-foot zinc pipe that had been gathering dust in their storage facility. Engraved with the name of its rank and discarded from some previous renovation, it had been lying in the corner for decades. Perfect! I met with a fine furniture maker, who was a member of our parish, and we designed a wooden casing to hold the organ pipe on the wall. It was about five inches wide and five feet long; the wooden case was both a little wider and taller, with beautiful carved accents. The pointed bottom of the pipe sat elegantly on a small shelf, and the top of the pipe was held in place by a slight hood. The names of the donors to the antiphonal organ were engraved and then blackened up and down on the actual organ pipe. Above the pipe was a small plaque—ten inches by ten inches—with an image of the new organ, its name (after the two lead donors), and some information about the organ. The whole donor wall—beautiful, interesting, three-dimensional, and made, mostly, of an old pipe, with the craftsmanship of a generous furniture maker—cost us 5 percent of what a conventional donor wall would have and was, in the end, a delight to the congregation. I loved to see people approach and reach out to touch the pipe with their hands. Kenton loved it. I watched him linger in front of it. He had made meaning. He left something behind that meant something to his life. That is what major-gifts fundraising can accomplish. Yes, we had a new organ, but what was even better and much more important, long-lasting, and impactful, was that we had helped an old man make meaning with his money. That was not his only major gift, but it was the one that authentically expressed his love of pipe organs, organ music, and liturgical music. He was of a generation that loves pipe-organ music, so he made sure it would live beyond him.

● ●

CHAPTER 5

Obstacles to Raising Major Gifts

Compassion for Human Fears

The art of leading a church around major gifts comes down to intentional compassion for people's fears. Many in our congregations are afraid of money, or they are afraid of not having enough. Fundraisers have a term for this fear among widows: "bag-lady syndrome." When something is true, we tend to coin a phrase for it. Bag-lady syndrome is a real thing. This syndrome has very little to do with how much money a person has. It is an irrational fear that if they give the money away, they will end up poverty-stricken and needing those funds. Young people are afraid of not being able to send their children to college. Middle-aged people are afraid of not having a funded retirement. Fear abounds.

The analogy that I would make is to the hospital. The church often has been referred to as either a gymnasium for strengthening or a hospital for healing. In a real hospital, anyone in the building and not on the staff will experience some fear. The doctors and nurses are fully aware that their patients are fearful, but it would not serve the caregivers or the patients to avoid conversations about illness so that nobody would be afraid. Indeed, doctors and nurses need to be honest with their patients and explain with compassion the real vulnerabilities at play. When the doctor diagnoses a malignant tumor that is causing pain in the stomach, she does not serve the patient well by explaining it away as indigestion. The doctor must tell the patient the truth. Though it is scary to hear the truth, it can also be a great relief.

"Well, okay—if that is the diagnosis, how do we proceed?"

Similarly, in our churches, we need to employ great compassion for the anxiety most of us feel about money. We need to move person to person, real situation to real situation, potential gift to potential gift, and not sugar-coat the anxiety many have about asking for money. Once members of the major-gifts team have had even a little experience (hopefully made effective by reading this and my other books first), they will make a few successful requests and find the work less frightening and more engaging and wonderful. But we need to tell the truth. This is human work. Major-gift fundraising employs tools and strategies that consider the great tenderness required when asking for a major gift or planned gift.

Some barriers do get in the way of donors making a major gift. Below are some examples:

Lack of Basic Trust between People

The wrong person was sent (or called) to ask for the wrong gift at the wrong time from the wrong person. Giving a major gift is based in trust. If there has been even a hint of financial or other mismanagement, then trust has been compromised, and a major gift will not be given. If there is doubt in the leadership of the vestry or of the rector, then a major gift will not be given. Relational misconduct between clergy and laity is the biggest problem, because it is not really actionable with discipline. Sexual and financial misconduct are easier to name and prove, but relational misconduct is much more challenging. It usually begins with ego and advances from there. It can seem slick, charming even. But underneath it slithers and hisses. A church in which the clergy, bishop, or leader has been repeatedly unkind or untruthful will be hard to motivate to give major gifts. Usually, major donors in this situation will simply smile and wait for the next leadership to arrive.

Failure to Show the Inherent Value

There needs to be a clear reason why a project is essential to the church and to the town or city in which the church sits. The value of the parish's mission, vision, and service must be clearly evident. The most common reason people do not give a major gift is that they have not been convinced that the project or parish or diocese is worthy. The case for support must be well-communicated and compelling. Deserve the gifts you ask for. I have seen too many bishops and clergy decide on a project as another "legacy," only to find out the hard way they were the only people who thought that "legacy" was a good idea. I have seen campaigns dry up and fizzle away, wasting hundreds of thousands of dollars on campaign consultants, only to realize, during the major-gifts phase, that nobody but the leader really wanted the project in the first place. Remember, in major-gifts fundraising you need a long runway and a short takeoff. Plan and test the plan with everyone, for years, before you actually start to raise money. If the project was not meant to be, then your donors will tell you. Let them tell you while you are planning and not while you are raising money and digging foundations.

A Lack of Urgency

When there is poor planning or communications, the sense of urgency that inspires a person to make a major gift is absent, and so the gift is not made. People do not give to a sinking ship; neither do they give to a program that does not seem to need their gift. Remember that most churches have a donor base that is 50 percent of the number of people on the rolls and about 80 percent of their Sunday attendance. If you have a hundred families who are members of your church, you probably have forty or fifty families who pledge to the annual pledge campaign that funds your budget. Those fifty families are probably the same people you see in your church each week. The other half—the people who do not attend or get involved (but who like to feel they are members by leaving their names on your list of members)—are a wonderful asset to you. Spend your time and effort, long before major-gifts fundraising begins, to find ways to communicate with them. You can do it with house visits, phone calls, a video sent by mail, or a booklet to explain what you are doing and why. But remember that most of those people are leading busy lives. Their views of your church, the local YMCA, and the local museum are ten years older than reality. Uninvolved people know your church for what it was ten years ago, not for what it is today. It is your job to teach them who you are today and why your mission and presence are vitally important.

Negativity

No donor will give a major gift to a campaign in dire circumstances, because they sense they are being asked to invest in poor management. If the request comes with a sinking-ship message to save a drowning organization from financial disaster, the request is doomed from the start. Nor can it come as a threat that staff or programs will be cut if the money is not raised. In an economic downturn, remember that prospects do not want to hear how the economic downturn is affecting your organization. They want to hear how your organization is helping people whose lives have been traumatized by economic downturn.

These are some of the barriers to the receipt of a major gift. One overriding issue in a major-gifts program is integrity. *Integrity* comes from the root from which we get *integer*—a whole number. Major gifts tend to flow freely and effectively when there is wholeness in the congregation and within the clergy. People want to be part of a good place, and they want to be led by a good person. They don't need a perfect place, nor do they need to be led by a perfect person, but the goodness, proven effectiveness, and kindness of the clergy and of the congregation are the best predictors in any church of major-gift program success.

There are many tasks involved in asking for a major gift. It is a process, not an event. The process is time-consuming and requires patience. If you skip steps or truncate what we have called the "engagement continuum" (the six to eight steps that help get donors ready to decide about a gift request), you will fail in requesting and in receiving major gifts, not to mention perhaps alienating the donor permanently. I have served in one church in which the clergy leader was so insecure, arrogant, and unkind that he single-handedly alienated the entire female philanthropist community and sent them all to two other local congregations, nearly doubling those congregations' average pledge in just a few years. In speaking to the senior warden of one of those churches, he laughed and remarked that *our* leader was *his* congregation's honorary stewardship chair. It was funny and sad at the same time.

If you manage the process carefully, donor by donor and step by step, you will be successful if your clergy are kind, honest, and effective, and your church is a whole, well place of mission—a place doing what Jesus would recognize as mission, were he to wander among you in disguise.

It may be that some churches need to get their act together before trying to raise major gifts. They may need a new rector or minister—one well-known for their kindness, honesty, integrity, and gentleness. It may be necessary to wait until a new vestry or church leadership board is elected so they can be intentional about getting honest, kind, effective, whole people into leadership, and gently moving unhealthy people into other, less destructive roles. It may also be necessary to host a series of organic conversations within your congregation—and here I do recommend using the Art of Hosting Conversations That Matter as your toolkit (see artofhosting.org). These tools make it harder for the megaphone voices to dominate and equally hard for the wallflower voices to recede. You will find some model documents on fearlesschurchfundraising.com. If you can inspire these conversations, using tools that dismantle hierarchy, power, control, and even order, then you can get into the "caordic space" (the overlap between chaos and order) where life gets messy and equally full of possibilities. If you can host that kind of conversation over time, and then if, from that conversation, a strategic plan emerges that puts meat on the bones of your mission, and if everyone feels their voices are heard, then your major-gifts program will be breathtakingly successful.

Facing Resistance

One of the most important spiritual and relational attributes of a good church fundraiser is their ability not to take resistance personally.

Our society is weighed down by money pressures, advertising, marketing, materialism, and social status that comes from possessions. That is a dangerous spiritual cocktail. There is terrible fear about not having enough, while, at the same time, we have no idea what enough is or will be in the future—in our old age. Sometimes the nightly news can be terrifying, sending us to bed with our adrenaline flowing and no way to metabolize it.

If the clergy and vestry decide it is necessary to raise money beyond keeping the lights on, then they can be sure that there will be natural resistance from some of the congregation—generally the portion whose spiritual depth is low and imagination atrophied. This is inevitable in a society that has so much fear about money and that allows for so little silence.

You will find that the members of your congregation that give small gifts will generally be those who also make the most vehement complaints about fundraising in church. This is partly because they are quite sure nobody will find out that their gifts are so small in relation to their income and capacity. Shame also plays a role. On the other hand, I've experienced that those who give the largest gifts are also those who make the fewest complaints.

There will always be people who do not want the church to raise money. Some operate out of the principle that Jesus lived a poverty-stricken life, as did Francis, and so should the church. Yet these people tend to be the ones who complain when the church is slightly too cold, too hot, too effective, too evangelical, or "too" anything. If you are going to resolve to raise major gifts in your church, then you are also going to have to resolve to face resistance from those who seek not so much a church, but rather a chapel of ease.

There is only one way, in my experience, to face resistance from your parishioners when they are upset about raising money. And that is to do what Jesus did when he was dominated by power, prestige, ambition, or manipulation. At these moments, Jesus did the following:

1. Jesus became very quiet.
2. Jesus kept going and stood up to the power, even in his silence.
3. Jesus may not have debated the people who had money or power around him, but he kept going every time.

And so must you. I would say that even when Jesus was nailed to a cross and died, and was buried in a rock tomb, even then Jesus kept going. Jesus did not let resistance hold him back from his mission. Is this not the story of Easter? Is not the resurrection God's ultimate refusal to back down when facing human resistance?

Go and do likewise.

An Exercise on Feelings about Money

Write a story from your life in which lack of money made you angry or afraid. What did it feel like? Where was God? What was it like to feel that vulnerability?

Now place yourself in the position of a wealthy donor asked for a major gift. What might they be feeling? What fears might they have? What disappointments might they have experienced when asked for a major gift? How might their money isolate them? What pain might result when a major donor feels that their priest, bishop, or fellow congregant will be angry or disappointed with them if they do not give?

Leadership Red Flags

1. A clergy or lay leader should never try to guide the conversation toward a specific gift that the parish church or diocese wants or needs.
2. Aggressive asking too soon in the process is abusive to the donor and will frighten them away, quite rightly, from making the gift.
3. People who ask for major gifts must never be abrasive, testy, hot-tempered, or irritable. They need to have a gentle, kind, polite demeanor and be more interested in the person than the money.
4. Major-gifts leaders should never be dismissive of people who are uncomfortable with emotions or self-centered in their conversation. It is helpful if those asking for major gifts have pastoral-care training. As I have said above, raising money is a pastoral initiative with logistical implications, not a logistical initiative with pastoral implications.

Facing Resistance to the Major-Gift Program— An Apology for the Return on Investment of Time

In general, it takes about four to eight visits with a person who could give a major gift before they are ready to be asked, which means clergy and lay leaders need to plan on the following time commitment.

1. It will take one hour to create a plan that leads toward the ask of a major gift.
2. It will take about six visits to build a relationship with the potential donor. Each visit will take approximately two hours, since these conversations are not as much about money as about that person's experience of life and church. This means that about twelve hours will be dedicated to relationship building.
3. Each visit will require time for travel, as well as for debriefing after each meeting and strategizing for the next. This adds up to an additional five hours.
4. When the conversations about meaning-making have happened and the donor is clearly ready to be asked for a major gift, the appointment in which the request is made will be quite brief. Plan for two hours to prepare and travel, and then twenty minutes for the request.

Let's say that the gift in question results from a successful request, and that the donor pledges ten thousand dollars to the church. This means that twenty hours was invested. Not only will the next gift require considerably less time for relationship building, this gift has resulted in a monetary value of about five hundred dollars per hour. Five hundred dollars per hour. Seriously. Most bake sales raise about four dollars per hour of allotted time.

My only point is that major-gift fundraising, even though time-consuming, is a very effective use of time. Not only has this donor moved closer to the church's mission by making this gift, but the gift will also provide needed resources.

I've seen many fundraising events (yard sales, talent nights, silent auctions, breakfast-burrito sales—the list is endless) designed to raise ten thousand dollars. There are many good reasons to have wonderful fundraisers. But when twenty people each spend two hours planning the fundraiser, then two hours shopping, then three hours prepping and setting up, then two hours at the event, and then, finally, one hour cleaning up, then those twenty people have just employed ten hours each and a total of two hundred hours to raise that ten thousand. Unlike the major-gift request that resulted in a five-hundred-dollar-per-hour time investment, the return on the time investment for this parish fundraiser is about fifty dollars per hour. There are great reasons to have a parish dinner, but do not pretend it is a fundraiser.

I would suggest that if the goal is fundraising, then the most effective use of time would be simply to ask for a major gift so that nineteen of those people could spend a week of evenings with their family. Of course, it is wonderful to host and attend a fundraiser, but, if you're trying to raise money, then the best use of time and energy is simply engaging and then asking for a major gift. Let the Girl Scouts sell cookies. Let the YMCA ask for membership dues. Let the hospitals have bake sales. The church should be teaching stewardship and asking for major gifts.

An Example of the Need for a Flexible "Case for Support"

I know of a church in a wealthy neighborhood seeking to add classrooms to its existing childcare center. One member of the congregation was a businessman who had earned his wealth by building sports centers around the world. For decades, he had created buildings out of glass and steel and, at a glance, could see any flaw in building plans.

It took the church a long time to gain access to this family that they knew would provide one of their major gifts and set the pace for the rest of the campaign. The right team had to be sent to visit. The team would include the rector of the church and the women who had made the largest gifts to the campaign. They had been meticulous to make sure that the binder had all the right pieces for the case for support: the donor list, a description of the project, the campaign plan, the childcare-center revenue plan, statements for donors who were his close friends, and the blueprints for the new building. There was even a proposal to name the most beautiful room after this man, from whom a major gift was being asked. The room that would bear his name was at the corner of the new building, with sloping lawns up to the glass entrance and soaring glass walls supporting a cathedral ceiling studded with skylights.

Everyone was on their best behavior, the binders were beautifully prepared, and the two people making the request were careful to establish exactly who would say what. They had practiced the meeting in the preceding days and were ready to ask for the flagship gift.

The major donor and his wife listened carefully, nodding from time to time to establish that they were paying attention. Once the presentation had been made, a review of the binder accomplished, and the ideas for the new building roundly complimented, the man considering the leadership gift asked for a red pen.

He spread the blueprints out on his grand piano and used the red pen to make sweeping lines, arrows, and notes around the room that was to be named for him, speaking as he went.

"I am sorry to disappoint you, but the way this grass line slopes down to the foundation, this room will be flooded every time it rains because there's no water egress. Furthermore, these beautiful glass walls will take on the afternoon sun and act like a magnifying glass on the poor children trying to play within those walls. The room is beautiful, but it needs to be placed on the other side of the building where it gets softer morning sun, broken by the trees along the road."

He smiled, the way only a southerner could smile after having made such a statement and covered the blueprints with red ink. The two people asking for the gift felt embarrassed and defeated. The had hoped for the leadership gift, and the request did not go well. The wealthy old man escorted the rector and the leader of the campaign to their cars, inviting them to return when the blueprints had been revised.

After a meeting with the architect, new drawings acknowledged all of the flaws the donor had seen in the originals. When the rector and the head of the campaign, in making a new case for support, returned to present this wealthy man with new drawings and a revised project description, he and his wife gladly gave the leadership gift, allowed their name on the building, and set off a chain reaction of support that raised the money in just a few days.

The case for support presented to the donor, along with the blueprints, needed to be flexible. This is why major donors need to be brought in on the ground floor of a campaign, in its planning phase, years before the asking begins. Because the case for support was in a binder, rather than printed in a slick and expensive brochure, there was flexibility.

The lesson from this story is that the conversation between a church (or a bishop at the diocesan level) and its major donors is a fluid and co-creative event that begins with the first inkling of an idea. Then, as the idea evolves with input from major donors and experts, the case and the project change (and sometimes are even abandoned or amplified). And as input is received so, too, engagement is deepened.

Asking for a major gift is like a novel. Most of the book concerns itself with development, in this case the developing relationship between the church and the major donor. The last chapter, and only the last chapter, contains the request for the gift. The many preceding chapters represent the undulating, creative, human conversation between the donor and the church. Like any good mystery novel, the exciting part—when the church asks for the gift—comes at the end and makes the whole read worthwhile.

Most people believe that asking for a major gift is nerve-racking, embarrassing, awkward, invasive, and frightening. If you jump the gun, nervously putting together the case for support so that the potential program looks good on paper but, in reality, has not been deeply discussed, then asking for the gift will indeed be nerve-racking. But it need not be. If relationship building happens over a long time, asking for the gift should be gentle and delightful.

Facing Resistance from the Pulpit— Pat's Sermon about the Realities

Recently, the future of the church I served was threatened by a massive annual deficit inspired by hubris and ignored though fantasy. This is the story of so many churches in which they spend money in hopes of revitalization when, in fact, a good, faithful church will revitalize itself as people recognize goodness and want to become involved. The problem is that most of our churches elect their vestry from middle management, and, when that happens, churches are managed as a business—and usually a financially unsuccessful one. Here is a good example of a turnaround.

Pat was a soft-spoken priest. He was gentle and kind with a mischievous grin and eyes that said you could trust him. He was appropriately vulnerable with people, and they trusted him deeply. I trusted him deeply. At one point as our interim dean, Pat mounted the pulpit and, instead of preaching a sermon, he read a "state of the church address." He told us we had been overspending for too long. He explained that our giving needed to increase and that we were too dependent on our endowment. We had given small pledges because we assumed the endowment would pay our bills.

Pat told us he loved us. He described what a powerful and wonderful congregation we were. He described our great potential even in the midst of our recent suffering, and he clearly and boldly said that if we did not begin to increase giving with annual pledges, will inclusion, and major gifts, we would spend down our endowment. The deficit meant we had about a decade or so left in the life of our parish.

There was a brief silence at the end of his sermon. For a moment, we wondered what would happen. "Was the congregation angry?" we thought. "Did he go too far? Was he too honest about the state of affairs in our church?" The congregation broke the silence with applause—a standing ovation.

I know many clergy and vestries who are anxious about talking about money and church. They do not want to offend. Pat's story reminds us that a good congregation is resilient and wants to be told the truth. It takes time to change the culture of a church. When we begin to try, we often face resistance. But try we must. The question I often ask when traveling among churches struggling to have a conversation about major gifts is: "I understand that you do not like talking about money and fundraising in church; but, with all due respect, your budget and mission are spiraling toward disaster. Is this plan to avoid fundraising and to avoid discussing money in church serving you well?"

QUICK-START SUGGESTIONS

1. Write a brief statement or covenant about daily spiritual practices to which the committees that raise money can agree. This may be vague, since different people enjoy different spiritual practices that connect them daily with God and their calling. However, I suggest that nobody should remain in leadership unless they have a spiritual practice that supports them when they face resistance in the church. The church is very anxious about money and members these days, and this anxiety will only increase as resources shrink with the death of older generations. Resistance is inevitable. But with an engaged spiritual practice, your leaders will be able to face resistance with grace, kindness, and courage.
2. Make resistance an agenda item when you need to discuss obstacles as a leadership group. An open, gentle, nonjudgmental discussion ending in prayer will often blow frustration and anxiety out of the room.
3. Write and add to a list of objections and resistance to what you are doing and planning. As a committee, write responses to each obstacle, so that everyone is saying the same thing when encountering resistance. Keep these responses kind, nonjudgmental, gentle, and brief.
4. Begin meetings with time to consider why you are raising this money. Remembering why you are doing this work will strengthen your resolve in the face of occasional resistance.

STUDY QUESTIONS

1. What topics of resistance might you face as leaders who seek to increase conversation about and success in raising money for your church's participation in God's mission?
2. What is your own resistance to this work?
3. What barriers have you experienced in raising money?

4. What is your "elevator speech" for people who say, "Why are we all of a sudden talking about money in church?" or, "Why do we need to raise money?—it has always been there for us, and it always will."

PRAYERS

A Prayer for Those Facing Resistance

Over and over again, Lord Christ, you faced deep resistance to your message and to your mission. Some of the deepest resistance you faced came from your own family and friends. And at one point, you even responded to your friend Peter with a verbal charge that Satan was fueling his resistance to your mission. Give us grace, gentle Lord Christ, to face resistance with the patience and determination you so often exhibited. And when we falter, send your Holy Spirit to pick us up, dust us off, and send us on our way with power and within your great glory. *Amen.*

*A Prayer for Those Who Express Resistance
to Stewardship and Fundraising Efforts*

Lord Jesus, when you faced resistance in the Gospel stories, we see so often that your response was simply to ask more questions. Occasionally, you even sensed the resistance and began with questions. Help us to see that the anxiety of the church around fundraising is simply a symptom and not the illness itself. Guide us to ask questions to engage conversation and then bring us, in this Word made flesh, to a willingness to listen to whatever is said. But, in the end, Sweet One, hold and comfort us in our distress at facing resistance, while holding and comforting the resisters in their distress. Your peace you leave with us. *Amen.*

A GIVING STORY:
CHUCK AND JANET—PLANNING A GIFT

By the time I met Chuck and Janet, they were both in their eighties. Life had been good to them. They had both worked very hard. Chuck had a career in finance and Janet had been a nurse. They were financially secure, but not what one might call wealthy. Chuck liked finances, spreadsheets, and investing, so he had built up an estate the way a potter might build a collection of bowls—one at a time, until there were many. Janet liked beautiful things. Her good taste and gentle personality served her well as she led the efforts in our church to care for its beauty. For decades, she led the Arts and Architecture Committee, taking care of what people could see as an extension of our ministry and mission. Scripture says, "Our eyes are the lamp unto our souls," so she cared for what our eyes saw on the walls, in glass cases, and in the sanctuary. Given their generation, Chuck and Janet loved the pipe organ of our church. The Silent Generation is well-known for working hard to preserve what the church has built over time, and Chuck and Janet were no different. They loved the great organ in our church, but they were deeply aware that, even after eighty years, the organ was only two-thirds complete.

Prior to World War II, when the main organ was installed in our church, it was known as a great instrument, attracting many for concerts and then inspiring them to consider joining our congregation. It was a pillar of evangelism in our church, a gateway to the melody and beauty of Jesus. People came to the church thinking they were coming to hear classical organ music, only for the Holy Spirit to sit on their shoulders tapping and whispering.

When the war began, the organ company folded because steel was needed for the war effort, and its labor force was drafted to fight. So the antiphonal organ (the register of pipes at the back of the church) was never built or installed, making it hard to hear the organ or sing the hymns in the back half of the long church nave. For eight decades, the church limped along with an organ that could not produce the needed sound. People got used to it. Other things were priorities. People forgot that the organ was unfinished. It was like buying a surround-sound set of speakers and getting home to find that you had only three of the five speakers in the box. You meant to go back and exchange the box for a new one, but you wanted the speakers for a movie that night and, after watching it, you never really got around to going back for the exchange. You just turned up the volume and made more popcorn.

But, like Kenton in the previous story, Chuck did not forget. He never forgot much of anything. His daughter and son-in-law were leaders in our church, and his grandson loved music and singing in our choir. One day, Chuck met me in the hall and asked to see me. We sat at a table in a quiet room. He was emotional. He wiped a tear in the elegant, gentlemanly way he always moved. "I want to honor Janet's life," he said in what was almost a whisper.

I asked him to please repeat himself.

"I want . . ." He paused. "I want to honor Janet's life with a gift to the church."

He knew that we had just found an antiphonal organ built by the same company that had built our organ during World War II. It was in a Presbyterian church, and they were selling their antiphonal organ for parts. If we were quick, we could buy the old organ, renovate it, and rebuild it in our gallery so that we had the organ the builders and original donors had imagined for our church. But we would need to move quickly, and we only had half the money raised. There were lots of things on our Saint John's meaning-making menu of major gifts—things our church really needed, such as a new roof, new kitchen, endowments to replace pledges lost to death, and an improved electrical system. But Chuck wanted this organ completed and installed before he died and before Janet died. He wanted to be a leadership donor, giving more than 30 percent of the cost of the new antiphonal organ, if I were willing to resurrect the major-gifts program to fund and complete it. It was a tall order. I wasn't sure that, even with his gift, we could raise the remaining money in time. We only had a year. Where would the other donors come from? How could we compete with other things for which we needed major gifts—more compelling things—more urgent needs—more modern needs? There were homeless people camping on our lawn, fifty feet from the organ inside our church. How could we raise money for an organ when we knew we needed to raise money to help the poor, the homeless, the suffering, and the destitute?

I remember looking Chuck directly in the eye and, before my confidence could waver, accepting his major gift and promising to raise the rest of the money—another four hundred thousand dollars—during an already challenging interim period. Though we were dreaming of the day when the trumpets of the antiphonal organ would rise during the Great Vigil and blast "Hail the Festival Day" to announce the end of death, this gift was the beginning of death for Chuck and Janet. They were fine, really. They were not dying any more than we all are, but they ached and were slowing down. They knew it was time to leave their money and possessions behind for the next generations. They know they were near the end of their lives, and they wanted this organ to be finished.

Chuck could not afford to give the gift outright as cash. He had established a charitable remainder trust about twenty-five years before, when he had retired, designating the proceeds for St. John's upon their deaths. There are many tools in planned giving, but this is one of the simplest. Chuck set up an irrevocable trust that set aside his gift to the organ and held no tax ramifications, because the money had already been reserved for philanthropy and for our church. They would lose the interest income since, now, the gift would transfer before their deaths, but they felt they did not need it for their day-to-day budget and, instead, wanted to make sure the organ was purchased, renovated, and rebuilt. This was their meaning-making.

Even now, it is hard for Chuck to talk about this gift. He gets emotional, and his emotion betrays his love for his wife and his love of beauty. It also indicates his love for Jesus, since the music praises the God whom he and Janet will meet one day in the not too distant future. The gift could never have been made from their monthly income, nor could it have been a major gift in the form of a check or money transfer. It needed to be a planned gift, coming from money he one day would no longer be able to control after his death and that of his gentle, kind wife.

What do we see in this beautiful story of a man and a woman who wanted to leave beauty behind for their church and who wanted to do so quickly in order that an opportunity was not lost? Sit with people and invite them to remember your church in their will. That is all. Just that. It can be a five-minute conversation, though I suggest it be an hour in which you both celebrate their life and the life and ministry of your church.

Chuck and Janet, in their soft, elegant way, taught me how to raise major gifts that are planned. Listen. Listen and rejoice in the lives lived and in the longing to leave something beautiful and meaningful behind. They wanted to leave a gift for a community that had loved them throughout their lives, a gift that would last long past their mortal bodies had returned to their maker in a reunion of love's youthful dancing, free of the constraints of flesh and blood. One must wonder what eternal life is like. I wonder if a small part of eternal life is the echo of love and generosity we leave behind us. The stories told by grandchildren. The glances at gifts we have given in life—that vase, that painting, that book. The wisdom that we have passed on to others. Perhaps even the sound of new organ trumpets ringing out from our church on Easter days for the next twenty decades. Will Chuck and Janet be able to hear those notes when they are newly and eternally lodged, years from now?

I do not know. I would like to think so, regardless of what theology and orthodoxy might have to say. I believe that part of our eternal life is like the echo of the last organ note sounded in a massive stone church.

CHAPTER 6

• •

Planned Giving as a Part of Major-Gifts Programming

It is true that the laws and regulations, the legal and accounting tools, the planning and execution of planned gifts in a person's last will and testament can be complex. Often, the wealthier a person is, the more complex their estate plan—what you and I will call their "will."

I, like many of us, will leave a simple will, one that a lawyer is drafting for me as this book is printed. My furniture, art, and money will be left to my sister when I die. There will be 20 percent left to my church, and my farmhouse will be left to Heartbeat, a nonprofit foundation founded by John Philip and Ali Newell, who have been friends and mentors since the first months of my ordination to the Episcopal priesthood. Heartbeat, a registered nonprofit, interfaith corporation, and foundation, supports the growth and advancement of the Celtic vision of listening for the heartbeat of the sacred in all things. This work is fostered by pilgrimages and action that inspire and continue the Celtic consciousness to which John Philip and Ali Newell have given their lives. Their work encourages level hierarchy in religious leadership, care for the planet, and pilgrimage to places like the island of Iona off the Scottish Hebrides' western coastline, to which I leave on retreat when this book is sent to the editors. The work of John Philip and his organization will revolutionize the church, just when the church and planet need it most. I have left my greatest asset to Heartbeat because their work overlaps with my own meaning-making—so it is that to which I want my assets to go (for more on Heartbeat, go to heartbeatjourney.org).

What is important to us will overlap with nonprofits like Heartbeat. But your meaning-making will be different from mine. You may find that your meaning-making is quilting and the beauty of art—so you may leave your house to a quilting museum. Or you may leave your assets to your parish church to endow the rector's salary. Others will find their meaning-making with a hospital that saved their life, while another might want their assets to go to the Nature Conservancy or to a diocesan initiative to care for those experiencing homelessness. The important thing is to find people whose meaning-making is the work of your church. It is within that overlap that we find the shimmering potential of a major gift.

My will is simple. It involves three gifts: to my sister, my church, and an agency I care about deeply. The will cost about five hundred dollars to produce, and it will also provide for my cremation. I will save some money by having one of my pottery urns contain the remains. My ashes will be scattered on beautiful land of my sister's choice. Simple. Easy.

The reality is, however, that those will be the largest gifts I ever make. I will be dead. I will have lived the best life I possibly could. I will have made many mistakes. I will have had many successes, though probably not as many as I'd hoped. And the money I leave behind will be simple and will in no way reflect the beauty of my life. It will just be residue. The important things I leave behind will be some kind words, a soft touch for friends or when I gave out communion wafers, good meals cooked in my gas-fired wok, hundreds of candles burned down to nothing after evenings with people I love, a beautiful dog's good life, and perhaps a few good sermons. But there will be a will. And it will provide for my three major gifts.

Since that last will and testament or estate plan form part of most people's lives, it serves the church well to remember to ask our members individually and corporately to remember our church in their will or estate plan.

As a priest in a church myself, I've had people asking me if they could give a major gift for a new organ or a renovated kitchen, to purchase new chalices or to sponsor a youth attending camp. That major gift is an important decision. And then there are others who cannot give anything more than a modest annual pledge, which is just fine, too. But everyone needs at some point to consider the reality that we will one day die. And so we next consider our meaning-making and what that last (and probably largest) gift will one day fund. For many, that largest gift goes to the government or some cousin, because they did not take time to write a will in life. And for others, consideration of their will and benefactors will take place on a deathbed or in great illness, which is also a difficult time to be considering meaning-making. However, I find that there are times—special thin-place times—while weeding our church gardens, polishing brass for the Christmas service, positioning flowers for an Easter service, or washing dishes after a potluck dinner, when people have turned to me and said, "Charles, I would like to be a part of the Saint John's planned-giving group. I'd like my name on that wall. I want to remember Saint John's in my will. This is where I want my money to go when I die."

It is hard for me to keep weeding, washing dishes, or positioning daffodils after a statement like that. Quite frankly, it is hard not to weep. And often I do. Just a tear or two, quickly wiped to save us both embarrassment. I never receive the news of a planned gift without getting a bit choked up. I hope I never receive the news without getting a bit choked up. It is a beautiful thing.

When a member of our congregation informs me that they have remembered or will soon remember our church in their will, I write a letter thanking them. As soon as I send the letter, I go downstairs and open the planned-giving wall, a series of shallow cabinets in which posters hang with the names of those who have or plan to remember the church in their wills. Each name is listed as the donor desires. The names are not formatted consistently, but that's okay with me. It is a donor-centric program. If they have already died, there is a small red, Canterbury cross by their name.

Gingerly, I remove the poster from the case. I burn it and replace it with a new poster. I hang it in the case with the new name on it. We always include. We do not ask for proof. We do not worry about whether they have already signed the will to include our church—we include the names both of people who have remembered us in their will and those who *intend* to do so. When they manage this process—a difficult process emotionally—is not our business. If they have not yet done their will, then it is the church's job to keep reminding them gently to do so, but, regardless, their name goes on the wall immediately. Our business is to say thank you, quickly and well, and to encourage them to get the will written by inspiring them with the vision for mission in which we include them. My chief concern as their pastor is their living will, which helps me and doctors know what they want when their life is in jeopardy or nearing its end. That I do ask for so that I can keep it in their file in case I need to lobby for their wishes as their priest.

Though I hate to disappoint any reader hoping this chapter would go into great detail about the ways people can leave planned gifts—beneficiary designations, transfer-on-death designations for stock portfolios, life-income gifts such as a charitable gift annuities or charitable remainder trusts, charitable lead trusts, retained life estates, outright or deferred gifts such as real estate, life insurance, possessions, oil or mineral rights, intellectual property—I will not be doing that here. Other books and experts are better suited to explain it all. If I start writing about the tax details of those gifts, you will stop reading, and I will lose the will to live. For now, the best thing is to make the request. Besides, a little knowledge is dangerous. Remember, your job is *only* to ask and get agreement on a will inclusion. The donor's job is to work out the financial details with their own experts—not with you or anyone affiliated with the church. If you or a staff or congregation member "helps" with the wills of your planned-giving members, you risk the liability of having advised them wrongly. That is very dangerous both to the relationship and to the gift.

Managing Your Planned-Giving Major-Gifts Program

As with your major-gifts program, planned giving is also a program, not a campaign. I have seen many churches use planned giving as part of a campaign to raise money for a building, renovation, program, or capital improvement. I have rarely seen it done well. In a large capital campaign, it is often advisable to include planned giving as an option for those who would like to participate in major gifts but do not have the ready assets to participate. Auditors will allow these gifts in a capital campaign if the donor is of a certain age and the gift is expected, well, rather soon.

For this reason, I suggest that churches maintain a planned-giving program alongside a major-gifts program. In smaller churches, this will be one initiative with two results. By *program* I mean a twelve-month, year-round effort. People will come forward at various times from your congregation to discuss planned gifts, simply because they have decided to have their will drawn up by a lawyer. Perhaps they are going away on vacation and would prefer to leave a will in case of an accident, since the children will be left with family while they're away. Other people are motivated to write their will because of a diagnosis, or because they know that having a will is a chore that big boys and girls do when they become adults. As with taxes, the work that goes into a will can be tedious. It can even be anxiety-producing, because it is difficult in our culture to talk about or even think about our own death. But we all will die, and we all must have a will.

Perhaps a parishioner mentions the desire to remember your church in their will. Their lawyer will ask them a series of questions as the will is being prepared that will assist in the drafting. One of the questions will be, "Are there any agencies or organizations to which you would like to give gifts, through your will, at the time of your death?" Most churches actively encourage planned gifts as part of their culture. Those who do receive planned gifts. Those who do not, do not receive planned gifts. If a member of your congregation volunteers in any one of the nearby nonprofits, they will be approached and encouraged to remember that agency in their will, because that agency knows that the average gift from a will to a nonprofit is about eighty thousand dollars. The time it takes to ask for inclusion in a person's will is about twenty-five minutes. From the point of view of time efficiency and nonprofit management, that is a great return on the investment of a cup of tea and a brief conversation. Since we know death will happen, and since the average churchgoer spends ten times more time in church then in any one of these agencies, it makes sense to me and hopefully to you that we proactively ask our members to remember our churches in their wills.

I am aware that some churches have lawyers set aside who will help people in the congregation create a will, if that person remembers the church in it. I am not a fan of doing business in the church. I nervously remember Jesus turning over tables in the temple in a fit of rage. Of course, the logistical problem is simple when someone asks for their will, when the will is simple and the gift generous, to be drawn up by one of the church lawyers. But what happens to that volunteer lawyer who ends up in a conversation with a member of your congregation whose will is more of an estate plan, requiring countless hours of detail work? The other problem, of course, is that many people write their will in their last years. It would be easy for family members of a deceased matriarch to charge that the church had undue influence and mixed motives when "helping" the grandmother with her will. There's also the possibility that the family might charge that their grandmother was suffering from dementia, a diagnosis most lawyers are not able to establish. There are pitfalls to this commingling of business and ministry.

Starting Up a Planned-Giving Program

At the risk of sounding rather anticlimactic and perhaps even flip, you only need two things to establish a planned-giving program.

1. You need to tell people you have a planned-giving program.
2. You need to keep a public list of those who have remembered your church in their will.

I know. "It can't be that simple," you may say. Well, it is. It's just that simple. Now if you have the resources, you can add some bells and whistles, a communications program, a committee and chairperson to help manage the process, a brochure that tells your congregation more about your vision for the use of these funds, and a brief description of some of the legal and financial tools they could use when leaving a gift.

A planned-giving insert model, if you need one, is on the fearlesschurch fundraising.com website.

Okay, so you have started your planned-giving program simply by telling people that you have one. Well done! You are now doing better than three-quarters of churches that have not even bothered to welcome bequests, let alone discuss them.

My brother-in-law is a fisherman. We spent time on his boat on the lakes of Virginia. He always says "the likelihood of catching a fish goes up substantially when I bother to put the hook and bait in the water." The likelihood of you receiving a bequest to fund the mission of your church goes up substantially when you bother to begin and manage a planned-giving program.

So, having started, as an extension of the major-gifts program, a planned-giving program with a little brochure, a letter to your congregation, a planned-giving Sunday to raise awareness, or an endowment that cannot be invaded, what do you do next?

What Gets Measured Gets Done

What you need to do now is manage the program. In some churches, planned giving and major-gifts programs are combined, but I recommend against it unless your church is very small (less than twenty-five on a Sunday.) Although the two initiatives—planned giving and major gifts—are very similar, they have different theologies, case stories, tools for engagement, and ethos. I suggest that you not combine these two programs, even if you are in a little church in which one person chairs major gifts and a different person chairs planned giving.

Form a small committee of the oldest, kindest, most trusted, connected people in your congregation, basically a committee just like the major-gifts advisory committee. Or, merge the two. Then draft a strategic plan using this chapter as an outline and get to work.

It is essential, as you receive the pledge cards during your annual pledge campaign, that when the major-gifts or planned-giving options has been checked by the donor, you call them immediately (*immediately!*) to thank them personally and to set an appointment. I know this is difficult, and that there's a lot going on during the fall as most of our campaigns are happening. And I have been guilty of leaving those pledge cards on my desk for days before remembering to deal with them. I am ashamed of that. Please do not do likewise. When a donor tells you that they have remembered your church in their will with a check mark on that card, this represents a massive gift. Please respond with a very quick "thank you." This will be the easiest major gift you solicit. Do not drop this ball.

Websites

Just as you have a Web page for supporting materials and an online pledge card for your annual pledge campaign, I suggest that you also have a Web page for the materials and secure pledge card related to planned gifts. Here's what I suggest you have on your website under planned giving:

- A brief letter from the minister inviting will inclusion and discussing the future of the church
- A brief description of the various giving tools (see the model bulletin insert above)
- Quotations and photographs from people who have already included the church in their will, describing how they feel about having done so
- Quotations from the children in your church (no names, no photographs) in which they describe their hope for your church's future and what it will mean to their families when they are grown up
- A secure location for a pledge or to request a visit. You can easily use the language I have suggested for pledge cards during the annual-giving campaign.

A Word about Vocabulary

Let's take a moment to look at vocabulary. Jesus Christ came to Earth as "the Word," so words are important. In my opinion, we need to update the vocabulary we are using for planned giving. The truth is, our planned-giving vocabulary is often classist.

More than I like to admit, I see churches acknowledging donors who remembered the church in their will with Edwardian language such as *society* and their involvement as donors with terms like *member*. I hope we can change this language. When we redid the donor wall for our planned-giving participants, we renamed that group. The John Smith Society (not the real name) originally had been named for the clergyperson who built our beautiful church. He had a strange-sounding name with a British spelling. The only portrait of him looks rather like Voldemort, the evil character in the Harry Potter novels. He was white, pale, with beady eyes, which makes you feel like you have done something wrong. So we updated our language as follows:

Before	Now
Balwyn Terrinton Society	Planned-giving participants
The Society Gala	Being Great Ancestors—A Party for the Future
"The Donor Wall"	"May We Rest in Peace and Rise in Glory"
Estate planning	Will inclusion

By making these and other changes to our language, we were able to improve the old messaging that "planned giving is for rich people, not for regular folk like me." The truth is, planned giving is for anyone who believes that they will one day die.

Looks Deceive: The Danger of Prejudgment about Capacity

One last word before I close this chapter. It is important not to prejudge what people can leave to a church in their will. As I said in earlier chapters about "prospect qualification," not everyone in the congregation is going to be able to make a major gift. However, everyone in the congregation will be able to make a planned gift. I have known people who left very little money behind because they spent it all on a lavish lifestyle, propping up a fragile self-esteem with trinkets and fine clothes. On the other hand, I've seen teachers who live in a one-thousand-square-foot World War II cinder-block house, who use a tea bag three times before they throw it away, and who leave millions to their church precisely because they have chosen a simple, humble lifestyle. Do not prioritize the people that you've visited to request will inclusion by how wealthy they do or do not seem.

Start with the oldest and most involved. Sit in their living room, listen to their wonderful stories about life in their church, and ask them to include your church in their will. It may take half an hour to drive to their house. It may take two hours in that living room listening to those wonderful stories. It may take another half-hour to drive home. Statistically speaking, most will agree to remember your church in their will. You have just spent three hours doing this work. If they say "yes," and they will (it's an easy "yes," given that taking the money with them after they die is not an option), then you have just raised eighty thousand dollars. This means that your time was worth twenty-six thousand dollars per hour, or $444 per minute. That is a good use of your time.

A Final Word on Planned Giving

It is sobering, but valuable, to do the following exercise. It will raise your awareness to the importance of asking members of your congregation to remember your church in their wills . . .

Count the funerals that you have done in the past twelve months. Then count the deaths of parishioners whose funerals were held elsewhere. Add the numbers together. The total is the number of eighty-thousand-dollar bequests that could have come to your church in the last twelve months had those people been approached and asked to include your church in their wills.

Now go back over your records and count the number of bequests that you received in the last twelve months.

Now compare the number of deaths in your parish to the number of bequests that you have received.

This exercise will give you the energy you need to get this job done. It is true that the hard work you do today in planned-giving solicitation in your church will probably not bring gifts for a number of years. It is therefore true that this hard work will benefit the budget of the future clergy, wardens, and congregations. But I would encourage you to stand in the middle of your church and look around. Let your eyes fall on all the windows, all those chairs or pews, all the artwork, all the brass and silver. As you look around, feel gratitude for the clergy and lay leaders who asked for those gifts decades ago. If you are so blessed as to have an endowment, look hard at the records that tell you who left that money and be grateful for the clergy and lay leaders who asked. Pray for them by name on the Feast of All Saints. Now get up, take a deep breath, and get to work, because you are the only one who can make that happen for the future of your church, among the congregation still needing to include your church in their wills.

The Annual-Giving Pledge Card

It is important that when you manage your annual pledge campaign, you include planned giving and major gifts as options on the pledge card. Each fall, as your parishioners decide about their pledges, they are thinking about their money and about their church. So it is important to include three questions at the bottom of your pledge certificate, which, by the way, I hope will be large and beautiful, on heavy stationery and full of color. A pledge of financial commitment deserves elegance. If parishioners can give you one thousand dollars, then you can spend twenty-five cents on their pledge card.

Here are the four questions to include on your annual pledge card and that refer to major gifts and planned giving:

___ I/we have remembered the church in my/our will(s).

___ I/we plan, one day in the future, to remember the church in my/our will(s).

___ I/we would like to make a major gift to the church beyond this annual pledge. Please visit me/us to discuss this gift.

___ I/we would like to remember the church in my/our will(s). Please visit me/us to discuss this.

This decision to include these options on your annual pledge card will serve you well as you work to change the culture of giving in your church.

The work you accomplish in planned giving over the next two decades (possibly just the next decade) will largely determine whether or not your church exists as a church (and by extension, your diocese) in the next fifty years and beyond. As generations shift, churches without endowments face difficult financial times. Not asking for planned gifts from your members now is a terrible betrayal of the future generations of your church—just as terrible as the one visited upon you by the last few generations of your church. So turn the tide and raise planned gifts.

RESOURCE

Sample—The Planned-Giving Committee Mission

The mission of the Planned-Giving Committee is to educate about the need and importance of planned giving, to encourage participation, and to ensure good stewardship through planned gifts to the ongoing and future mission of the parish.

The mission of the Major-Gifts Advisory Committee is to manage the process by which the parish members consider, discern, and make major gifts to the mission of the church. The committee, in coordination with the Planned-Giving Committee, will identify members who can make such gifts and will oversee the process by which major donors are informed, encouraged, and invited to invest in the mission of the parish now and into the future.

RESOURCE

Sample—A Strategic-Plan Outline

Create a tracking system that will allow you to record the people who have been asked to remember your church in their wills. This is the most valuable thing you can do. At the end of each month, count how many people in your congregation were asked. If you track the number, then you can see, with your own eyes, whether or not you have accomplished your goal. This can be as simple as a list on a piece of paper or as complex as data entry. But the most important thing to remember is that this is a chronological record of requests of and responses from congregation members, asked to remember the church in their will or estate plan. Because we only do what gets measured, it is important to log the actual requests made of your congregation for will inclusion. One easy way to accomplish this task is to create a binder insert for each adult member. Then create a top page that chronicles, by date, the name of the person asked and the name of the person who asked for will inclusion.

Host an annual event for those who have remembered the church in their will *and* for all others curious to do so. Make this an event for the entire congregation and be sure to invite effectively. (People need eight "taps" in order to remember to put something on their calendar: a postcard to save the date six months out, a letter invitation three months out, a card invitation one month out, announcements in church every week for one month and in all communications venues, a letter one week out, and so on.) This event should be fun, playful, inexpensive, and should point to the future of the church and its mission.

Have a "Future Party." It can be a lot of fun to go back fifty or one hundred years and remember how odd the current year must have seemed to members of your congregation. The church from which I write this book today was founded 150 years ago on the second floor of a saloon in "Denver City." Downstairs were "ladies of the night" in corsets and cowboys slinging beer and scotch with someone pounding on the piano. Gunshots rang out from time to time, and the collection for our church that first day was $2.45. Could they have imagined the city of Denver 150 years later? Could they have seen the impact our church would have on the homeless, food justice, or gun control? Get dressed up in costumes. Have historians write articles and have futurists discuss our society in thirty years. (For example, Danish and Dutch futurists who study societal change predict that, in thirty years, the chief malady in the West will be social isolation due to technology. We already don't know our next-door neighbors. They say that churches will be the one place in which people connect. So imagine the needs of your church in the future and talk openly about funding that future.) Talk about what it means to "be great ancestors to the future." Get creative about this event. Whatever you say will be the "case for support" that inclines people to change or write their will.

Host an annual "Planned-Giving Sunday" in which the whole experience is crafted around will inclusion. Place folded cards in each bulletin and pens on each seat. Invite people to tell you that they have or will one day include your church in their will. Have them place that card in the collections plate. If they say they "will one day soon" remember the church in their will, immediately add those new names to the donor wall and to your records. Then treat them just like any other planned giver who *has* already remembered your church in their will (except visit them, and keep visiting them, until you have helped them to make good on this intention). As soon as someone becomes a member of the planned-giving donor group (we will talk about the name of this group shortly), it becomes *the responsibility of the staff and clergy,* not just the donor, to help them ratify their pledge to get a will and include the church. Do *not* block membership simply because they have not yet seen a lawyer, paid for a will, or added a codicil to include your church. You *first* include them in this group with radical hospitality and then let them include you in their will with equal hospitality and generosity later, when it is convenient for them. Remember, this is donor-centric fundraising, not church-centric fundraising.

Sample—A Communications Plan

So that you are careful and intentional about reminding the congregation to remember your church in their wills, you may want to develop a strategic plan for communications. This planned-giving communications plan could involve the following:

1. A monthly bulletin insert
2. A quarterly newsletter article
3. A quarterly adult forum or class to discuss end-of-life planning. (Note: I am not a fan of will clinics and panels. Every person's estate is different, and they should be going to their own advisers and not listening in on all sorts of advice that may or may not be pertinent to their situations.)
4. A quarterly sermon (remember the reference in the Book of Common Prayer on page 445)
5. A monthly e-news article (an e-mail newsletter)
6. A monthly announcement by the clergy or wardens
7. A quarterly direct-mail letter or card
8. One sermon a year, by the youth, in which they express their hopes and longings for the future of your church and the hope that parishioners include the church in their wills so that the church has a strong future
9. One Sunday a year in which everybody who has remembered the church in their will wears a special badge or name tag that says, "Ask me about why I remembered this church in my will." And get people talking after church.
10. Create and maintain a planned-giving donor wall so families that have remembered your church in their wills are clearly recognized for their major gifts. You may also keep nearby a "Book of Remembrance" in which the names of donors who have made major gifts (not planned gifts) are listed in a beautifully bound book, and in beautiful calligraphy. Each week, you can turn the page to honor those names. The proximity of the donor wall, and this book of remembrance, will link the two kinds of gifts (major and planned) in the minds of your members.

One Planned-Giving Donor— An Example

Benjamin Franklin loved life, but his greatest achievement was his last will and testament. It is so great that you can buy a copy at your local bookstore. He loved to live, was raucous and controversial, and he planned for death. Everything was a curiosity to him. How did things work? What made this do that? Always inventing. Always seeing potential in things that others saw as stagnant. He understood giving, and he understood planned giving and major gifts. He took two years' worth of his lowest annual salary—money paid to him for a civil post—and set it aside. It was about twenty pounds sterling in 1790, or about four thousand dollars in today's money.

His will directed that it be kept in a bank account to be withdrawn two hundred years after he died. The money was made available to his beloved community, the city of Philadelphia, on April 17, 1990. This bequest had grown to four million dollars because of the interest compounding over the two hundred years it was held by his estate. He thought that in the future—after he died—there might still be a problem with the education and employment of the financially poor. That money built schools and clinics all over Philadelphia and provided training for countless kids who would otherwise be in prisons, brothels, crack houses, and on the streets. That gift also taught this nation and its philanthropists a lesson. Today, Americans are the most generous philanthropists on the planet.

A Valuable Testament to Your Mission Being Known in Your Town

In the 1970s, a wealthy woman in a city in which I ministered employed her tax accountant as the executor of her estate. She was the heiress of a large fortune, and she had remembered a school for girls that she attended by placing a bequest to the school in her will. By the time of her death, nine decades later, the girls' school had closed, leaving no foundation in its wake. She was an Episcopalian, and so her will stipulated that, in the event that any of the agencies to which she gave money had closed before her death, those funds should be redirected to a local church well-known for doing good work among the poor and the marginalized. The executor of her estate was well-informed of the good work our church was undertaking, so, in keeping with her wishes, the money was designated to our church. The gift was more than seven million dollars. Our church had been financially fragile until that moment, and, without an endowment of such magnitude, our church might indeed have had to close or sell off its large building, a masterpiece of beautiful architecture in our town—indeed, the city cathedral. But because one tax accountant knew about our church by reputation—knew we were doing good work—we received a gift that transformed our mission overnight and set our church on a course of tremendous success for decades to come. The donor was not a member of our church. No one is even sure if she ever attended once. But because the person who was managing her will and its bequests knew about our parish, we received that gift.

The lesson to be learned here is that a simple mail-merged letter to financial planners throughout your town or city on an annual basis would be a profoundly important investment of time and energy, not to mention stationery and stamps.

Sample Tracking System
for Requests for Will Inclusion

Parishioner	Solicitor	Visit date	Outcome	Next step
John Smith	Rev. Jones	1/19/20__	Inclusion	Recognition
Sarah Winters	Sr. Warden	2/23/20__	Inclusion	Recognition
Harrold Hallock	Joe Wright	2/29/20__	Declined (ill)	Revisit 4/25
Sam & Sue Johnson	Rev. Jones	4/19/20__	Inclusion	Recognition

Sample Planned-Giving Participants' Welcome Letter (for New Members)

Sent with the large-format planned-giving *Stewards of God's Bounty* magazine and brochure for use with their financial planner.

Dear _____:

Thank you for your generous willingness to remember Saint Mergatroid's in your will. The parish's ministry is a good investment of your philanthropy, and we are mindful of the great responsibility to use this gift for the work Christ would have us do in the future.

Many have gone before us as ancestors to establish what we now enjoy as a parish church, and what now serves the city of Molene in so many ways and for so many communities of human need. Those who went before us remembered the parish in their wills; and, so now, as we do the same thing, we are providing for future ministries among future generations with our planned gifts.

As you make decisions about everything from living wills to planned-giving financial tools, we are able and willing to assist in any way we can. Your financial and legal advisors will advise you as to what best suits your needs and your philanthropic interests; however, I have enclosed a brochure called *Stewards of God's Bounty* so that you have ready access to a summary of various tools and issues in making this planned gift.

Please feel most welcome to attend the annual Planned-Giving Participants' luncheon on June 14 after the 10:00 service in the church's gardens and in Severin Hall. And please do not hesitate to contact me if there is anything I can do to assist you in this process of discernment and this act of great generosity. I will follow up this letter with a phone call in order to set an appointment to visit you. I would like to hear more about why you have taken this tremendous step into the mission of our church, and I would, quite frankly, like to get to know you better.

Warmly and with gratitude,

(live, blue-ink signature of leader or clergy)

A Story of Missed Opportunity—
Mrs. Symington's Last Question

When I was curate in my first church, I was called to the bedside of an old and sick lady who was dying. I did not know her, and she did not know me. She had heard me preach a few times, and she knew that I had come to her home a few times to bring her communion. She knew my name.

I arrived with my oil stock securely attached to my key ring—its usual location, so that I always have it handy. I had my Book of Common Prayer, and I said the prayers indicated for the time of death. She thanked me with a shallow voice. She told me that there was nobody left in her family to sit with her and thanked me for doing so. The hospice nurse said that it would be a matter of hours. So I waited. She held my hand.

About an hour later, she awoke and told me she once had a dog, and knew that I had had one. She asked me about him. A moment passed, and she told me that she left her whole estate to the Society for the Protection of Cruelty to Animals (SPCA) in our town. I stroked her hand and told her they would do good things with the money. She smiled gently. Then she cocked her head slightly and said wistfully, "I wish the church had asked me. I would have given it to you—all of it. We just never had the conversation." After an increase in medicine, she dozed off. An hour later, she died peacefully in her sleep.

I've never forgotten that day. The SPCA received a gift of $250,000. It was the value of her home and a small savings account. It was true that the SPCA would use that money well, but part of me wished my church had asked her for a planned gift—in part because it was clear that she had wished that as well.

I hope that reading this inspires you to realize how easy and wonderful this work is. If you do not raise major gifts from your church members, then I promise you that members able to give major gifts will give them to non-profits in your town or city. Some people give large major gifts, and some people give small major gifts; the national average for a major gift is about seventy thousand dollars. If you have a hundred families in your congregation, and ten of them could give major or planned gifts, then, over the next two decades, you could raise seven hundred thousand dollars from those families. I suppose the question is this: could you use that kind of money for your ministry and mission and its future? What would it be like to bring joy to the people who give the money away?

Sample Donor Wall

© William Roberts, CutWood Workshop, cutwoodworkshop.com

QUICK-START SUGGESTIONS

Here are a few things to get going right now as you plan your planned-gifts programming:

1. Buy or have a small wooden case built, like a deep picture frame that opens. If you are low on funds, simply buy a large poster or picture frame and hang it on the wall. Insert into it the list of your planned-giving donors with a small red cross next to names of the deceased. Ask your donors how they want their name listed. Different styles are fine—let your doors decide. Hang this in a prominent place so that

people moving into and out of your sanctuary will see it often and will consider adding their names.

2. At all entrances, have brochures offering more information about planned-giving tools and options. Many fine companies produce these brochures and will print your church name and contact person, or you may simply affix your own labels to the back. Spend the money. The first planned gift you receive will reimburse the budget tenfold. Be sure that a specific person and their contact information are listed as a means by which an interested member of your congregation may include your church in their will.

3. Set a date for a planned-giving Sunday at which each member of the congregation receives an interest card to identify their willingness to participate or that they have already done so. Simply have them mark the card, print their contact information (have pens in the pews), and drop it in the collection plate. If only one person does so, then you have just raised an (on average) a one-hundred-thousand-dollar planned gift.

STUDY QUESTIONS

1. What are your fears about asking someone for will inclusion?
2. What does it feel like to imagine your possessions and your money benefiting other people after you are dead?
3. What is your "elevator speech" if someone were to ask you, "Why should I include this parish in my will?"
4. Close your eyes and imagine the headlines of the local newspaper twenty-five years from now. Imagine that your church receives a bequest twenty-five years from now, a bequest that you requested this year. Imagine that bequest is equal to 10 percent of your church's annual budget. Imagine the headline is about the wonderful thing you are going to do with that bequest. Write the headline and write the story. Playfully imagine how planned gifts could benefit human life twenty-five years from now because they were left to and used by your church.
5. How would you design your donor wall if you were not too concerned about money?
6. Is there one story from the history of your church that clearly shows how wonderful it is for a church to receive a planned gift that provides money needed for mission? Tell that story.

PRAYERS

A Prayer for Those Considering a Planned Gift

It was in deep darkness that the women came to the tomb that night with pounds of costly spices, bandages, and syrupy myrrh with which to wrap and bless your body in that cold tomb. But an angel told them you were not there, that you were risen and back among humanity. Help those who are considering their own death. Bring them peace when they are afraid. And, Lord Christ, if they are considering remembering this church in their will, give them the joy of your Holy Spirit as they imagine a funded future of mission and ministry. *Amen.*

A Prayer for Those Asking for Will Inclusion

We give thanks for those willing and able to ask others to remember our church and its mission in their wills. Give them a quiet confidence to tell their own story of having made that decision for their own will. Then give them the courage to ask others to remember their church in the same way. This is holy work, more ministry than praxis. So dwell within those beautiful souls willing to ask for our church's future. This we pray in the name of Christ, the gift you gave even beyond the grave. *Amen.*

A GIVING STORY:
DAVID BALL—THE CHAIRPERSON

I first met David in a hospital. It was my first week on staff at a new church, and I was nervous. Every face was new, and I was still grieving the loss of old friends from my last parish and chaplaincy to the State Senate. My job in this new church was to be a good parish priest, but I also had the responsibilities of stewardship, membership growth, and fundraising. The work of a fundraiser in a church or any other organization takes time, because you have to build relationships and trust. I remember my first day on the job at the YMCA when the chief executive officer introduced me to the staff and said, "This is Charles. He is our new fundraiser. He will do a great job, but do not expect any increases in fundraising for two years. It will take him that long to be trusted, and it will take that long to build relationships. But, come two years from now, watch out! He's going to raise a lot of money." And we did.

Now I was making my first pastoral visit as a parish priest in a new church, standing in front of a man lying in a hospital bed. David was a jovial, gentle soul. He was the kind of person everyone in the church liked and respected. He was universally trusted. "David," I thought as I stood there, "would make a great stewardship chairperson." It would not be until three years later, after some painful failures in lay leadership for stewardship, that I would ask him to be the chairperson of the stewardship commission, and that he would kindly agree. It was a great day both for the church and for me, personally.

David was a lawyer by trade, but he also had a brief career as a fundraiser for an environmental nonprofit. He had also led our church in a lawsuit against a group of picketers who were harassing our congregation—a lawsuit he won and won, all the way to the Colorado Supreme Court. David was soft-spoken and gentle, but his brain was always watching carefully to see where there was truth, and where there was not. David had suffered a lot, but his suffering had forged his soul. His rivers ran deep as did his great kindness and gentleness. He and his family attended our church regularly and were well-known and respected in the congregation. He was a generous donor, giving to the full capacity of his income and beyond.

David was an ideal chairperson for stewardship in our church. His deep integrity and legal mind contributed to his ability to manage the stewardship of our time and talent. He was meticulous about invitations to meetings and energetic about the details of agendas. He cared deeply about the process—making sure the right thing followed the right thing. And he was deeply caring about the people involved—how they were feeling, what they were thinking, how deeply they were involved, what they were producing, who needed to be thanked, encouraged, and even challenged.

I remember one day he asked me to describe the perfect stewardship chairperson. I said, "You need someone who can engage the people who need to be engaged, challenge the people who suffer from resistance, and thank the people who need to be thanked." I still stand by that statement. David's grace and kindness combined with his lacerating intelligence and missional passion brought stewardship in our church to a new and stunning level. The power in the combination of a deeply trusted lay leader and clergyperson cannot possibly be underestimated. If you do everything in this book, but make a mistake in the lay leadership of stewardship, then the book will be of little help.

I am an Episcopal priest. The word *Episcopal* has in its etymology the word *scope*—also in *telescope, microscope,* and *periscope.* The name of our denomination and the names we give our elected leaders emerge from the word used for "looking closely." A good bishop will look closely enough to care for their flock. I say without reservation that when a member of the clergy, lay leader, or warden wants to have and maintain an effective stewardship program, in which money is raised and hearts are warmed to philanthropy, the single most important contribution is the careful choice of the layperson to lead this effort. If you make a poor choice, either of clergy or lay leader, you will find that raising money is like walking through tar. On the other hand, if you do the hard work of discernment, carefully choosing the chairperson of your stewardship and major-gift programs, you will have taken the most important step in moving toward a successful resource-development ministry.

David had the playfulness and delight of a ten year old, with the wisdom of a ninety year old. When he smiled and laughed, the whole room lit up a bit. But it took only a glance at the spreadsheet or a donor report for him to see a problem, inconsistency, or potential and to address it.

David and I were an amazing team. True, it inspired some envy—and the politics of envy are not to be ignored. But we loved working together. We knew each other, and we trusted each other. We could each sense when something was wrong, and, when we did, we asked each other about it. He was willing to challenge me to do my best work as a priest and fundraiser, as he was willing to protect me from out-of-control goal increases and reckless attempts to make fundraising magically solve immediate budgetary problems (a grotesque misuse of power, triangulating any fundraiser). The components of resource development in the church are not unlike the pieces of a mobile. When you touch one thing, all the other things move. Touch the annual fund, and planned giving shifts. Touch major gifts, and the annual fund shifts. An effective leader in church stewardship is honest, kind, gentle, strong, and brilliant. Find that person and don't settle for less. There is a lot at stake. The most important choice you will make when working to build a stewardship program is the choice of your leaders. Make good choices of clergy, bishops, and lay leaders, or your campaigns will fail. If you make quick or poor choices, your carelessness will be expensive and painful. If you choose well, by prayer and discernment, patience, and careful observation, then everything else will fall into place.

David and I were friends. I realize that, as clergy, I am only a spiritual friend, but we were friends. We supported each other. We liked each other. We trusted each other, and we had each other's back. We were willing to say hard things without fear of anger or resentment. And we were very good at the occasional high five when we raised a major gift or blasted through a campaign goal to fund the mission to which Jesus was calling our church. Our friendship was a reminder of the single most essential aspect of any fundraising, but especially in major gifts: it is all, always, and primarily about relationships.

CHAPTER 7

●●●

Programming and Stewarding

Why Is the Work in This Chapter Important?

If you know how to do the isolated tasks in this book, but do not form them into a program that flows through the year's calendar and strategic plan, you will find your major-gifts work to be sporadic and ineffective. This work is like dieting or exercise—you must keep it slow and steady. If it is sporadic and done only when you have time, you will find that the fits and starts will be frustrating and bear little fruit. It is better to set a small goal at first— "I will visit one person per week with the intention of engaging them into deepening willingness to make a major gift." At least you know that measurable steps will be taken. They will result in money raised and given. But if you do not track that work, writing it down so that you can see it at the end of the month, you will find yourself walking in circles or stalled in resistance.

Clergy are trained in theology, pastoral care, scripture, and liturgy, but, when they get their first church job, they often find they have a nonprofit agency to manage without the skills to effect change. Sure, anyone may, if they choose, super-spiritualize church work and say that it is not a nonprofit agency, but they are dead wrong. Jesus never super-spiritualized anything— he led men and women. This book works to teach clergy and lay leaders how to lead men and women.

Leadership in the twenty-first century is becoming organic. Each piece fits into the other, and, like a mobile, when you touch one piece the others move. Effective program management allows for all the parts to speak to each other. This chapter seeks to help leaders to integrate resource development into the whole work and leadership of a church.

We are often so anxious about major-gifts work that we isolate the brave souls willing to do it, but that siloing only weakens the system. Program management integrates and connects. Stewardship inspires confidence and repeat gifts.

The biggest barrier in major-gifts fundraising in any church is the anxious thinking that breeds the thought, "I do not have time for this." If you are in clergy or lay leadership in these days, you must do this work.

About Programming

If you are anything like most of the clergy who read this book in its early phases, you might admit to being a little bit overwhelmed. If you're not used to raising major gifts and are perhaps a bit frightened of it, you may feel anxious. I beg you to reconsider. I'm always amazed at the suffering we create for ourselves simply because we believe our thoughts. Friendly reader, do not believe your thoughts. They are just thoughts. If they're anxious thoughts, then inquire about them. If you think that you cannot do this work, that you do not have time, courage, or resources, then I beg you to realize that those are just thoughts. Can you let them go, so that you're peaceful again? Effective? Successful in God's vineyard?

This work can be time-consuming; we've discussed that in previous chapters. The results that you get in major-gift fundraising are a significant return on the investment of your time. You will never have to have another bake sale.

If you create a major-gifts program, you are going to have to manage the programming that results. You're going to have to create a system by which you get the work done. Whether you are the cardinal rector of a massive church, the minister of a megachurch, or the pastor of a tiny parish, it all works the same way. You can say, "I don't have time for this," but that is just a thought.

The only way to do major-gifts fundraising in a church is to manage the engagement of your major-gift prospects, occasionally asking for a large gift. There are only two tools you need: first, you need the integrity of a great mission, set in the context of a great strategic plan; second, you need to track the engagement encounters and the requests made in living rooms. Yes. Count them. Measure your effectiveness. Vestries, church leaders . . . measure your clergy's work in financial development. Hold them accountable. It is part of their job.

Let's say, for example, that a clergyperson's Sabbath day is Friday. On Thursday afternoon, about four o'clock, they should sit down at their desk, thank God for a week of work well done, and, by reviewing their calendar, write down the engagement-continuum events they or others participated in that week. How many living-room visits were made? How many were asked for a gift? These numbers should be part of each vestry or board meeting. What gets measured gets done. If you want clergy to raise money, then measure what they do to raise it. If you do not measure this work on a monthly basis, then you, the leadership, are responsible for mismanagement and deserve the poor income you will inevitably get from your stewardship program.

About the Stewardship of Received Gifts

Woven into the days, weeks, and months of your year, in this tapestry that is your work, whether you are clergy or a lay leader, is the stewardship of the gifts you receive in your church. Institutional stewardship is an essential aspect of fundraising. Just as programming is important to managing the process, stewardship is important nutrition for the process. When you are a good steward of the money given to you, and when the community and your donors notice that you are a good steward, you will find that the second and third requests are exponentially easier. The gifts get significantly larger and the planned giving nearly miraculous.

Every donor giving a major gift is managing the stewardship of what God gave them. It is a spiritual act. That act is made no less spiritual by the second reality that every donor is making a philanthropic investment, and they would like to see a return on the investment. Jesus often spoke in parables about sowing seeds, planting vineyards, and reaping harvests. Jesus was not being unspiritual, he was simply aware of the reality for the people with whom he walked and spoke. We must be aware of the reality in the lives of the major donors from whom we seek major and planned gifts. We are shooting ourselves in the foot, or, worse, we wiggle out of the responsibility of raising major gifts when we overspiritualize the work.

I have seen clergy turn up their noses when major donors ask for earthly things such as strategic plans, long-range plans, campaign budgets, program budgets, site and facility studies, if-you-build-this-what-will-happen-to-the-budget reports, blueprints, and lists of donors already committed. It is not unspiritual for them to ask for these things. Indeed, having this material ready and available, accurate and readable, is part of good stewardship of the philanthropy you have received. It will grease the skids for the philanthropy you hope to receive, and it is basic, good leadership.

I often wonder about the women who followed Jesus and "gave out of their resources," as Luke says. I expect the kinds of things they saw Jesus doing inspired their confidence and gifts. Jesus was stewarding the gifts. So must we. Please be heartened, because great stewardship of the annual, major, and planned gifts is best done by simply being a good, kind, honest, and authentic church. You are probably doing great stewardship of philanthropy without even realizing it, because you are a good church leader. It is that simple. And it has to be that intentional.

If a church is asking its congregation to be good stewards of the money God has given them, then the church must also be a good steward by inspiring major and annual donors to make gifts. Once you have raised a major gift, it must be carefully stewarded and the donor repeatedly thanked. The last step in the receipt of a gift is the thanks you offer to the donor, and the first step in asking for the next gift is that same thanks.

Leadership recruitment, strategic planning, mission authenticity, and effective communications will be foundational to your success. The last component is essential, and it is how we thank those who give to the church. This is one area in particular in which the church diverges from the average nonprofit. We do not list our donors in the bulletin, nor do we put their names on special-events posters.

Much is made in scripture and tradition of holy numbers. The number seven is often touted as a number with mystical weight. It is, in my opinion, a good approximation of how many times a person should be thanked per year. You cannot thank people too much for their gift. You can thank them too expensively—that will get you in trouble. You can thank them carelessly—late or with misspelled names—and that also will get you in trouble. But you cannot thank people too much for their gifts. If your program is robust, it will have an effective thank-you component. In fundraising, this is called "donor recognition." In church, this is more usually called "stewardship acknowledgment." Do not get too worried about terminology, but be attentive to doing it right, because donor acknowledgment—thanking people effectively for their gifts—is a bridge to the next gift . . . and so on.

Let's look at a few "thank you" tools in a stewardship and major-gifts program. Effective donor recognition for the annual pledge campaign that funds your annual mission and ministry is the cornerstone of a major-gifts program. Scripture says that those who are trustworthy with little can be trusted with much—a good motto for donor acknowledgment in church stewardship programming. Take great care in how you thank people for the annual giving campaign, and it will pay dividends when you need to raise major gifts. The phone call checking in on every member begins the next annual pledge process along with the warm-up letter as the campaign unfolds.

Once you are absolutely sure that you have thanked people robustly for their annual pledge, you need to thank them for any major gift. There are three phases to the major gift: the promise, the payment, and the spending (church's stewardship) of the gift. Each phase should have a donor thank-you attached to it. The more personal the thank-you, the better. Avoid expensive gifts. Just call people, visit them, and send videos and photos of the ministry their gift has made possible. Donors want a personal touch, and they want human engagement. It is what won you the gift, and it is the best way to thank them for the gift.

Toward Regeneration

When a major donor has given a major gift, and you have done an effective job both stewarding the gift and thanking the donor, then the art of major-gift fundraising is to know when to ask for the next gift. The entire process of donor engagement begins over again in consideration of the next possible gift. If someone has been taken through five or seven engagement events, is asked for and gives the major gift, then the entire process begins again, and these questions are asked, again, about the prospect (within the confidentiality of the major-gifts advisory committee):

1. To what do we believe they would like to give next?
2. What steps need to happen to deepen their engagement with this church, provide further discernment, and lead up to another request for their next major gift?
3. Who should be involved in these next steps?
4. What are the ways we thanked them for the last gift? Were they done effectively?
5. What are the names and dates on the engagement continuum? What are the measurable objectives? What tasks are assigned to what people? What are the deadlines?
6. Who is going to keep an eye on this process to make sure we do not skip any steps and to make sure that this unfolds in a timely fashion—neither too quickly, nor too slowly?

The last word about the programming and stewarding of the major gift in a church is the question of conscience. People who are raising money, especially major gifts, are necessarily the conscience of the church that is raising the money. A fundraiser is always the conscience of the nonprofit for which they are raising money, because it is they who must look the donor in the eye and say, "This gift is a good philanthropic investment." If there is relational, financial, or missional misconduct, then the fundraiser is triangulated between the failure of nerve and the donor. The clergy and lay leaders leading major-gifts fundraising must never cease in their vigilance. If it appears to you, as leaders, that there is any hint of mismanagement of funds, abuse of relationships, or misconduct of any kind, you must address it quickly and thoroughly. Otherwise, you will jeopardize the integrity of the church, which will, in turn, jeopardize its health and the likelihood of receiving major gifts. To some extent, those responsible for major gifts in a church are watchdogs and whistle-blowers. To blow the whistle on any form of misconduct, to deal with it appropriately and quickly, is to secure the viability of any major-gift program.

Major-gift fundraising in a church is not a campaign. Though a campaign may exist in the midst of it, major-gifts fundraising needs to be woven into all of the other programs managed in your church—day in and day out.

We end as we began, and I began by saying that fundraising is not secular, sinful, dirty or in any way unspiritual. *Fundraising* is good work that leadership does in a church to raise money. *Stewardship* is the good work of helping the donor to discern their gift to God's mission in the context of their financial blessings.

Major-gifts fundraising is no less spiritual or important than spiritual formation, liturgical practice, hospitality, pastoral care, or any other primary function of the church. Any church's strategic plan (and every church should have one) needs to have major-gift components woven through it, alongside the plan for annual pledges, planned giving, and membership growth—with dedicated, effective, faithful, kind leadership shepherding the process.

When you're choosing leadership for the major-gifts program, you are also, inevitably, making a choice about the integrity and stewardship of the major gifts you will receive, so make those choices very carefully. Choices about the chairperson of your major-gifts and annual pledge programs are some of the most important decisions you will make. Discern and make them well, and you will enjoy tremendous success.

RESOURCE

A Sample Weekly Major-Gifts Report to the Major-Gifts or Stewardship Committee

Saint John's Church, Werington, New Jersey
Week of April 16, 20__

1. Sally Smith: I took her to lunch (2.1 hours)
2. John Harrington: the senior warden took him on a tour of the church's old kitchen (phone call, 3 minutes)
3. Susan Jones: invited her over lunch in three weeks to see the old kitchen and the blueprints for the new kitchen (phone call, 5 minutes)
4. Harold Williams: set a date, April 29, 11:00 A.M., to visit his living room to discuss remembering the church and his will (phone call, 15 minutes)
5. Sarah Johnson: wrote her a thank-you note for the meeting we had this week (4 minutes)
6. Sarah Johnson: set up a tour of the old kitchen and time to view the blueprints May 3 (3 minutes)
7. Sally Heming: encouraged senior warden to visit her last month, which ended in a request for her to consider including the church in her will. Called to set appointment for May 5. On the telephone, Sally mentioned that she has included the church in her will. (Note: The mean planned gift to a church in 2017 is about $80,000) (phone call, 25 minutes)
8. Susan Roosevelt: made first visit to home. Spent two hours chatting (3 hours) (Note: Susan sent me home with a check for the food pantry, $2,000, and made first pledge to annual fund, $1,000)

Money raised: $83,000
Major gifts in process, not yet given: $600,000
Time spent: 7 hours of the 50 I worked this week
Engagement-continuum accomplishment this week: Eight steps
Major donors engaged: 8 of the 27 major-donor prospects in our church
Report to vestry: engaged 8 major-donor prospects, managed one request,

received will inclusion (estimated value, $80,000), received major designated gift, raised an annual pledge

Note: As you can see from the above sample, in which the clergyperson evaluates the week's major-gifts work, this work is simply about shepherding a process and maintaining public accountability for the engagement-deepening actions by which vestries evaluate clergy and by which diocesan councils and convention clergy evaluate bishops for effective, measurable major-gifts work. Some weeks you will only engage two or three donors. Some weeks you will engage eight or ten. Some weeks there will be no engagement.

What gets measured gets done. The key to programming major-gifts fundraising into the mission of your church is *tracking the engagement events*. If you track each engagement event, both by clergy and by other lay leaders, and if you record that engagement, then you will indeed weave the major-gifts work into your schedule. This will not only help your donors to give to the church they love (primary benefit), but you will also raise the money your mission needs and that your church needs for the future (secondary benefit).

A Sample Letter—What to Do When Stock Is Being Given

Inform the church regarding your intention to donate stock to Saint James' Church. They will record your address, telephone number, the name of your broker, the name of the corporation issuing the security, and the number of shares you will be transferring. Our contact information is (give them the name and contact information for whomever handles stock gifts).

Instruct your broker to contact the church to verify your name, the name of the security, and number of shares being transferred, as well as the expected transfer date.

Provide your broker with the following information for transfer of shares:

Account name	Saint James' Church Gift Account
Trustee	Name your church's bank representative receiving the funds
Trustee's telephone number	305-864-____
Transfer agent	Bank of New York
DTC number	720
For credit to	Bank of Oklahoma
Account number	010471
For further credit to	St. James' Church Gift Account
FFC account number	720964023

Important advisory: Please let the church office know by e-mail, phone call, or letter that you have given stock to Saint James' Church by informing us directly of your intentions. Your gift will be gratefully acknowledged, together with the market information of the shares transferred by the trustee on the day of receipt.

QUICK-START SUGGESTIONS

1. Take good care of the leaders who lead planned, annual, and major-gifts work in your church. They work very hard, often on top of busy personal and business lives. They need to be thanked often and well.

2. Never try to balance a budget by forcing more from the stewardship efforts. Live within your means and let stewardship grow naturally based on interest and improvement. Stewardship programming is not there to rescue poor planning by the finance committee or the budget process.

3. Do not set and measure goals by numbers. Set and measure goals by programmatic function. Do not set a goal for dollars raised. Set a goal for work accomplished to raise the pledges and publicly hold clergy, lay leaders, and bishops accountable for this work so that they are measured on time spent engaging in measured face-to-face major-gift engagement-deepening and thanked for their hard work.

4. Be sure that you have a detailed strategic plan that measures all aspects of financial development and stewardship formation in your church. If possible, this plan should be related to the church's master plan, and each should have a general seven-year version, a more specific three-year version, and a very detailed one-year version, which is broken down by month with measurable objectives.

5. As with feasts and fasts of the church, the committees that serve your resource development (raising money and raising people) need to feast from time to time. Be sure that you have a calendar (it may be part of your strategic plan) and that those calendars include times for celebration, good food, and fellowship to rejoice over the work you are doing to raise money for mission.

6. Be sure to have a *year-round calendar* and program for financial development in your church. Winter is for evaluation and planning. Spring is for membership growth and annual-giving materials production. Spring is also a fine time for living-room visits for major gifts and planned giving. Fall is generally taken up with new programming and the pledge campaign, and then the cycle begins again. Set all your meetings in advance with rosters and meeting dates in the hands of all lay and clergy leaders. Cancel if you must, but have the dates and times preset so that time does not slip away from you.

STUDY QUESTIONS

1. What do you consider to be the most-valued traits of the leaders in your church? What do you look for in the lay leadership and the lay leader of a major-gifts program?

2. Discuss your church's strategic planning and the prayer that goes into the discernment of your plan. What does your written, strategic plan look like? Is it vague, or does it have measurable objectives? How is major-gift programming woven into the strategic plan for your church or diocese?

3. In what ways are you a good steward of the money that God gives to you? And, by extension, in what ways is your church a good steward of the major gifts that are, or could be, given to your church?

4. What is the provision for a safe form of whistle-blowing in the event of a lack of integrity that could threaten a major-gifts program and the confidence of your donors?

5. If your bishop invites a gift from your church to a diocesan capital project, what is your discernment around that gift? How will you enthusiastically raise money for it, or how would you politely decline to be part of a project you deem to be a managerial or case-development (missional) failure?

6. What would a written "thank-you program" for the major gifts your church receives look like?

7. If you are the clergyperson, bishop, or lay leader responsible for raising major gifts, what would you consider to be a month of work well-done on major gifts? How many visits would you make? Would you track your progress in writing? If you fail one month to engage major donors, what would that look like? What accountability exists for measuring accomplishment?

8. Draft a job description for the chairperson of major gifts in your church. What would it look like? What components would you include? How would you measure success?

PRAYERS

A Prayer for the Stewarding of Gifts in Mission

Lord God, giver of all good things, inspire us with the power of your Holy Spirit to take great care in the stewarding of the major gifts given to us. When a person gives a major gift to our church, help us to hold that gift tenderly and carefully. Give us an awareness of the integrity with which we must spend that gift. Help us remember that to whom much is given, much is expected; help us remember that every donor who gives to our church expects us to use their gift with great care. Give us the grace to be as mindful of the process by which we spend the money as we were mindful of the process by which we raised it. *Amen.*

CONCLUSION

. . . .

Loving the Lord our God with all our heart, mind, and soul is not just something we do in our head on a Sunday morning at church or while being super-spiritual on a retreat, or during our prayer time. Love is a verb. It requires action. And part of the love we have and express for our God is stewardship—how we oversee what has been given to us. And part of that work is philanthropy. So, inspiring major gifts for the mission of a church or nonprofit agency is a very real, tangible, and measurable part of loving God.

Similarly, loving other humans as we love ourselves is also an action verb. When we make ourselves breakfast or earn the money we need for a bed and a home, we are loving ourselves. When we connect with other humans and socialize in church or outside of it, we are loving ourselves. When we eat well and exercise, rest, work, or play, we are loving ourselves. However, we are also called to love others *as ourselves*. So, we encourage, support, and call for *philanthropy*—a word that means "loving humans."

Making a good life involves loving God, others, and ourselves. Other books (some by this author) exist to help us love God. But this book is designed to help with the important work of loving other humans—philanthropy. Raising major gifts helps us to love other humans by transferring money from those who have it to those who need the help such gifts can provide in the nonprofit sector and in the church's mission. However, what I hope this book has also conveyed is that inspiring meaning-making is an act that participates in the important work of loving ourselves. We humans need to make meaning of our lives. We can see in the nightly news what happens to humans when they are not making real meaning.

This book was written so that the church and nonprofit sector might do better work when raising major gifts to fund their missions. Major-gifts work is the most effective and efficient way to raise money and is as simple as the relationship between two people and a worthy mission. But major-gifts work is also helping the donor make real, lasting meaning in their lives. So sure, I love that people doing good work in major-gifts fundraising are raising money to alleviate suffering. But I admit, in these final words, that my great hope, and the reason this book needs to be read and used, is that it will transform the lives of the donors whose gifts will be requested by you, the reader.

The harvest is indeed plentiful, and the workers, especially in fundraising within our church, are few. Clergy (and bishops who were, let's face it, once parish priests) were not taught how to raise money, even though their missions depend on it. And, of course, fundraising (especially major-gifts fundraising) requires vulnerability that, in turn, requires humility. It shows vulnerability to ask for a gift, and many do not have the humility to do so. This work demands a certain spiritual depth not often extant in many clergy and bishops today, though it can and will be found in the best of them—and often is.

May this book inspire the workers in the vineyards of church and non-profit sectors to raise money for mission. May it also inspire and midwife meaning-making in those who give their money away as philanthropy, so that we may, indeed, love God, love others, and love ourselves. And may all manner of thing be well.

We think major-gifts fundraising is difficult. It is not. We too often think that people are greedy, materialistic, or stingy. We are not. We are exhausted and frightened—our greed is simply the way we have decided to scream. But doing great work in meaning–making and in mission will heal all our wounds—the wounds of those whose suffering is soothed by the church's mission and the wounds of those whose soul needs to make meaning on this planet.

Our life is short.

Midwife generosity.

Then use the money to restore the world.

Do not be afraid.

ABOUT THE AUTHOR

. . . .

The Reverend Canon Charles LaFond is an Episcopal priest, speaker, author, and blogger who works to help churches help people give their money to Jesus' mission. He provides basic resource development materials to churches, nonprofits, and judicatory bodies such as dioceses as a public service, without any website-access or download fees required, ever, by anyone, at any time. These downloadable templates, along with related teaching videos, are available at fearlesschurchfundraising.com as a gift and an extension of this text. Charles also writes regular articles on *Episcopal Café* (episcopalcafe.com) under the title "Fearless Fundraising" as support to clergy and nonprofit and lay leaders.

Fearless Church Fundraising was the first in a series of three books on annual pledging, major gifts, and membership growth. *Fearless Major Gifts: Inspiring Meaning-Making* is the second in the series.

As Canon Steward at The Cathedral of Saint John's in the Wilderness, Charles is a potter, beekeeper, priest, retreat leader, speaker, theologian, blogger, and author on spiritual depth and philanthropy. He spent a decade as a corporate nonprofit development officer and a second decade as an Episcopal priest and monk. Charles lives in Denver, where he raises money and membership at Saint John's in the Wilderness. He blogs on spiritual life, stewardship, food, hospitality, and generosity at thedailysip.org, which is syndicated, along with a new series of weekly articles on church financial development called "Fearless Fundraising," on episcopalcafe.com, an online news service. Charles offers considerable resources for parish financial development, including videos and manuals, on his personal website, charleslafond.net.

Charles divides his time between Denver and farms in rural New Hampshire and New Mexico and lives with a companion English black lab named Kai.